Democracy and the Global Order

For T. G. and J. B. T.

Democracy and the Global Order

From the Modern State to Cosmopolitan Governance

David Held

Polity Press

First published in 1995 by Polity Press
in association with Blackwell Publishers Ltd.

Reprinted 1996, 1997

Editorial office:
Polity Press
65 Bridge Street
Cambridge CB2 1UR, UK

Marketing and production:
Blackwell Publishers Ltd
108 Cowley Road
Oxford OX4 1JF, UK

ISBN 0–7456–0055–7
ISBN 0–7456–0056–5 (pbk)

A CIP catalogue record for this book is available from the British Library.

Phototypeset in 11 on 12 pt Caslon
by Intype, London
Printed in Great Britain by
TJ International, Padstow, Cornwall

This book is printed on acid-free paper.

CONTENTS

Preface

There is a daunting challenge facing democratic theory and practice today. The key traditions of democratic thinking, above all those which stem from republicanism, liberalism and Marxism, appear to be severely strained in the face of major twentieth-century developments. Among these developments are to be counted the dynamics of a world economy which produce instabilities and difficulties within states and between states which outreach the control of any single polity; the rapid growth of transnational links which have stimulated new forms of collective decision-making involving states, intergovernmental organizations and international pressure groups; the expansion and intensification of transnational communication systems; the proliferation of military technologies and arms as a 'stable' feature of the contemporary political world; and the development of pressing transnational problems – involving, for instance, environmental challenges like acid rain, damage to the ozone layer and the 'greenhouse effect' – which do not acknowledge national boundaries and frontiers.

Moreover, the form of international governance which dominated world politics for over four decades – the Cold War international system – has disintegrated; no alternative has yet developed, while debates about alternatives have all too often been stymied by old state interests and strategic concerns. However, with the end of the geopolitical divisions created in the aftermath of the Second World War, a new fluidity has been established in international affairs which heralds the possibility of a new fluidity in political thought. These circumstances present significant opportunities for the establishment of an international order based upon the principles of constitutionality and democracy – opportunities which need to be grasped if the current revival of sectarian politics and of the use of force, evidenced in the resurgence of right-wing politics in Europe, the intensification of racism and the spread of ethnic and political separatism throughout the world, are to be checked.

While democratic theory has debated at length the challenges to democracy that emerge from within the boundaries of the nation-state – for instance, the development of mass bureaucratic parties, the preoccupation of parties with their own particular ends and ambitions, the fragmentation of political power, the problem of 'overloaded government' – it has not seriously questioned whether the nation-state itself can remain at the centre of democratic thought. The rapid growth of complex interconnections and interrelations between states and societies – often referred to as the process of 'globalization' – along with the intersection of national and international forces and processes pose questions that remain largely unexplored. These centre on the challenges to democracy deriving, on the one hand, from the world political economy and the web of relations and networks which stretch across national borders and, on the other, from the divergence that sometimes exists between the totality of those affected by a political decision and those who participated in making it (however indirectly) within a democratic state.

If democratic theory is concerned with 'what is going on' in the political world and, thereby, with the nature and prospects of democracy, then a theory of democratic politics today must take account of the place of the polity within geopolitical and market processes, that is, within the system of nation-states, international legal regulation and world political economy. The pursuit of political knowledge on old disciplinary grounds is not adequate to this task. For too long the concerns of political theory, political economy, international relations and international law have been kept separate, with persistently disappointing outcomes. Significant beginnings have been made in recent times to reintegrate elements of these disciplines, but a great deal of ground remains to be covered. At issue is rethinking the nature, form and content of democratic politics in the face of the complex intermeshing of local, national, regional and global relations and processes.

The pursuit of the following questions is central to this enterprise: is the idea of democratic politics progressively comprised by the intersection of national and international forces and pressures? Is the notion of national self-determination becoming an anachronism in a world of interconnected political authorities and power centres? What is the contemporary meaning of citizenship and citizenship rights? Is the principle of territorial representation the single most appropriate principle for the determination of the basis of political representation? Are there duties beyond borders? If so, what are the political and legal implications of these duties? How should agencies that cut across nation-state boundaries be regulated? What is the appropriate level of democratic control – the local, national, regional, global?

Democratic political theory has to be rethought, and along with it the actual underlying principles and practices of democratic politics. The explosion of interest in democracy in recent times has all too often left unquestioned whether democracy must be conceived as liberal democracy, whether democracy can only be applied to 'governmental affairs' (and not to the economic, social and cultural realms as well), and whether the most appropriate locus for democracy is the nation-state. These terms of reference are all critically addressed in this book. By examining how the conditions of democracy are changing on national and international levels, and by rethinking some of the central principles and concerns of democratic theory, it is hoped it is possible to reconfront the problems faced by democracy in the contemporary global order.

Democracy and the Global Order is divided into four parts. Part I addresses why conventional accounts of the nature and meaning of democracy will no longer do, and introduces the issues which inform the volume as a whole. Part II offers an analysis of the nature and the development of the modern state. Different state forms are explored and an explanation is offered for why the liberal democratic nation-state became the predominant form of the modern state. Key stages in the formation of the international order – the states system and the United Nations Charter framework – are then examined and a map is provided of the dense network of regional and global relations in which states and societies are enmeshed. Against this background, the changing role of the nation-state, and of the idea of a national democracy, is assessed. It is argued that, in an era in which the fates of peoples are deeply intertwined, democracy has to be recast and strengthened, both *within* pre-established borders and *across* them. The particular conditions which created the impetus to the establishment of the liberal democratic nation-state are being transformed and, accordingly, democracy must be profoundly altered if it is to retain its relevance in the decades ahead.

How democracy might be altered within borders, on the one hand, and across them, on the other, are the subjects of, respectively, parts III and IV. Unlike part II, which offers an historical and empirical analysis of the changing form and context of the modern state, part III engages in a reconstruction of some of the core concepts of political theory. It begins by examining the tensions between the idea of the modern state, as a circumscribed system of power which provides in principle a regulatory mechanism and check on rulers and ruled alike, and the idea of democracy, as a political association in which citizens are able to choose freely the conditions of their own association. Among the matters raised are questions about the proper form and scope of supreme political power; the conditions and limits of democratic participation; and the legitimate range and scope of democratic decision-making. The case is made that democracy entails a commitment to what I call the 'principle of autonomy' and a set of 'empowering rights and obligations' – rights and obligations which must cut across all those sites of power, whether rooted in politics, economics or culture, which can erode or undercut autonomy, for individuals and groups. Such a principle and set of rights and obligations create the possibility of what is referred to as a 'common structure of political action'. Such a structure, it is suggested, needs to be entrenched and enforced in a 'democratic public law' if it is to be effective as the basis of a fair and circumscribed system of power. I explore lines of argument which seek to show how the ideas of democracy and of the modern state can be coherently linked through the notion of a 'democratic legal order' – an order which is conditioned and shaped by democratic public law in all its affairs.

Part IV elaborates this position. In particular, it argues that democracy can only be adequately entrenched if democratic public law is enacted in the affairs of nation-states and in the wider global order – that is, as cosmopolitan democratic law – and if a division of powers and competences is recognized at different levels of political interaction and interconnectedness. I contend that democratic politics needs to be reshaped at local, national, regional and global levels, for each of these levels is appropriate for a different set of public problems and issues. Thus, a democratic political order must embrace diverse and distinct domains of authority, linked both vertically and horizontally, if it is to be a creator and servant of democratic practice. The discussion focuses on the idea of a cosmopolitan model of democracy, and its short- and long-term implications. Such a model, it is maintained, provides a basis for thinking that democracy might become an enduring and stable framework for the politics of our times, although the obstacles to the realization of it are formidable. However, the nation-state was not built in a day, and cosmopolitan democracy, assuming for a moment that it can find a broad range of advocates, will certainly not be either!

In the preparation of this book many friends and colleagues have provided invaluable support and criticism of earlier drafts, among others, Daniele Archibugi, Richard Falk, David Goldblatt, Joel Krieger, Anthony McGrew, Jonathan Perraton, Quentin Skinner and Rob Walker. I am indebted to them all. I should also like to acknowledge the support and inspiration I have had from an older and a younger generation: from my father, Peter Held, and from my children, Rosa and Joshua Stanworth Held. In addition, I have been aided in numerous ways by Michelle Stanworth, who provided many sharp commentaries on the text as it developed and much encouragement throughout. Julia Harsant, Gill Motley, Nicola Ross, Fiona Sewell, Pamela Thomas and Rhona Richard also contributed to the production of this volume; I am extremely grateful for their help. Finally, I want to mention the generosity, advice and constructive criticism I have received on this book and over the years from my friends Anthony Giddens and John B. Thompson, to whom this volume is dedicated.

DH
January 1995

Part I

Introduction

1

STORIES OF DEMOCRACY: OLD AND NEW

Democracy seems to have scored an historic victory over alternative forms of governance. Nearly everyone today professes to be a democrat. Political regimes of all kinds throughout the world claim to be democracies. In an age in which many traditional ways of resolving value disputes are treated with the utmost caution – especially those which appeal, for instance, to other-worldly teachings, or to doctrines about the natural order of rank and hierarchy, or to claims about the proletarian interest – it seems as if political choices can only begin to be adequately recognized, articulated and negotiated in a democracy. Democracy bestows an aura of legitimacy on modern political life: laws, rules and policies appear justified when they are 'democratic'. But it was not always so. The great majority of political thinkers from ancient Greece to the present day have been highly critical of the theory and practice of democracy. A widespread commitment to democracy is a very recent phenomenon. Moreover, democracy is a remarkably difficult form of government to create and sustain. The history of twentieth-century Europe alone makes this clear: fascism, Nazism and Stalinism came very close to obliterating democracy altogether.

Against this background, it is unsettling that some recent political commentators have proclaimed (by means of a phrase borrowed most notably from Hegel) the 'end of history' – the triumph of the West over all political and economic alternatives. The revolutions which swept across Central and Eastern Europe at the end of 1989 and the beginning of 1990 stimulated an atmosphere of celebration. Liberal democracy was championed as the agent of progress, and capitalism as the only viable economic system: ideological conflict, it was said, is being steadily displaced by universal democratic reason and market-orientated thinking (see Fukuyama, 1989, 1989/90; cf. Held, 1993a, 1993b). But such a view is quite inadequate in a number of respects.

In the first instance, the 'liberal' component of liberal democracy cannot be treated simply as a unity. There are distinctive liberal traditions which embody quite different conceptions from each other of the individual agent, of autonomy, of the rights and duties of subjects, and of the proper nature and form of community. In addition, the 'celebratory' view of liberal democracy neglects to explore whether there are any tensions, or even perhaps contradictions, between the 'liberal' and 'democratic' components of liberal democracy; for example, between the liberal preoccupation with individual rights or 'frontiers of freedom' which 'nobody should be permitted to cross', and the democratic concern for the regulation of individual and collective action, that is, for public accountability. Those who have written at length on this question have frequently resolved it in quite different directions. Furthermore, there is not simply one institutional form of liberal democracy. Contemporary democracies have crystallized into a number of different types, which makes any appeal to a liberal position vague at best (see, for example, Lijphart, 1984; Dahl, 1989). Moreover, they have crystallized at the intersection of national and international forces which have profoundly affected their nature and efficacy. To neglect these issues is to leave unanalysed a wide spectrum of questions about democracy and its possible variants.

This introductory chapter seeks to address this lacuna, first, by examining the development of different models of democracy and their conditions of application; secondly, by exploring the meaning of democracy in the context of the progressive enmeshment today of states and societies in regional and global networks; and thirdly, by considering a number of leading approaches to the understanding of transnational and international phenomena. The result, it is hoped, is a step towards the specification of an historical and theoretical framework for the problems and issues addressed in the volume as a whole.

1.1 Models of democracy

Within the history of democratic theory lies a deeply rooted conflict about whether democracy should mean some kind of popular power (a form of politics in which citizens are engaged in self-government and self-regulation) or an aid to decision-making (a means of conferring authority on those periodically voted into office). This conflict has given rise to three basic variants or models of democracy. First, there is direct or participatory democracy, a system of decision-making about public affairs in which citizens are directly involved. This was the 'original' type of democracy found in ancient Athens, among other places. Secondly, there is liberal or representative democracy, a system of rule embracing elected 'officers' who undertake to 'represent' the interests or views of citizens within delimited territories while upholding the 'rule of law'. Thirdly, there is a variant of democracy based on a one-party model (although some may doubt whether this is a form of democracy at all). Until recently, the Soviet Union, East European societies and many developing countries were committed to this conception. The following discussion deals briefly with each of these models in turn. Although it offers a guide to what will be familiar territory to some readers, it develops concepts and issues which will be drawn upon in later argument.

The active citizen and republican government

Athenian democracy has long been taken as a fundamental source of inspiration for modern Western political thought. This is not to say that the West has been right to trace many elements of its democratic heritage exclusively to Athens; for, as recent historical and archaeological research has shown, some of the key political innovations, both conceptual and institutional, of the nominally Western political tradition can be traced to older civilizations in the East. The city-state or *polis* society, for example, existed in Mesopotamia long before it emerged in the West (see Bernal, 1987; Springborg, 1992). Nonetheless, the political ideals of Athens – equality among citizens, liberty, respect for the law and justice – have been taken as integral to Western political thinking, and it is for this reason that Athens constitutes a useful starting point.

The Athenian city-state, ruled as it was by citizen-governors, did not differentiate between state and society. In ancient Athens, citizens were at one and the same time subjects of political authority and the creators of public rules and regulations. The people (*demos*) engaged in legislative and judicial functions, for the Athenian concept of citizenship entailed their taking a share in these functions, participating *directly* in the affairs of 'the state'.[1] Athenian democracy required a general commitment to the principle of civic virtue: dedication to the republican city-state and the subordination of private life to public affairs and the common good. 'The public' and 'the private' were intertwined. Citizens could properly fulfil themselves and live honourably only in and through the *polis*. Of course, who was to count as a citizen was a tightly restricted matter; among the excluded were women and a substantial slave population.

The Athenian city-state – eclipsed ultimately by the rise of empires, stronger states and military regimes – shared features with republican Rome. Both were predominantly face-to-face societies and oral cultures; both had elements of popular participation in governmental affairs; and both had little, if any, centralized bureaucratic control. Furthermore, both sought to foster a deep sense of public duty, a tradition of civic virtue or responsibility to 'the republic' – to the distinctive matters of the public realm. And in both polities, the claims of the state were given a unique priority over those of the individual citizen. But if Athens was a democratic republic, contemporary scholarship generally affirms that Rome was, by comparison, an essentially oligarchical system (Finley, 1983, pp. 84ff). Nevertheless, from antiquity, it was Rome which was to prove the most durable influence on the dissemination of republican ideas.

Classical republicanism received its most robust restatement in the early Renaissance, especially in the city-states of Italy (see Rahe, 1994). The meaning of the concept of 'active citizenship in a republic' became a leading concern. Political thinkers of this period were critical of the Athenian formulation of this notion; shaped as their views were by Aristotle, one of the leading critics of Greek democracy, and by the centuries-long impact of republican Rome, they recast the republican tradition. While the concept of

[1] When referring to the Greek *polis*, some scholars prefer to use the term 'city-republic' on the grounds that the concept of the state was an early-modern formulation. For some of the issues underpinning this preference see Held, 1987, ch. 2.

the *polis* remained central to the political theory of Italian cities, most notably in Florence, it was no longer regarded as a means to self-fulfilment (see Pocock, 1975, pp. 64–80). Emphasis continued to be placed on the importance of civic virtue but the latter was understood as highly fragile, subject particularly to corruption if dependent solely upon the political involvement of any one major grouping: the people, the aristocracy or the monarchy. A constitution which could reflect and balance the interests of all leading political factions became an aspiration. Niccolò Machiavelli thus argued that all singular constitutional forms (monarchy, aristocracy and democracy) were unstable, and only a governmental system combining elements of each could promote the kind of political culture on which civic virtue depends (see Machiavelli, 1983, pp. 104–11). The best example of such a government was, he proclaimed, Rome: Rome's mixed government (with its system of consuls, Senate and tribunes of the people) was directly linked to its sustained achievements.

The core of the Renaissance republican case was that the freedom of a political community rested upon its accountability to no authority other than that of the community itself. Self-government is the basis of liberty, together with the right of citizens to participate – within a constitutional framework which creates distinct roles for leading social forces – in the government of their own common business.[2] As one commentator put it, 'the community as a whole must retain the ultimate sovereign authority', assigning its various rulers or chief magistrates 'a status no higher than that of elected officials' (Skinner, 1989a, p. 105). Such 'rulers' must ensure the effective enforcement of the laws created by the community for the promotion of its own good; for they are not rulers in a traditional sense, but agents or administrators of justice.

In Renaissance republicanism, as well as in Greek democratic thought, a citizen was someone who participated in 'giving judgement and holding office' (Aristotle, 1981, p. 169). Citizenship meant participation in public affairs. This definition is noteworthy because it suggests that theorists within these traditions would have found it hard to locate citizens in modern democracies, except perhaps as representatives or office holders. The limited scope in

[2] The republican view emphasizes, in short, that the freedom of citizens consists above all in their unhindered pursuit of their self-chosen ends. The highest political ideal is the civic freedom of an independent, self-governing republic.

contemporary politics for the active involvement of citizens would have been regarded as most undemocratic (see Finley, 1973b). Yet the idea that human beings should be active citizens of a political order – citizens of their states – and not merely dutiful subjects of a ruler has had few advocates from the earliest human associations to the early Renaissance (see chapters 2 and 3).[3]

The demise in the West of the idea of the active citizen, one whose very being is affirmed in and through political action, is hard to explain fully. But it is clear enough that the antithesis of *homo politicus* is the *homo credens* of the Christian faith: the citizen whose active judgement is essential is displaced by the true believer (Pocock, 1975, p. 550). Although it would be misleading to suggest that the rise of Christianity effectively banished secular considerations from the lives of rulers and ruled, it unquestionably shifted the source of authority and wisdom from this-worldly to other-worldly representatives. During the Middle Ages, the integration of Christian Europe from the Eastern Atlantic seaboard to the Balkans came to depend above all on two theocratic authorities: the Roman Catholic Church and the Holy Roman Empire. There was no theoretical alternative to their account of the nature of power and rule (Bull, 1977, p. 27; cf. Black, A., 1992). Not until the end of the sixteenth century, when it became apparent that religion had become a highly divisive force and that the powers of the state would have to be separated from the duty of rulers to uphold any particular faith, did the nature and limits of political authority, law, rights and obedience become a preoccupation, from Italy to England, of European political thought (Skinner, 1978, vol. 2, p. 352).

[3] The concern with aspects of 'self-government' in Renaissance Italy had a significant influence in seventeenth- and eighteenth-century England, France and America. The problem of how civic life was to be constructed, and public life sustained, was faced by diverse thinkers. While the meaning of the ideal of active citizenship was progressively altered – and denuded of many of its most challenging implications – threads of this ideal remained and continued to have an impact. It is possible to trace 'radical' and 'conservative' strains of republicanism throughout the early modern period (cf. Wood, 1969; Pocock, 1975).

Liberal representative democracy

This preoccupation became the hallmark of modern liberal theory, which constantly sought to justify the sovereign power of the state while at the same time justifying limits on that power. The history of this attempt is the history of arguments to balance might and right, power and law, duties and rights. On the one hand, states must have a monopoly of coercive power in order to provide a secure basis on which family life, religion, trade and commerce can prosper. On the other hand, by granting the state a regulatory and coercive capability, liberal political theorists were aware that they had accepted a force that could, and frequently did, deprive citizens of political and social freedoms.

How this dilemma was addressed in early-modern political theory is explored in chapter 2, which sets out the scope of the early formulation of the concept of political sovereignty and the idea of the modern state, alongside rival accounts of these notions found in the work of Bodin and Hobbes, and Locke and Rousseau. However, important as these accounts were to the development of the discourse of the modern state, it was not until later that a new model of democracy was fully articulated – liberal representative (or simply representative) democracy – by those who subsequently became known as liberal democrats. For the latter, representative democracy constituted the key institutional innovation to overcome the problem of balancing coercive power and liberty. The liberal concern with reason, lawful government and freedom of choice could only be upheld properly by recognizing the political equality of all mature individuals. Such equality would ensure not only a secure social environment in which people would be free to pursue their private activities and interests, but also a state which, under the watchful eye of political representatives accountable to an electorate, would do what was best in the general or public interest. Thus, liberal democrats argued, the democratic constitutional state, linked to other key institutional mechanisms, particularly the free market, would resolve the problems of ensuring both liberty and authority.

Two classic statements of the new position can be found in the philosophy of James Madison and in the work of one of the key figures of nineteenth-century English liberalism: Jeremy Bentham. In Madison's account, 'pure democracies' (by which he means societies 'consisting of a small number of citizens, who assemble and administer the government in person') have always been intolerant, unjust and unstable (Madison, 1966, no. 10, p. 20). By contrast, representative government overcomes the excesses of 'pure democracy' because regular elections force a clarification of public issues, and the elected few, able to withstand the political process, are likely to be competent and capable of 'discerning the true interest of their country'.

The central concern of Madison's argument is not the rightful place of the active citizen in the life of the political community but, instead, the legitimate pursuit by individuals of their interests, and government as a means for the enhancement of these interests. Although Madison himself sought clear ways of reconciling particular interests with what he called modern 'extended republics', his position signals a clear shift from the classical ideals of civic virtue and the public realm to liberal preoccupations (1966, no. 10, pp. 21–2). He conceived of the representative state as the chief mechanism to aggregate individuals' interests and to protect their rights. In such a state, he believed, security of person and property would be sustained and politics could be made compatible with the demands of large nation-states, with their complex patterns of trade, commerce and international relations (see Krouse, 1983, pp. 58–78).

In parallel with this view, Bentham held that representative democracy 'has for its characteristic object and effect . . . securing its members against oppression and depredation at the hands of those functionaries which it employs for its defence' (1843, p. 47). Democratic government is required to protect citizens from the despotic use of political power, whether it be by a monarch, the aristocracy or other groups. The representative state thus becomes an umpire or referee while individuals pursue in civil society, according to the rules of economic competition and free exchange, their own interests. The free vote and the free market are both essential, for a key presupposition is that the collective good can be properly realized in most domains of life only if individuals interact in competitive exchanges, pursuing their utility with minimal state interference. Significantly, however, this argument has another side. Tied to the advocacy of a 'minimal state', whose scope and power need to be strictly limited, there is a strong commitment to certain types of state intervention: for instance, intervention to regulate the behaviour of the disobedient, and to reshape social relations and institutions if, in the event of the failure of *laissez faire*, the greatest happiness of the greatest number is not achieved – the only defensible criterion, Bentham held, of the public good.

From classical antiquity to the seventeenth century, democracy, when it was considered at all, was largely associated with the gathering of citizens in assemblies and public meeting places. By the early nineteenth century, in contrast, it was beginning to be thought of as the right of citizens to participate in the determination of the collective will through the medium of elected representatives (Bobbio, 1989, p. 144). The theory of representative democracy fundamentally shifted the terms of reference of democratic thought: the practical limits that a sizeable citizenry imposes on democracy, which had been the focus of so much critical (anti-democratic) attention, were practically eliminated. Representative democracy could now be celebrated as both accountable and feasible government, potentially stable over great territories and time spans (see Dahl, 1989, pp. 28–30). It could even be heralded, as James Mill put it, as 'the grand discovery of modern times' in which 'the solution of all difficulties, both speculative and practical, would be found' (quoted in Sabine, 1963, p. 695). Accordingly, the theory and practice of popular government shook off its traditional association with small states and cities, opening itself to become the legitimating creed of the emerging world of nation-states. But who exactly was to count as a legitimate participant, or a 'citizen' or 'individual', and what his or her exact role was to be in this new order, remained either unclear or unsettled. Even in the work of John Stuart Mill ambiguities remained: the idea that all citizens should have equal political weight in the polity remained outside his actual doctrine, along with that of most of his contemporaries (see Held, 1987, ch. 3).

It was left by and large to the extensive and often violently suppressed struggles of working-class and feminist activists, frequently in complex coalitions with other groups (notably, sectors of the middle class), to accomplish in the nineteenth and twentieth centuries a genuinely universal suffrage in some countries (see Rueschemeyer, Stephens and Stephens, 1992). Their achievement remained fragile in places such as Germany, Italy and Spain, and was in practice denied to some groups, for instance, many African-Americans in the US before the civil rights movement in the 1950s and 1960s. However, through these struggles the idea that the rights of citizenship should apply equally to all adults became slowly established; many of the arguments of the liberal democrats could be turned against existing institutions to reveal the extent to which the principles and aspirations of equal political participation remained unfulfilled. It was only with the actual achievement of citizenship for all adult men and women that liberal democracy took on its distinctively contemporary form: a cluster of rules and institutions permitting the broadest participation of the majority of citizens in the selection of representatives who alone can make political decisions, that is, decisions affecting the whole community.

This cluster includes elected government; free and fair elections in which every citizen's vote has an equal weight; a suffrage which embraces all citizens irrespective of distinctions of race, religion, class, sex and so on; freedom of conscience, information and expression on all public matters broadly defined; the right of all adults to oppose their government and stand for office; and associational autonomy – the right to form independent associations including social movements, interest groups and political parties (see Bobbio, 1987, p. 66; Dahl, 1989, pp. 221 and 233). The consolidation of representative democracy, thus understood, has been a twentieth-century phenomenon; perhaps one should even say a late twentieth-century phenomenon. For it is only in the closing decades of this century that democracy has been (relatively) securely established in the West and widely adopted in principle as a suitable model of government beyond the West.

Marxism and one-party democracy

The struggle of liberalism against tyranny, and the struggle by liberal democrats for political equality, represented a major step forward in the history of human emancipation, as Karl Marx and Friedrich Engels readily acknowledged. But for them, and for the Marxist tradition more broadly, the great universal ideals of 'liberty, equality and justice' cannot be realized simply by the 'free' struggle for votes in the political system together with the 'free' struggle for profit in the market-place. Advocates of the democratic state and the market economy present these institutions as the only ones under which liberty can be sustained and inequalities minimized. However, according to the Marxist critique, the capitalist economy, by virtue of its internal dynamics, inevitably produces systematic inequality and massive restrictions on real freedom. The formal existence of certain liberties is of little value if they cannot be exercised in practice. Therefore, although each step towards formal political equality is an advance, its liberating potential is severely curtailed by inequalities of class.

In class societies the state cannot become the vehicle for the pursuit of the common good or public interest. Far from playing the role of emancipator, protective knight, umpire or judge in the face of disorder, the agencies of the liberal representative state are enmeshed in the struggles of civil society. Marxists conceive of the state as an extension of civil society, reinforcing the social order for the enhancement of particular interests. Their argument is that political emancipation is only a step towards human emancipation; that is, the complete democratization of both society and the state. In their view, liberal democratic society fails when judged by its own promises.

Among these promises are, first, political participation, or general involvement mediated by representatives in decisions affecting the whole community; secondly, accountable government; and thirdly, freedom to protest and reform (Bobbio, 1987, pp. 42–4). But 'really existing liberal democracy', as one Marxist recently put it, 'fails to deliver' on any of these promises (Callinicos, 1991, pp. 108–9). For it is distinguished by the existence of a largely passive citizenry (significant numbers of eligible citizens do not vote in elections, for example); by the erosion and displacement of parliamentary institutions by unelected centres of power (typified by the expansion of bureaucratic authority and of the role of functional representatives); and by substantial structural constraints on state action and, in particular, on the possibility of the piecemeal reform of capitalism (the flight of capital overseas, for example, is a constant threat to elected governments with strong programmes of social reform).

Marx himself envisaged the replacement of the liberal democratic state by a 'commune structure': the smallest communities, which were to administer their own affairs, would elect delegates to larger administrative units (districts, towns); these in turn would elect candidates to still larger areas of administration (the national delegation) (Marx, 1970a, pp. 67–70). This arrangement is known as the 'pyramid' structure of 'delegative democracy': all delegates are revocable, bound by the instructions of their constituency, and organized into a 'pyramid' of directly elected committees. The post-capitalist state would not, therefore, bear any resemblance to a liberal, parliamentary regime. All state agencies would be brought within the sphere of a single set of directly accountable institutions. Only when this happens will 'that self-reliance, that freedom, which disappeared from earth with the Greeks, and vanished into the blue haze of heaven with Christianity', as the young Marx put it, gradually be restored (1844).

In the Marxist-Leninist account, the system of delegative democracy is to be complemented, in principle, by a separate but somewhat similar system at the level of the Communist Party. The transition to socialism and communism necessitates the 'professional' leadership of a disciplined cadre of revolutionaries (see, for example, Lenin, 1947). Only such a leadership has the capacity to organize the defence of the revolution against counter-revolutionary forces, to plan the expansion of the forces of production, and to supervise the reconstruction of society. Since all fundamental differences of interest are class interests, since the working-class interest (or standpoint) is the progressive interest in society, and since during and after the revolution it has to be articulated clearly and decisively, a revolutionary party is essential. The party is the instrument which can create the framework for socialism and communism. In practice, the party has to rule; and it was only in the 'Gorbachev era' in the Soviet Union (from 1984 to August 1991) that a pyramid of councils, or 'Soviets', from the central authority to those at local village and neighbourhood level, was given anything more than a symbolic or ritualistic role in the post-revolutionary period.

Democracy, the state and society

What should be made of these various models of democracy today? The classical participatory model cannot easily be adapted to stretch across space and time (see Held, 1987, chs 5 and 8). Its emergence in the context of city-states, and under conditions of 'social exclusivity', was an integral part of its successful development. In complex industrial societies, marked by a high degree of social, economic and political differentiation, it is very hard to envisage how a democracy of this kind could succeed on a large scale without drastic modification (see Budge, 1993; and chapter 12 of this volume).

The significance of these reflections is reinforced by examining the fate of the conception of democracy advocated by Marx and Engels and their followers. In the first instance, the 'deep structure' of Marxist categories – with its emphasis on the centrality of class, the universal standpoint of the proletariat, and a conception of politics which is rooted squarely in production – ignores or severely underestimates the contributions to politics of other forms of social structure, collectivity, agency, identity, interest and knowledge. Secondly, as an institutional arrangement that allows for mediation, negotiation and compromise among struggling factions, groups or movements, the Marxist model does not stand up well under scrutiny, especially in its Marxist-Leninist form. A system of institutions to promote discussion, debate and competition among divergent views – a system encompassing the formation of movements, pressure groups and/or political parties with independent leaderships to help press their cases – appears both necessary and desirable. Further, the changes in Central and Eastern Europe after 1989 seem to provide remarkable confirmatory evidence of this, with their emphasis on the importance of political and civil rights, a competitive party system, and the 'rolling back of the state' – that is, the freeing of civil society from state domination.

In the chapters which follow, therefore, I shall argue that a defensible account of the proper meaning of democracy must acknowledge the importance of a number of fundamental liberal and liberal democratic tenets. Among these are the centrality, in principle, of an 'impersonal' structure of public power, of a constitution to help protect and safeguard rights, and of a diversity of power centres within and outside the state, including institutional fora to promote open discussion and deliberation among alternative political viewpoints and platforms (see chapters 3 and 7 especially). However, to make these points, I shall also contend, is not to affirm any one liberal democratic model as it stands. For by focusing on the proper form and limits of government, liberal democrats have failed to explore and specify adequately, on the one hand, the conditions for the possibility of political participation and, on the other, the set of governing institutions capable of regulating the forces which actually shape everyday life. The requirements of democratic participation, the form of democratic control, and the scope of democratic decision-making are all insufficiently examined in the liberal democratic tradition (see chapters 7–9).

Accordingly, if a justifiable account of democracy is to be established, it is not enough to inquire into the proper principles and procedures of democracy and of the liberal democratic state, important though this is. An inquiry into the conditions of enactment of these principles and procedures is also necessary; that is, an inquiry into the character and dynamics of different types of power and their impact on democratic arrangements. Such an investigation must ask how and why one particular type of power

– political power – crystallized and became embedded in the state, and how and why democracy came to be associated with this site of power, above all others. How it was that democracy became established as, and became almost synonymous with, liberal democratic government needs clarification, as do the consequences of this for collective decision-making and the nature of accountability. At issue, it will be seen, is an attempt to understand the nature of the modern state, its reach over social and economic affairs in a given territory, and the implications of this for the form and efficacy of democracy. However, democracy has another side which also requires specification if its contemporary meaning is to be grasped fully. The problems of democracy extend beyond state borders.

1.2 Democracy, globalization and international governance

Throughout the nineteenth and twentieth centuries theorists of democracy have tended to assume a 'symmetrical' and 'congruent' relationship between political decision-makers and the recipients of political decisions. In fact, symmetry and congruence have often been taken for granted at two crucial points: first, between citizen-voters and the decision-makers whom they are, in principle, able to hold to account; and secondly, between the 'output' (decisions, policies and so on) of decision-makers and their constituents – ultimately, 'the people' in a delimited territory.

Even contemporary critics of modern democracies have tended to share this assumption; following the narrative of democracy as conventionally told, they have thought of the problem of political accountability as, above all, a national problem. Representative structures are, they hold, insufficiently responsive to their citizens; and, in discussing various forms of direct democracy, or in interpretations of the continuing relevance of republicanism, they place emphasis on making the political process more transparent and intelligible, more open to, and reflective of, the heterogeneous wants and needs of 'the people' (see Macpherson, 1977; Barber, 1984; Pateman, 1985).

But the problem, for defenders and critics alike of modern democratic systems, is that regional and global interconnectedness contests the traditional national resolutions of the key questions of democratic theory and practice. The very process of governance can escape the reach of the nation-state. National communities by no means exclusively make and determine decisions and policies for themselves, and governments by no means determine what is appropriate exclusively for their own citizens (Offe, 1985, pp. 286ff). To take some topical examples: a decision to increase interest rates in an attempt to stem inflation or exchange-rate instability is most often taken as a 'national' decision, although it may well stimulate economic changes in other countries. A decision to permit the 'harvesting' of the rainforests may contribute to ecological damage far beyond the borders which formally limit the responsibility of a given set of political decision-makers. A decision to build a nuclear plant near the frontiers of a neighbouring country is a decision likely to be taken without consulting those in the nearby country (or countries), despite the many risks and ramifications for them. A decision by a government to save resources by suspending food aid to a nation may stimulate the sudden escalation of food prices in that nation and contribute directly to an outbreak of famine among the urban and rural poor. These decisions, along with policies on issues as diverse as investment, arms procurement and AIDS, are typically regarded as falling within the legitimate domain of authority of a sovereign nation-state. Yet, in a world of regional and global interconnectedness, there are major questions to be put about the coherence, viability and accountability of national decision-making entities themselves.

Further, decisions made by quasi-regional or quasi-supranational organizations such as the European Union (EU), the North Atlantic Treaty Organization (NATO) or the International Monetary Fund (IMF) diminish the range of decisions open to given national 'majorities'. The idea of a community which rightly governs itself and determines its own future – an idea at the very heart of the democratic polity itself – is, accordingly, today deeply problematic. Any simple assumption in democratic theory that political relations are, or could be, 'symmetrical' or 'congruent' appears unjustified (see chapters 4–6).

If the inadequacy of this assumption can be fully shown, issues are raised which go to the heart of democratic thought and practice. The idea that *consent* legitimates government and the state system more generally has been central to nineteenth- and twentieth-century liberal democrats (Hanson, 1989, pp. 68–9). The latter have focused on the ballot box as the mechanism whereby the individual citizen expresses political preferences and citizens as a whole periodically confer authority on government to enact laws and regulate economic and social life. The principle of 'majority rule', or the principle that decisions which accrue the largest number of votes should prevail, is at the root of the claim of political decisions to be regarded as worthy or legitimate (cf. Dahl, 1989, chs 10 and 11). But the very idea of consent through elections, and the particular notion that the relevant constituencies of voluntary agreement are the communities of a bounded territory or a state, become problematic as soon as the issue of national, regional and global interconnectedness is considered and the nature of a so-called 'relevant community' is contested. Whose consent is necessary and whose participation is justified in decisions concerning, for instance, AIDS, or acid rain, or the use of non-renewable resources, or the management of transnational economic flows? What is the relevant constituency: national, regional or international? To whom do decision-makers have to justify their decisions? To whom should they be accountable? Further, what are the implications for the idea of legitimate rule of decisions taken in polities, with potentially life-and-death consequences for large numbers of people, many of whom might have no democratic stake in the decision-making process?

Territorial boundaries demarcate the basis on which individuals are included in and excluded from participation in decisions affecting their lives (however limited the participation might be), but the outcomes of these decisions often 'stretch' beyond national frontiers. The implications of this are considerable, not only for the categories of consent and legitimacy, but for all the key ideas of democracy: the nature of a constituency, the meaning of representation, the proper form and scope of political participation, and the relevance of the democratic nation-state, faced with unsettling patterns of relations and constraints in the international order, as the guarantor of the rights, duties and welfare of subjects.[4] Of course, these considerations would probably come as little surprise to those nations and countries whose independence and identity have been deeply affected by the hegemonic reach of empires, old and new, but they do come as a surprise to many in the West.

It could be objected that there is nothing new about global interconnections, and that the significance of global interconnections for democratic theory has in principle been plain for people to see for a long time. Such an objection could be developed by

[4] It was decisions of the European Court of Justice, for instance, which led to changes in British law in the 1980s on issues as far ranging as sexual discrimination and equal pay.

stressing that a dense pattern of global interconnections began to emerge with the initial expansion of the world economy and the rise of the modern state (see Wallerstein, 1974a; Anderson, P., 1974a). Four centuries ago, as one commentator succinctly put it, 'trade and war were already shaping every conceivable aspect of both domestic politics and the international system' (Gourevitch, 1978, p. 908). Domestic and international politics are interwoven throughout the modern era: domestic politics has always to be understood against the background of international politics; and the former is often the source of the latter. Whether one is reflecting on the monarchical politics of the sixteenth or seventeenth centuries (the question of whether, for instance, the king of France should be a Catholic or a Protestant), or seeking to understand the changing pattern of trade routes from East to West in the fifteenth and sixteenth centuries (and the way these changed the structure of towns, urban environments and the social balance), the examination of patterns of local and international interdependence and interpenetration seems inescapable (Gourevitch, 1978, pp. 908–11).

These considerations are concisely reflected in a classic study of diplomacy in Europe, *On the Manner of Negotiating with Princes*, published by Callières in 1716. As he wrote:

> To understand the permanent use of diplomacy, and the necessity for continual negotiations, we must think of the states of which Europe is composed as being joined together by all kinds of necessary commerce, in such a way that they may be regarded as members of one Republic, and that no considerable change can take place in any one of them without affecting the condition, or disturbing the peace, of all the others. The blunder of the smallest of sovereigns may indeed cast an apple of discord among all the greatest powers, because there is no state so great which does not find it useful to have relations with the lesser states and to seek friends among the different parties of which even the smallest state is composed. (1963, p. 11)

The complex interplay between state and non-state forces and actors is hardly a new or recent development: it would be quite misleading to maintain that political thought today faces a wholly novel set of political circumstances (Bull, 1977, pp. 278–80).

However, it is one thing to claim that there are elements of continuity in the formation and structure of modern states, economies and societies, quite another to claim that there is nothing new about aspects of their form and dynamics. For there is a fundamental difference between, on the one hand, the development of particular trade routes, or select military and naval operations or even the global reach of nineteenth-century empires, and, on the other hand, an international order involving the conjuncture of: dense networks of regional and global economic relations which stretch beyond the control of any single state (even of dominant states); extensive webs of transnational relations and instantaneous electronic communications over which particular states have limited influence; a vast array of international regimes and organizations which can limit the scope for action of the most powerful states; and the development of a global military order, and the build-up of the means of 'total' warfare as an enduring feature of the contemporary world, which can reduce the range of policies available to governments and their citizens. While trade routes and empires could link distant populations together in long loops of cause and effect, these links took a substantial period to establish and were only maintained with some difficulty (see Abu-Lughod, 1989). They were heavily dependent on face-to-face communication and, in its absence, on the direct movement of people, goods and messages using (what we would now consider) very slow systems of transportation and communication. Up to the 1830s, for example, a letter posted in England took between five and eight months to reach India, and an exchange of letters could take up to two years if affected by the monsoon seasons (see Thompson, 1995, ch. 5). By contrast, contemporary developments in the international order link people, communities and societies in highly complex ways and can, given the nature of modern communications, virtually annihilate distance and territorial boundaries as barriers to socio-economic activity.

Developments putting pressure on democratic polities are often referred to as part of the process of 'globalization'. Although the use of the term globalization will be subject to qualification later (see chapters 5 and 6), globalization can be taken to denote the stretching and deepening of social relations and institutions across space and time such that, on the one hand, day-to-day activities are increasingly influenced by events happening on the other side of the globe and, on the other, the practices and decisions of local groups or communities can have significant global reverberations. Accordingly, globalization can be conceived as 'action at distance' (see Giddens, 1990). The particular form of action at distance that is of concern here is engendered by the stretching and deepenin of relations across the borders of nation-states and at increasing intensity.

Globalization, thus interpreted, implies at least two distinct phenomena. First, it suggests that many chains of political, economic and social activity are becoming world-wide in scope. And, secondly, it suggests that there has been an intensification of levels of interaction and interconnectedness within and between states and societies (see McGrew, 1992a, pp. 1–28). What is new about the modern global system is the stretching of social relations in and through new dimensions of activity – technological, organizational, administrative and legal, among others – and the chronic intensification of patterns of interconnectedness mediated by such phenomena as modern communications networks and new information technology. Politics unfolds today, with all its customary uncertainty and indeterminateness, against the background of a world shaped and permeated by the movement of goods and capital, the flow of communication, the interchange of cultures and the passage of people (Kegley and Wittkopf, 1989, p. 511).

There is, accordingly, a striking paradox to note about the contemporary era: from Africa to Eastern Europe, Asia to Latin America, more and more nations and groups are championing the idea of 'the rule of the people'; but they are doing so at just that moment when the very efficacy of democracy as a national form of political organization appears open to question. As substantial areas of human activity are progressively organized on a global level, the fate of democracy, and of the independent democratic nation-state in particular, is fraught with difficulty. In this context, the meaning and place of democratic politics, and of the contending models of democracy, have to be rethought in relation to overlapping local, national, regional[5] and global structures and processes.

If the case for rethinking democracy in relation to the interconnectedness of states and societies is established successfully, a new agenda will have been created for democratic theory and practice.

[5] By a region, I mean here a cluster of nation-states in a geographical area which enjoy a high degree of interaction (relative to extra-regional interactions), share a number of common concerns and may cooperate with each other through limited membership organizations. Thus within Europe it is possible to identify the EU with the political and economic boundaries of an emerging regional community of states and societies, whilst in Southeast Asia the Association of South East Asian Nations (ASEAN) defines the boundaries of a developing regional complex.

It is important to be clear about the meaning of 'new' in this context. The agenda will not be new in the sense of being without precedent; others before have sought to understand the impact of the international order on the form and operation of domestic politics within democratic states. Others before have also sought to set out the normative implications of changes in the international order for the role and nature of democratic government. Nor will the agenda be new in the sense that traditional questions of democratic theory will be wholly displaced. On the contrary, questions will remain about the proper form of citizenship, the nature of individual rights and duties and the extent of participation and representation, for instance. But the agenda will be new to the extent that the case is made that a theory of democracy (whether focused on empirical or philosophical concerns) requires a theory of the interlocking processes and structures of the global system. For a theory of democracy must offer, it will be maintained, an account both of the changing meaning of democracy within the global order and of the impact of the global order on the development of democratic associations. Democratic institutions and practices have to be articulated with the complex arena of national and international politics, and the mutual interpenetration of the national and international must be mapped. Political understanding, and the successful pursuit of democratic political theory, are dependent on the outcome of these tasks.

In an age in which there are many determinants of the distribution of power, many power centres and authority systems operating within and across borders, the bases of politics and of democratic theory have to be recast. The meaning and nature of power, authority and accountability have to be re-examined. In what follows, I seek to do this and to argue that the concept of legitimate political power or authority has to be separated from its exclusive traditional association with states and fixed national borders, and that the conditions of its successful entrenchment depend on an international framework of political life, given form and shape by what I call 'cosmopolitan democratic law' or simply 'cosmopolitan law' (see chapters 10 and 11). I hasten to add, to avoid misunderstanding, that this does not entail abandoning the modern state as such – it will be with us for the foreseeable future – but rather coming to appreciate it as an element in a wider framework of political conditions, relations and associations. It will be argued, ultimately, that democracy can result from, and only from, a nucleus, or cluster, of democratic states and societies.

Or, to put the point differently, national democracies require an international cosmopolitan democracy if they are to be sustained and developed in the contemporary era. Paradoxically, perhaps, democracy has to be extended and deepened within and between countries for it to retain its relevance in the future. The chapters which follow provide, if they are compelling, an account of the form and limits of this new democratic project.

1.3 The limits of democratic political theory and international relations theory

The starting point of part II of the volume – the formation of the modern state – requires clarification. Ideas such as sovereignty, liberty and representative democracy, and the embodiment of these notions in institutions, laws and procedures, still carry with them the marks of their earliest formulation during the epoch in which the modern nation-state was being forged. Accordingly, if the nature and limits of the modern polity – that is, its 'reach' within territorial boundaries and its 'stretch' across them – are to be understood, it is important to grasp this historical context. However, the context of the modern polity has altered in many important respects over time, raising questions about the validity and continuing relevance of some of the core concepts of modern political thought. Part II addresses these changing conditions while parts III and IV unfold their implications for contemporary political theory and practice.

Unfortunately, the conceptual resources for such an exercise are not readily found in the traditions of either democratic political theory or international relations theory. It is evident, as already indicated, that nineteenth- and twentieth-century democratic political theory generally regarded the world beyond the state as a given – subject to a *ceteris paribus* clause.[6] The 'sovereignty' of the state was rarely questioned. It was generally assumed that the representative democratic state had control over its own fate, subject only to compromises it must make and limits imposed upon it by groups and forces operating within its territorial boundaries, and by agencies and representatives of other nation-states. Most of the leading perspectives on political and social change assumed,

[6] Among the honourable exceptions are the works of Laski, 1932, pp. 237ff; and Figgis, 1913, pp. 54–93. See also Hirst, 1989.

moreover, that the origins of societal transformation were to be found in processes internal to society (see Giddens, 1985; Mann, 1986; Dunn, 1990, pp. 123–41; cf. Weber, 1923, 1972a; Hintze, 1975). Change was presumed to occur via mechanisms 'built in', as it were, to the very structure of a given society, and governing its development. The world beyond the nation-state – the dynamics of the world economy, the intensification of transnational links, international law and institutions, for example – was barely theorized.

It is intriguing to note that conceptions of the state were not always like this. Early modern theorists of 'international society' – such as Grotius and Kant – sought to develop an understanding of the state in the context of the 'society of states' (see Bull, 1977, ch. 1; and chapter 10 of this volume). They explored the conditions and requirements of coexistence and cooperation among states, focusing in particular on the nature and extent of law-governed relations. These thinkers provided a crucial stimulus to the development of international law and to international political theory. While elements of their work survived in international law and international relations theory, they were all too often lost to political theory as a whole.[7] Given the deficiencies in the latter, it is hardly surprising if a political theorist or social scientist seeking to understand the position of the modern democratic polity in the global order turned to the well-established frameworks of international relations theory.

For much of this century the study of international relations has been dominated by the realist tradition (see Smith, S., 1987; Holsti, 1988). This tradition has often been referred to as 'statist', because it is almost exclusively concerned with how the global states system conditions the behaviour of individual states (Morgenthau, 1948; Waltz, 1979). Within realist thinking, the complex interplay of internal and external forces remains largely unexplored. For in the context of a global states system, the state is conceived principally as a sovereign, monolithic entity whose primary purpose is to promote and defend the national interest. At its simplest, the realist tradition views the state as a vehicle for securing national and international order through the exercise of national power. In some respects, the state is almost taken for granted, with its goals assumed and little or no internal differentiation among its

[7] For a fuller discussion of this thesis, see Held and McGrew, 1993, pp. 277–82, from which the following five paragraphs are adapted.

elements. Moreover, the categories 'state', 'nation-state' and 'nation' are often used interchangeably even though these terms should be reserved for distinct phenomena (see chapters 2 and 3 below).

However, realism has not completely failed to acknowledge the significance of processes of globalization (see, for example, Gilpin, 1981, 1987). Some elaborate explanations of the emergence of international regimes and intergovernmental cooperation have been developed (see Keohane, 1984a; cf. Mastanduno, Lake and Ikenberry, 1989, pp. 457–74). Behind this work is a strong sense of the continued primacy of the liberal democratic state in world politics combined with an explicit rejection of those accounts which interpret the intensification of global interconnectedness as portending a 'crisis of the modern nation-state'. But whilst 'neo-realism' has revived intellectual interest in 'the state' amongst international relations scholars, this has so far not been expressed in any systematic theoretical inquiry. Only in more sophisticated neo-realist analyses has the notion of 'the state' come to be explored with any rigour. Yet, even here, the state is conceived as little more than a sovereign, rational, egoistic actor on the global stage (Waltz, 1979; Keohane, 1986; Buzan, Jones and Little, 1993). Accordingly, there is not much evidence to suggest that realism and neo-realism possess a convincing account of the enmeshment of states with the wider global order, of the effects of the global order on states, and of the political implications of all this for the modern democratic state.

Some attempts to consider seriously the modern state within its web of global interconnectedness can be found in the rather diffuse literature which has its philosophical roots in the 'liberal-idealist' tradition in international relations (see Howard, 1981). The common thread uniting this particular school of thought is the assumption that increasing global interconnectedness is transforming the nature and role of the state in the global system (see Morse, 1976; Rosenau, 1988, 1990; Brown, 1988). In essence, this 'transformationalist' literature portrays the modern state as trapped within an extensive web of global interdependence, heavily permeated by transnational networks and forces, and increasingly unable to fulfil its core functions without recourse to international cooperation. A world of 'complex interdependence', it is argued, has dramatic implications for the sovereignty, autonomy and accountability of the state. Interdependence involves a sensitivity and vulnerability to external developments, compromising the independence of states, and crucially eroding the boundaries between the internal and external domains (see Keohane and Nye, 1989). Moreover, the growth of regional and global institutions is interpreted as further evidence of the limited capacity of the state to resolve independently the key policy problems which confront it.

But while such observations may be valid to a degree, the transformationalist literature has so far failed to provide a convincing or coherent account of the modern state itself. In particular, it tends to exaggerate the erosion of state power in the face of globalizing pressures and fails to recognize the enduring relevance of the modern state, both as an idea and as an institutional complex, in determining the direction of domestic and international politics. The degree to which the state enjoys 'autonomy' under various conditions is underestimated and, therefore, a key basis for a systematic and rigorous account of the modern state is too hastily put aside.

Many of the same developments which gave rise to the 'transformationalist' critique of realism have also provided fresh stimulus to radical approaches to international relations. World systems theory, and associated neo-Marxist projects, have engaged with the globalization of capitalism (see Wallerstein, 1974a, 1979, 1983, 1990, 1991; Sunkel and Fuenzelida, 1979; Cox, 1987). At the intellectual core of these approaches is an account of the modern state which stresses its limited autonomy from the dictates of transnational capital or from the structural requirements of the global capitalist order. States are thus conceived as partially autonomous political entities (Cox, 1987; Gill and Law, 1989). But while neo-Marxist attempts to confront the ramifications of economic globalization have led to a more sophisticated conceptualization of the state's relation to economic forces, significant issues remain largely unaddressed. In particular, the emphasis given to the relative autonomy of the state from transnational and national economic interests arises out of a recognition that the global states system has its own internal logic and imperatives. Yet, the formation and development of states tend to be explained primarily in terms of the global expansion of capitalism or Western-led modernization, that is, the state is conceived as an epiphenomenon (see Skocpol, 1977; Zolberg, 1981; Tilly, 1990). This failure to explore systematically the independent dynamics of the states system and to assess its relation to the operations of the world capitalist economy is a profound difficulty in many neo-Marxist analyses.

The traditional literature of democratic political theory and the existing frameworks of international relations theory have complementary limitations – limitations which must be overcome if a satisfactory understanding of the nature and prospects of democratic political power is to be achieved. Simply stated, there cannot be an account of the modern democratic state any longer without an examination of the global system and there cannot be an examination of the global system without an account of the democratic state. The way forward is to transcend the endogenous and exogenous frameworks of the theoretical traditions which have informed hitherto the analysis of the modern polity and international relations.

Accordingly, the chapters which follow in part II have four overall purposes: first, to introduce the fragmented and conflict-ridden context which forms the background conditions for the development of the modern state; secondly, to explore the question of why the liberal democratic nation-state became the supreme form of the modern state; thirdly, to examine the development of the inter-state system; and, fourthly, to assess the extent to which both the modern state and the inter-state system face erosion and decay in the face of globalizing structures and forces. These objectives are clearly wide-ranging; but by devoting attention to all four some light can be shed on the key formative processes of the modern state and on the contemporary controversies about its future. However, several steps need to be taken back in time before addressing contemporary political matters.

Part II

Analysis: The Formation and Displacement of the Modern State

2
The Emergence of Sovereignty and the Modern State

The formation of the modern state needs to be understood against the backdrop of the political divisions and religious conflicts which followed the break-up of the medieval world, and the new controversies about the nature of political authority which emerged at this time. This backdrop makes it possible to appreciate the key institutional and conceptual innovations of the modern state, and thus to highlight how discussion about the proper nature and form of political community developed. The concept of sovereignty mediated the rise of the modern state and framed the development of democracy and the processes by which it was consolidated. The aim of this chapter is to sketch these relationships. By doing so, the basis is provided for exploring, in the following chapter, how the modern state became the primary focus of public decision-making and how the liberal democratic nation-state became the dominant form of the modern state over time.

The central point of reference will be the making of the modern state in Europe. There are a number of important reasons for this geographic restriction. In the first instance, the story of the formation of the modern state is in part the story of the formation of Europe, and vice versa. The development of a distinctive 'European' identity is closely tied to the creation of Europe by states. Moreover, the states system of Europe has had extraordinary influence in the world beyond Europe: European expansion and development have had a decisive role in shaping the political map of the modern world. Furthermore, debates about the nature of the modern state in large part derive from European intellectual traditions, although to recognize this is by no means to claim, of course, that everything of importance about the state has been said in Europe alone.

It needs to be emphasized that 'Europe' was the creation of many complex developments at the intersection of 'internal' and 'external' processes and forces. A thousand years ago Europe as such did not exist. The roughly thirty million people who lived across the European land mass did not conceive of themselves as an interconnected people (Tilly, 1990, p. 38). The larger power divisions which crystallized in 'Millennial Europe' to some extent masked the area's fragmented and decentred nature (see McEvedy, 1961, p. 53). Those who prevailed over territories did so above all as military victors and conquerors, exacting tribute and rent to support their endeavours; they were far from being heads of state governing clearly demarcated territories according to formal law and procedure.

Yet one can talk about the beginnings of a recognizable states system at the Millennium. In the Italian peninsula, the pope, the Holy Roman emperor and the Byzantine emperor claimed most of the territory, even though these claims intermingled and were contested routinely by many localized powers and independent and semi-autonomous cities. But the political map of Europe was to be shaped and reshaped many times. For example, the European map of the late fifteenth century included some five hundred more or less independent political units, often with ill-defined boundaries. By 1900 the number had dwindled to about twenty-five (see Tilly, 1975). Although it took a long time for national states to dominate the political map, as § 2.1 shows, the era they ushered in was to change fundamentally the nature and form of political life itself.

2.1 From divided authority to the centralized state

The political system of overlapping power and divided authority which dominated Europe between the eighth and the fourteenth centuries – better known as feudalism – assumed many forms. But it is probably fair to say that it was distinguished in general by a network of interlocking ties and obligations, with systems of rule fragmented into many small, autonomous parts (Poggi, 1978, p. 27). Political power was local and personal in focus, generating a 'social world of overlapping claims and powers' (Anderson, P. 1974a,

p. 149). Some of these claims and powers conflicted; and no ruler or state was sovereign in the sense of being supreme over a given territory and population (Bull, 1977, p. 254). Within this system of power, tensions were rife and war was frequent.

Within the medieval world the economy was dominated by agriculture, and any surplus generated was subject to competing claims. A successful claim constituted a basis to create and sustain political power. But the web of kingdoms, principalities, duchies and other power centres which depended on these arrangements was complicated further by the emergence of alternative powers in the towns and cities. Cities and urban federations depended on trade and manufacture and relatively high accumulations of capital. They developed different social and political structures and frequently enjoyed independent systems of rule specified by charters. While Florence, Venice and Siena were to become among the best-known cities, hundreds of urban centres developed across Europe. Nowhere, however, did they (and the web of feudal relations in the countryside) alone determine the pattern of rule or political identity. For in the Middle Ages 'Europe' more accurately meant 'Christendom'. And the papacy and the Holy Roman Empire gave Christendom what overarching unity it had.

The Holy Roman Empire existed in some form from the eighth until the early nineteenth century. At its height, it represented an attempt, under the patronage of the Catholic Church, to unite and centralize the fragmented power centres of Western Christendom into a politically unified Christian empire. The countries federated under the empire spread from Germany to Spain, and from northern France to Italy. However, the actual secular power of the empire was always limited by the complex power structures of feudal Europe on the one hand, and the Catholic Church on the other. The Church itself was the chief rival power to feudal and city networks. Throughout the Middle Ages, it consistently sought to place spiritual above secular authority, and to shift the source of recognized authority and wisdom from this-worldly to other-worldly representatives. The Christian world-view transformed the rationale of political action from an earthly to a theological framework; it insisted that the good lay in submission to God's will.

In medieval Europe there was no alternative 'political theory' to the theocratic positions of pope and Holy Roman emperor. The integration of Christian Europe came to depend above all on these authorities. This order has been characterized as the order of 'international Christian society' (Bull, 1977, p. 27; cf. Kennedy, 1988, ch. 1). International Christian society was conceived as being Christian first and foremost; it looked to God for the authority to resolve disputes and conflicts; its primary political reference point was religious doctrine; and it was overlaid with assumptions about the universal nature of human community. It has been succinctly depicted by Gierke:

> the Constitutive Principle of the Universe is in the first place Unity. God, the absolutely One, is before and above all the World's Plurality, and is the one source and one goal of every Being. Divine Reason as an Ordinance for the Universe (*lex aeterna*) permeates all apparent plurality. Divine Will is ever and always active in the uniform government of the World, and is directing all that is manifold to one end only. (1987, p. 8)

It was not until Western Christendom was under challenge, especially from the conflicts generated by the rise of national states and by the Reformation, that the idea of the modern state was born, and the ground was created for the development of a new form of political identity – national identity.

Some date the crisis of feudalism as early as 1300. But whether or not one accepts this date, the decay of feudalism can be detected over a substantial period as competing claims to more extensive and penetrating political power were fought out in the context of the structural economic problems of the fourteenth century.[1] From the fifteenth to the eighteenth century two different forms of political regime crystallized in Europe: the 'absolute' monarchies in France, Prussia, Austria, Spain and Russia, among other places, and the 'constitutional' monarchies and republics found in England and Holland. There are important conceptual and institutional differences between these regime types, although in terms

[1] For over two hundred years the population of Europe had expanded without significant increases in agricultural productivity, generating economic, ecological and demographic pressures. Good agricultural land was in short supply and labour was plentiful. Against the background of the Black Death of the 1340s and 1350s, however, the balance of power shifted between feudal nobility and serfs: labour became scarce, the capacity to extract dues from tenants was reduced, land was abandoned by growing numbers of peasants (especially in the East), and agricultural relations went through a period of dramatic change (see McNeil, 1977; cf. Anderson, P., 1974a, pp. 182–209). The fragmentation of the feudal polity was underwritten by a diminution of feudal economic power.

of the history of state/society relations some of the differences have been more apparent than real. Constitutional states will be discussed later, while the focus in the first instance will be on absolutism.

Absolutism signalled the emergence of a form of state based upon: the absorption of smaller and weaker political units into larger and stronger political structures; a strengthened ability to rule over a unified territorial area; a tightened system of law and order enforced throughout a territory; the application of a 'more unitary, continuous, calculable, and effective' rule by a single, sovereign head; and the development of a relatively small number of states engaged in an 'open-ended, competitive, and risk-laden power struggle' (Poggi, 1978, pp. 60–1). Although the actual power of absolutist rulers has often been exaggerated, these changes marked a substantial increase in 'public authority' from above.[2] Certainly, absolutist rulers claimed that they alone held the legitimate right of decision over state affairs. One of the most remarkable statements of this view has been attributed to Louis XV:

> In my person alone resides the sovereign power, and it is from me alone that the courts hold their existence and their authority. That... authority can only be exercised in my name.... For it is to me exclusively that the legislative power belongs.... The whole public order emanates from me since I am its supreme guardian.... The rights and interests of the nation... are necessarily united with my own and can only rest in my hands. (quoted in Schama, 1989, p. 104)

The absolutist monarch claimed to be the ultimate authority on all matters of human law, although it is important to note that this broad writ was understood to derive from the law of God. The king's legitimacy was based on 'divine right'. In this very particular sense, political authorities were regarded as being as much under the law as any other corporate institution (Benn and Peters, 1959, p. 256).

The absolutist monarch was at the apex of a new system of rule which was progressively centralized and anchored on a claim to supreme and indivisible power: sovereign power or sovereignty (see § 2.2. below). This system was manifest in the monarch's

[2] Instructive contrasts can be drawn between the nature of absolutism in the West and East; see Anderson, P., 1974b.

'public' personage and in the routines and rituals of courtly life. However, linked to the latter there developed a new administrative apparatus involving the beginnings of a permanent, professional bureaucracy and army (Mann, 1986, ch. 14). If the French monarchy of the seventeenth century represents the best example of an absolutist court, Prussia under the Hohenzollern dynasty provides the best example of the 'prototypes of ministries' (Poggi, 1990, p. 48). These 'prototypes' increased the state's involvement in the promotion and regulation of a hitherto unparalleled diversity of activities. This shift towards the vertical integration of political power involved an alliance between the monarchy and some key social groups, notably the nobility, who sought to consolidate an infrastructure of military and revenue-raising capacity in the face of a more independent peasantry, and the emerging centres of urban power and wealth.

Six ensuing developments were of great significance in the history of the states system: (1) the growing coincidence of territorial boundaries with a uniform system of rule; (2) the creation of new mechanisms of law-making and enforcement; (3) the centralization of administrative power; (4) the alteration and extension of fiscal management; (5) the formalization of relations among states through the development of diplomacy and diplomatic institutions; and (6) the introduction of a standing army (see Anderson, P., 1974b, pp. 15–42; and Giddens, 1985, ch. 4). Absolutism helped set in motion a process of state-making which began to reduce the social, economic and cultural variation *within* states and expand the variation *among* them (Tilly, 1975, p. 19).

By the end of the seventeenth century Europe was no longer a mosaic of states. For the gradual consolidation of the independent sovereignty of each state was at the same time part of a process of the development of the inter-state system (see chapters 3 and 4). A concomitant of each and every state's claim to uncontestable authority was the recognition that such a claim gave other states an equal entitlement to autonomy and respect within their own borders. The development of state sovereignty was part of a process of mutual recognition whereby states granted each other rights of jurisdiction in their respective territories and communities.

Absolutism and the inter-state system it initiated were the proximate sources of the modern state. In condensing and concentrating political power in its own hands, and in seeking to create a central system of rule, absolutism paved the way for a secular and national system of power. Moreover, in claiming sovereign authority exclusively for itself, it threw down a challenge to all those groups and classes which had had a stake in the old order, and to all those with a stake in the developing order based on capital and the market economy. It forced all these collectivities to rethink their relationship to the state, and to re-examine their political resources. In addition, the myriad battles and wars fought out in the inter-state system altered fundamentally the boundaries of both absolutist states and the emerging modern states – the whole map of Europe changed as territorial boundaries gradually became fixed borders.

However, the formation of the *idea* of the modern state itself probably received its clearest impetus from the bitter struggles between religious factions which spread across Western Europe during the last half of the sixteenth century, and reached their most intense expression during the Thirty Years War in Germany (see Sigler, 1983). The theocratic concepts of authority which had dominated medieval Europe were challenged in the wake of the Reformation. The Reformation did more than just question papal jurisdiction and authority across Europe; it raised concerns about political obligation and obedience in a most stark manner. Whether allegiance was owed to the Catholic Church, a Protestant ruler or particular religious sects was not an issue easily resolved. Very gradually it became apparent that the powers of the state would have to be differentiated from the duty of rulers to uphold any particular faith (Skinner, 1978, vol. 2, p. 352). This conclusion alone offered a way forward through the dilemmas of rule created by competing religions, all seeking to secure for themselves the kinds of privilege claimed by the medieval church.

It was only when political rights, obligations and duties were no longer closely tied to religious tradition or property rights that the idea of an impersonal and sovereign political order – a legally delimited structure of political power – could predominate. Similarly, it was only when human beings were no longer thought of as merely dutiful subjects of God, an emperor or a monarch that the notion could begin to take hold that they, as 'individuals', 'persons' or 'a people', were capable of being active citizens of a new political order – citizens of their state. The emergence of the modern state signalled a new discursive terrain, embodying claims to sovereignty, independence, representativeness and legitimacy, which radically recast traditional understandings of law, community and politics.

2.2 The modern state and the discourse of sovereignty

The core of the idea of the modern state is an impersonal and privileged legal or constitutional order, delimiting a common structure of authority, which specifies the nature and form of control and administration over a given community (see Skinner, 1978, vol. 2, p. 353).[3] This order was announced, most notably by Jean Bodin and Thomas Hobbes, as a distinct form of public power, separate from both ruler and ruled, and constituting the supreme political reference point within a specific community and territory.[4] And it was an idea constructed, at least initially, with the clear purpose of both denying a people the right to determine their own political identity independently of their sovereign (whether their motives were secular or religious), and denying a sovereign the right to act with impunity against a given population or people (see Dunn, 1992, pp. 247–9). As a result, the state came to be defined as a phenomenon independent of subjects and rulers, with particular properties of its own. In the language of the times, it was an 'artificiall Person', quite distinct from the person or assembly who must bear or represent it. Moreover, it was in the name of this 'Person' that rulers could legitimately rule and demand loyalty from their subjects, and subjects could legitimately expect secure and non-arbitrary government. This 'Person' could, thus, be understood as the subject of sovereignty – a determinate structure of laws and institutions with a life and standing of its own.

The idea of sovereignty is closely linked to the idea of the modern state. While the concept of sovereignty can be traced to the Roman Empire, it was not until the second half of the sixteenth century that it developed as a major theme in political thought.

[3] The discussion of the idea of the modern state which follows is indebted to Quentin Skinner (1978, vol. 2, 1989a, 1989b). His account of this idea has been a point of orientation in my attempt to rethink the foundations of modern democratic governance.

[4] To what extent this new form of political control was actually conceived as extending over a bounded territory is, in early-modern political theory at least, a somewhat open and controversial question (see Baldwin, 1992).

Sovereignty became a new way of thinking about an old problem: the nature of power and rule. When established forms of authority could no longer be taken for granted, it was the idea of sovereignty which provided a fresh link between political power and rulership. In the struggle between church, state and community, sovereignty offered an alternative way of conceiving the legitimacy of claims to power. In the debate about sovereignty which ensued, differing accounts were offered of the proper locus of 'supreme power' in society, the source of authority for that power, limitations upon that power, and the ends to which that power might or should be directed. But as the theory of sovereignty developed from Bodin to Hobbes, from Locke to Rousseau, it became a theory of the possibility of, and the conditions of, the rightful exercise of political power. The theory developed two overriding preoccupations: a concern with where sovereign authority properly lay; and a concern with the proper form and limits – the legitimate scope – of state action (Hinsley, 1986, pp. 222–3). It became, thus, the theory of legitimate power or authority and, as such, is of crucial significance to the arguments which follow concerning the role and locus of political authority, and the relationship between the state and democracy, in a more secular age.

State sovereignty

Reflecting on the religious and civil conflicts of the sixteenth century, Bodin contended that they could only be solved if it was possible to establish the existence of a supreme power competent to overrule all religious and customary authorities. He argued strenuously that an 'ordered commonwealth' depended upon the creation of a central authority which could wield decisive power within a specified community. While Bodin was not the first to make this case (see Machiavelli, 1983, especially book 1), he developed this notion into what is commonly regarded as the first statement of the modern theory of sovereignty: that there must be within every political community or state a determinate sovereign body whose powers are recognized by the community as the rightful or legitimate basis of authority.

Bodin developed one of the most celebrated definitions of sovereignty. Sovereignty, in this account, is the untrammelled and undivided power to make laws. It is the supreme power over subjects; 'the right to impose laws generally on all subjects regardless of their consent' (1967, 1, 8, p. 32). Law is, accordingly, 'nothing else than the command of the sovereign in the exercise of his sovereign power' (1967, 1, 8, p. 35). The sovereign has the capacity to make and alter the law for all his subjects. 'There are none on earth, after God, greater than sovereign princes, whom God establishes as His lieutenants to command the rest of mankind' (1967, 1, 10, p. 40). The sovereign 'cannot be subject to the commands of another', for it is the sovereign that 'makes law for the subject' (1967, 1, 8, p. 28). Sovereign power is properly exercised if it is exercised 'simply and unconditionally' (1967, 1, 8, p. 26).

Sovereignty, in Bodin's thought, is the defining characteristic or constitutive power of the state. While the sovereign is the rightful head of the state, he is so by virtue of his office not his person. A ruler exercises power in the light of his possession of sovereignty, which is a temporary 'gift' and not a personal attribute (Skinner, 1989b, lecture 2). Different types of state can be differentiated according to the locus of this supreme power – monarchy, aristocracy and democracy. However, Bodin's clear preference was for a monarchical polity with a just form of government: a monarchy which would temper power with respect for law and justice. Sovereignty properly exercised, or good government, is subject to the laws of God and of nature as well as to the fundamental or customary rights and laws of the political community (1967, 1, 8, pp. 29 and 33). Sovereignty may be unlimited, but the sovereign is bound in morals and religion to respect the laws of God, nature and custom.[5]

It was Hobbes, however, who was the first to grasp fully the nature of public power as a special kind of institution – an 'Artificiall Man', defined by permanence and sovereignty, 'giving life and motion' to society and the body politic (1968, p. 81). In his famous 'thought experiment' about the 'Warre of every one against every one', individuals discover that life is 'solitary, poor, nasty,

[5] In maintaining this position – in championing, on the one hand, the exercise of supreme power to make and enforce the law and, on the other, necessary limits upon this power – Bodin has been charged with inconsistency. However, this particular criticism misses the mark; for Bodin's primary concern is with lawful government (see, for example, 1967, 1, 8, p. 36). An additional suggestion made by Bodin, that sovereignty can and ought to be limited by constitutional laws, raises further difficulties for the coherence of his position, but even these do not necessarily raise decisive problems (Bodin, 1967, 1, 8, p. 31; see Benn, 1967; King, P., 1974; Parker, 1981).

brutish and short' and, accordingly, that to avoid harm and the risk of an early death, let alone to ensure the conditions of greater comfort, the observation of certain natural laws or rules is required (1968, ch. 13). The latter are things the individual ought to adhere to in dealings with others if there is sufficient ground for believing that others will do likewise. Hobbes says of these laws that 'they have been contracted into one easy sum, intelligible even to the meanest capacity; and that is, *Do not that to another which thou wouldest not have done to thyself*' (see 1968, chs 14 and 15).

Hobbes holds that individuals ought willingly to surrender their rights of self-government to a powerful single authority – thereafter authorized to act on their behalf – because, if all individuals do this simultaneously, the condition would be created for effective political rule, and for security and peace in the long term. A unique relation of authority would be created – the relation of sovereign to subject – and a unique political power would be established: sovereign power or sovereignty – the authorized, hence rightful, use of state powers by the person or assembly established as sovereign. The sovereign's subjects would have an obligation and duty to obey the sovereign; for the office of 'sovereign' is the product of their agreement, and 'sovereignty' is a quality of this agreed position rather than of the person who occupies it.

The conferment of the rights of self-government is the basis, Hobbes argued, of the 'unity of all' – a unity which must be borne or carried by the sovereign (1968, p. 220). Conferment constitutes 'the person of the commonwealth', the 'artificiall Person' or state which itself must be brought to life through a process of impersonation or representation (1968, p. 217). While sovereignty is created by the act of conferment, the office of sovereign is formed through the conferment of the right of impersonation (pp. 227–8). Sovereignty inheres in the distinctive form or 'Person' of public power; the sovereign acts in the name of this person, that is, in the name of the state (Skinner, 1989b, lecture 2).

The sovereign has to have sufficient power to ensure that the laws governing political and economic life are upheld. Since, in Hobbes's view, 'men's ambitions, avarice, anger and other passions' are strong, the 'bonds of words are too weak to bridle them . . . without some fear of coercive power': 'covenants, without the sword, are but words, and of no strength to secure a man at all' (1968, p. 223). Beyond the state's sphere of influence there will always be the threat of constant warfare; but within the territory controlled by the state, with its laws, institutions and coercive powers, social order can be sustained. States can, in principle, be peaceful and prosperous islands within seas of potential conflict.

It is important to stress that, in Hobbes's opinion, sovereignty must be self-perpetuating, undivided and ultimately absolute (1968, pp. 227–8). The justification for this is '*the safety of the people*' (1968, p. 376). By 'safety' is meant not merely minimum physical preservation. The sovereign must ensure the protection of all things held in property: '[T]hose that are dearest to a man are his own life, and limbs; and in the next degree, (in most men) those that concern conjugall affection; and after them riches and means of living' (1968, pp. 382–3). Hobbes affirms repeatedly certain clear delimitations on the range of the sovereign's actions: the sovereign has the warrant neither to injure individuals nor to harm the basis of their material wellbeing, and should recognize that authority can be sustained only so long as protection is afforded to all subjects (see 1968, ch. 21). Indeed, government can be judged to the degree to which it produces 'the Peace, and Security of the people', for which end it was instituted (1968, p. 241).

With Hobbes, the justification of state power received its fullest articulation. At issue were the conditions of a political order free of strife and internal disturbance – an order that could endure beyond the clamourings of religious interests and the pursuit of sectional aims. Hobbes was not seeking to persuade his contemporaries to enter into a contract to create a state, but to accept that there were good grounds for acting as if they had and, thus, good grounds for accepting a full obligation to the sovereign state (Macpherson, 1968, p. 45). But Hobbes's position was, of course, controversial and challenged on at least two grounds (see Hinsley, 1986, pp. 144ff). The first of these raised the fundamental question of where sovereignty properly lay, with the state, the ruler, the monarch or (as was increasingly to be argued) the people; the second was concerned with the proper form and limits, the legitimate scope, of state action.

Popular sovereignty

Elements of an alternative to the theory of state sovereignty can be found in the arguments of John Locke, who, among others, sought to provide an account of both public and private right. Locke approved of the revolution and settlement of 1688 in England, which imposed certain constitutional limits on the authority of the crown. In Locke's view, the formation of a governmental apparatus does not signal the transfer of all subjects' rights to the political realm (1963, pp. 402–3, para. 135 and pp. 412–13, para. 149). As he famously put it: 'This is to think that Men are so foolish that they take care to avoid what Mischiefs may be done them by *Pole-Cats*, or *Foxes*, but are content, nay think it Safety, to be devoured by *Lions*' (1963, p. 372; see also n. 36 on the same page). While the rights of law-making and enforcement (legislative and executive rights) are rightly transferred, the whole process should be conceived as conditional upon government adhering to its essential purpose: the preservation of 'life, liberty and estate'. The institutions of government are properly founded if they serve to protect citizens; that is, if they uphold individuals' rights to pursue their own objectives, to dispose of their own labour and to possess their own property.

It is important to emphasize that, in Locke's account, political authority is bestowed by individuals on government for the purpose of pursuing the ends of the governed; and should these ends fail to be represented adequately, the final judges are the people – the citizens – who can dispense both with their deputies and, if need be, with the existing form of government itself. The government rules, and its legitimacy is sustained, by the 'consent' of individuals. 'Consent' is a crucial and difficult notion in Locke's writings. It could be interpreted to suggest that only the continually active personal agreement of individuals would be sufficient to ensure a duty of obedience, that is, to ensure a government's authority and legitimacy (see Plamenatz, 1963, p. 228). However, Locke seems to have thought of the active consent of individuals as having been crucial only to the initial inauguration of a legitimate state.[6] Thereafter, consent ought to follow from majority decisions of 'the people's' representatives, so long as they uphold the rule of law and earn the trust of citizens (cf. Lukes, 1973, pp. 80–1; Dunn, 1980, pp. 36–7). Faced with a series of tyrannical political acts, rebellion to form a new government might be not only unavoidable but justified. For if a ruler puts himself into a state of war with his subjects, by using force against their interests outside the framework of what is legally permissible, he destroys his own authority; and under these circumstances, each subject has the right to resist him as they would any other unjust aggressor

[6] Strictly speaking, one should refer here to a legitimate 'civil association', for Locke never wrote of 'the state' as such.

(Dunn, 1984, p. 54). 'Where-ever Law ends Tyranny begins' (Locke, 1963, p. 448, para. 202).

With these arguments Locke fashioned a doctrine which was at odds in fundamental respects with the Hobbesian concept of the state, and which was to have considerable influence on the world of democratic politics. For it stipulated that supreme power was the inalienable right of the people; that governmental supremacy was a delegated supremacy held on trust; that government enjoyed full political authority so long as this trust was sustained; and that a government's legitimacy or right to rule could be withdrawn if the people judged this necessary and appropriate, that is, if the rights of individuals and the 'ends of society' were systematically flouted.

However, with these arguments Locke's position also ran into distinct difficulties, difficulties common to all those positions which invest, in the last instance, untrammelled authority in 'the people'. For he did not resolve, or explore systematically, tensions between the sovereignty of the people – the idea of the people as the active sovereign body with the capacity to make or break governments – and government – as the institution with the right to make and enforce the law. At the root of this problem lay a failure to draw an effective contrast between the power of the people and the powers of the state (Skinner, 1989a, p. 115). As Locke put it, 'the *Community* perpetually *retains a Supream Power*' over its prince or legislature (1963, p. 413; see also p. 477). Accordingly, what constitutes the precise autonomy or independence of state powers remains unspecified. If government is entrusted with the power of the people, what can be its distinctive claim to independence and impartiality, if any? Must not government be entrusted with the powers of the state in order to offer, as Bodin and Hobbes held, a coherent account of itself, as a law-maker and political arbiter?

Contrary to the terms of this question, Rousseau insisted, perhaps more forcefully than anyone before or after him, that a coherent account of political power requires an explicit and formal acknowledgement that sovereignty *originates* in the people and ought to *stay* there. In his judgement, sovereignty cannot be represented or alienated (1968, p. 141). For the very essence of sovereignty is the creation, authorization and enactment of the law according to the standards and requirements of the common good. And the nature of the common good can only be known through public discourse, deliberation and agreement. Only citizens themselves can articulate 'the supreme direction of the general will' –

it is the sum of their publicly generated judgements about the common good (1968, pp. 60–1). Moreover, Rousseau maintained that citizens can only be fully obligated to a system of laws and regulations they have prescribed for themselves with the general good in mind (1968, p. 65; cf. p. 82). In order to grasp Rousseau's position, it is important to distinguish the 'general will' from the 'will of all': it is the difference, he argues, between the sum of judgements about the common good and the mere aggregate of personal fancies and individual desires (1968, pp. 72–3 and 75).

Taking arguments about sovereignty in a new direction, Rousseau held that, ideally, individuals should be involved directly in the creation of the laws by which their lives are regulated. For sovereign authority is formed by the general will – the deliberative judgements about the common good made by people in their capacity as citizens. All citizens should meet together to decide what is best for the community and enact the appropriate laws. The ruled should be the rulers: the affairs of the state should be integrated into the affairs of ordinary citizens (see 1968, pp. 82 and 114, and for a general account, book 3, chs 1–5). Rousseau was critical of the Athenian conception of direct democracy because it failed to incorporate a division between legislative and executive functions and, consequently, became prone to instability, internecine strife and indecision in crisis (1968, pp. 112–14 and pp. 136ff). But while he wished to defend the importance of dividing and limiting 'governmental power', the executive or government in his scheme was legitimate only to the extent to which it fulfilled 'the instructions of the general will'. The 'artificiall Person' was the general will – generated by the people and 'impersonated' by the executive. In so arguing, Rousseau follows Hobbes in holding that executive power is derived from the conferment of the right of impersonation, but he represents an opposing position to Hobbes in the debate about the locus of sovereignty.

However, both Hobbes and Rousseau cast their arguments in such a way as to face a common objection: that they projected models of political power with potentially tyrannical implications. Hobbes placed the state in a practically all-powerful position with respect to the community; although the sovereign's activities were in principle circumscribed by an obligation to maintain the safety of the people, the people's rights to self-government were wholly alienated and the community left with no effective checks against the rule of 'mortall gods'. Hobbes defined sharply the idea of the modern state, but the relationship of this idea to the people, that is, the relationship between the powers of the state and the power of the people, was resolved only by surrendering the latter to the former. Ultimately, the state was pre-eminent in all spheres, authorized to represent all individuals, and in danger of absorbing all public and private right. Rousseau, by contrast, placed the community (or a majority thereof) in a position to dominate individual citizens – the community was all-powerful and, therefore, the sovereignty of the people could easily destroy the liberty of individuals (Berlin, 1969, p. 163).

Just as Hobbes failed to articulate the principles and institutions necessary to delimit state action and hold it to account, so Rousseau assumed that minorities ought to consent to the decisions of majorities, and posited no limits to the reach of the decisions of a democratic majority, and therefore to political intervention. Thus, Rousseau undermined the distinction between the state and the community, the government and the people, but in the opposite direction to Hobbes. The state was reduced to a 'commission'; 'the public' absorbed all elements of the body politic.

In sum

The centralized state was initially the domain of rulers who claimed formidable powers for themselves. But the discourse of sovereignty set in motion a debate about this claim and about the standing of the state in relation to other corporate bodies and collectivities. As the idea of state sovereignty became more clearly articulated and as the state's sphere of authority expanded, there were effects beyond the concentration of political power at the apex.

The idea of state sovereignty was the source of the idea of impersonal state power. But it was also the legitimating framework of a centralized power system in which all social groups in the long run wanted a stake. How elements of both state and popular sovereignty were to be combined coherently remained far from settled. As the next chapter shows, the modern state became the primary site in which competing collectivities and groups sought to struggle over rule systems and scarce resources; and it also became the organizational basis on which rulers and subjects mobilized in their competitive struggles with groups beyond their boundaries. While the concept of the modern state projected the possibility of impartial administration and accountability within communities, it did not make the extension of these notions across peoples and nations a central part of the meaning of the new conception of political community. Political community had come to be linked – if not by all early modern political theorists,[7] then by changing political and social circumstance – to fixed borders.

[7] Rousseau, for instance, explored the possibility of connecting Europe's political communities together in a union of European states, although he was sceptical about the feasibility of such an idea (see 1962). For a survey of Rousseau's views, and of those of his contemporaries interested in similar questions, see Archibugi, 1992.

3

THE DEVELOPMENT OF THE NATION-STATE AND THE ENTRENCHMENT OF DEMOCRACY

Modern states developed as nation-states – political apparatuses, distinct from both ruler and ruled, with supreme jurisdiction over a demarcated territorial area, backed by a claim to a monopoly of coercive power, and enjoying legitimacy as a result of a minimum level of support or loyalty from their citizens. This conception of the modern state underscores a number of its most prominent innovations, including:

1 *Territoriality.* While all states have made claims to territories, it is only with the modern states system that exact borders have been fixed.
2 *Control of the means of violence.* The claim to hold a monopoly on force and the means of coercion (sustained by a standing army and the police) became possible only with the 'pacification' of peoples – the breaking down of rival centres of power and authority – in the nation-state. This element of the modern state was not fully attained until the nineteenth century, and remained a fragile achievement in many countries.
3 *Impersonal structure of power.* The idea of an impersonal and sovereign political order – that is, a legally circumscribed structure of power with supreme jurisdiction over a territory – could not prevail while political rights, obligations and duties were conceived as closely tied to religion and the claims of traditionally privileged groups. This matter remained in

contention in Europe in the eighteenth and nineteenth centuries, and still remains so in those countries today where the 'rule of law' is in question.

4 *Legitimacy*. It was only when claims to 'divine right' or 'state right' were challenged and eroded that it became possible for human beings as 'individuals' and as 'peoples' to win a place as 'active citizens' in the political order. The loyalty of citizens became something that had to be *won* by modern states: invariably this involved a claim by the state to be legitimate because it reflected and/or represented the views and interests of its citizens.

Of course, the above conception of the modern state, like all definitions in political analysis, is controversial. It is controversial because it tends to run together the two notions of the modern state, noted in the previous chapter, which in principle ought to be kept separate – the notion of the modern state as a circumscribed system of power which provides a regulatory mechanism and check on rulers and ruled alike, and the notion of the modern state as a democratic political community in which 'rulers' are representatives of, and accountable to, their citizens. But the possible tensions between these ideas will simply be noted here; for they will be addressed and explored later (see part III). The justification for postponing this discussion is that in the making of the modern state itself these ideas were often linked, if not elided, especially in what eventually came to be the dominant form of the modern state: the liberal democratic nation-state.

A further clarification should be made at this juncture. The concept of the nation-state, or national state, as some prefer, ought not to be taken to imply that a state's people necessarily 'share a strong linguistic, religious, and symbolic identity' (Tilly, 1990, pp. 2–3). Although some nation-states approximate to this state of affairs, many do not (for example, Britain, where significant differences in national tradition remain). It is therefore important to separate out the concepts of 'nation-state' and 'nationalism'. One commentator has made the point succinctly: 'what makes the "nation" integral to the nation-state . . . is not the existence of sentiments of nationalism but the unification of an administrative apparatus over precisely defined territorial boundaries' (Giddens, 1987, p. 172). The concept of 'nationalism' – denoting the existence of symbols and beliefs which create patterns of ethnic, or religious, or linguistic commonality and political ambition – should be reserved for highlighting particular types of configuration of peoples and states (cf. Hont, 1994).

It has been argued that the difference between absolute and modern states is not as great as conventionally thought, for two reasons (see Mann, 1986, pp. 450–99). First, absolutist states had less power over civil society than is frequently claimed. Second, modern states are rarely 'bounded' by their constitutions and borders and, hence, have often behaved like arrogant 'absolutist' states, especially in their dealings with peoples and cultures overseas. Both points carry weight and need to be borne in mind in what follows. However, neither point negates fully the conceptual and institutional innovations introduced by the modern state. In order to highlight these, it is useful to draw attention to a number of forms of the modern state itself. These are the constitutional state, the liberal state, the liberal democratic state, and the single-party polity.

Forms of the modern state

1 *Constitutionalism* or the *constitutional state* refers to implicit and/ or explicit limits on political or state decision-making, limits which can be either procedural or substantive; that is, specifying how decisions and changes can be made (proceduralism), or blocking certain kinds of change altogether (substantivism) (see Elster, 1988). Constitutionalism defines the proper forms and limits of state action, and its elaboration over time as a set of doctrines and practices helped inaugurate one of the central tenets of European liberalism: that the state must be restricted in scope and constrained in practice in order to ensure the maximum possible freedom of every citizen.
2 The *liberal state* became defined in large part by the attempt to create a private sphere independent of the state, and by a concern to reshape the state itself, that is, by freeing civil society – personal, family, religious and business life – from unnecessary political interference, and simultaneously delimiting the state's authority (Held, 1987, chs 2–3). The building blocks of the liberal state became constitutionalism, private property, the competitive market economy and the distinctively patriarchal family (see Pateman, 1988). While liberalism celebrated the rights of individuals to 'life, liberty and property', it was generally the male property-owning individual who was the focus of so much attention; and the new

freedoms were first and foremost for the men of the new middle classes or the bourgeoisie. The Western world was liberal first, and only later, after extensive conflicts, liberal democratic; that is, only later was a universal franchise won which in principle allowed all mature adults the chance to express their judgement about the performance of those who govern them (Macpherson, 1966, p. 6).

3 The third variant of the modern state is *liberal* or *representative democracy*. Liberal democracy means that decisions affecting a community are taken not by its members as a whole, but by a sub-group of 'representatives' who have been elected by 'the people' to govern within the framework of the rule of law. In the arena of national politics, liberal democracy is distinguished by the presence of a cluster of rules and institutions all of which are necessary to its successful functioning; without any one of these, liberal democracy cannot exist. The rules and institutions are: (a) the constitutional entrenchment of control over governmental policy in elected officials; (b) the establishment of mechanisms for the choice and peaceful removal of elected officials in frequent, fair and free elections; (c) the right to vote for all adults in such elections (unless legitimately disbarred due to severe mental illness or criminal conviction); and (d) the right to run for public office. In addition, there must be (e) an effective right for each citizen to freedom of expression, including the freedom to criticize the conduct of government and the socio-economic system in which it is embedded; (f) accessible sources of information other than those controlled by government or by any other single body or group; and, finally, (g) an established right to form and join independent associations, whether they be political, social or cultural, that could shape public life through legitimate, peaceful means (Dahl, 1989, p. 221 and p. 233). The number of countries with these rules and institutions has increased greatly in the twentieth century, consolidating liberal democracy as the dominant form of the modern state (see Ware, 1992; Held, 1993c).[1]

4 Finally, there is the form of the state known as the *one-party* or *single-party polity*. Until recently, the Soviet Union, East European societies and many Third World countries have

[1] To say this is not to claim, of course, that there are no distinct types of liberal democracy (see Lijphart, 1984; cf. Ware, 1992, pp. 137–40).

> been governed by this system. The principle underlying one-party polities is that a single party can be the legitimate expression of the overall will of the community. Voters have the opportunity to affirm the party's choice of candidate, or occasionally to choose from among different party candidates.

Little further will be said about the single-party polity until later in the volume. There is a fundamental question as to whether it constitutes a legitimate form of the modern state at all, since a single-party system may compromise the idea of a circumscribed and impartial system of power, separate from both ruler and ruled.[2] Accordingly, the arguments below focus on elements of the first three forms of the modern state. In particular, they address how the modern state developed as the nation-state, how democracy became sedimented within the nation-state as representative liberal democracy, and how this type of democracy came to predominate in the political world. Although many factors and processes are involved in this account, the prime consideration will be three 'macro-patterns': war and militarism, the emergence of capitalism, and the struggle for citizenship. These macro-patterns all involve deeply structured processes of change taking place over long periods; they cannot be collapsed into a single historical narrative, because they all developed according to different historical time scales, the intersection of which helped generate the rise of the modern liberal democratic state.

3.1 War and militarism

It has already been suggested that the nature and form of the modern states system crystallized at the intersection of 'international' and 'national' conditions and processes (the terms in inverted commas are so expressed because they did not take on their contemporary meaning until the era of fixed borders, that is, the era of the nation-state). In fact, it is at this intersection that the

[2] It is possible to meet this objection in theory (a single-party system may uphold a clear conception of the powers of the state, subscribe to the rule of law and maintain a rigorous defence of a constitution which delimits power and demarcates procedures for the administration of justice), although it has generally not been met by communist (or fascist) states in practice.

'shape' of the state was largely determined – its size, external configuration, organizational structure, ethnic composition, material infrastructure and so on (see Hintze, 1975, chs 4–6 and 11). At the heart of the processes involved was the ability of states to secure and strengthen their power bases and, thereby, to order their affairs, internally and externally. What was at issue, in short, was the capacity of states to organize the means of coercion (armies, navies and other forms of military might) and to deploy them when necessary. How important this element of state power has been to the history of modern states can be gleaned by examining the case of England.

From an analysis of state finances over several centuries, it can be shown that 'the functions of the state appear overwhelmingly military and overwhelmingly geopolitical rather than economic and domestic' (Mann, 1986, p. 511; see also Mitchell and Deane, 1962; Mitchell and Jones, 1971). From about the twelfth to the nineteenth century, between 70 and 90 per cent of the English state's financial resources were continuously devoted to the acquisition and use of the instruments of military force, especially in international wars. For most of this period the state grew slowly and fitfully (although when it did grow it was due to warfare and related developments), and its size, measured in relation to the resources of the economy and its impact on the daily life of most people, was small. But in the seventeenth and eighteenth centuries the state's real finances grew rapidly, largely in response to the escalating costs of the means of 'coercive power'; in this case, the costs of growing, professional, standing armies and navies. Expenditures on non-military civil functions remained relatively minor.

Reliable annual sets of accounts are available for central government expenditure in Britain for the period after 1688. These figures confirm hypotheses made for previous centuries on the basis of sketchier data: state finances were dominated by foreign wars. As warfare changed and was marked by the engagement of more professional and permanent forces, so the state grew both in overall size and (probably) in terms of its size in relation to 'civil society' (Mann, 1986, pp. 485–6; cf. Black, J., 1991).[3]

[3] The significance of these remarks is highlighted further if it is recalled that they bear on the activities and functions of a constitutional state. In fact, over the broad period of the eighteenth and early nineteenth centuries, whether a state was 'constitutional' or 'absolutist' made little difference to the proportion of its expenditure devoted to

The above remarks are not an argument for 'military determinism'; that is, for a view which asserts that changes in war and the military are the exclusive source of change in the state and the states system. However, they do indicate that the development and maintenance of a coercive capability were central to the development of the state: if states wished to survive they had to fund this capability and ensure its effectiveness. Precisely what this involved can be analysed further by means of figure 3.1. (The discussion which follows concentrates initially on the left-hand column of the figure.)

The process of state-making, and the formation of the modern states system, was to a large degree the result, as Poggi has observed, 'of the strenuous efforts made by rulers, each by means of his/her apparatus of rule, to widen and secure their power base and to increase their own effectiveness and discretion in managing and mobilizing societal resources' (1990, p. 101). State-makers were locked into an open-ended and ruthless competition in which, as Tilly put it, 'most contenders lost' (1975, p. 15). The successful cases of state-making such as Britain, France and Spain were the 'survivors'.

The competition among states was driven not just by the ambitions of rulers and internal or domestic considerations, but also by the very *structure* of the international system: individual states, pursuing their own security, had to be prepared for war, a process which itself generated insecurity in other states, which sought to respond in kind. In short, states armed and became militaristic partly to ensure their own safety, and in so doing they ensured the insecurity of others, who armed in turn – thus making all states less secure. This vicious circle of mutual insecurity can be referred to as the 'security dilemma' of the state. It led to a situation in which each state seemed to adopt, as one observer succinctly put it, 'a *national* security policy and an *international* disarmament policy', but no country pursued 'an *international* security policy and a *national* disarmament policy' (Øberg, 1983,

---

the military. Sketchier evidence appears to confirm a similar pattern of income and costs for France, Prussia and Russia, although each had its peculiarities. However, there is evidence that the general growth of the state in relation to civil society (measured by ratios of state expenditure to gross domestic product and by state employment to population size) was checked later in the nineteenth century (see Mann, 1993, ch. 11).

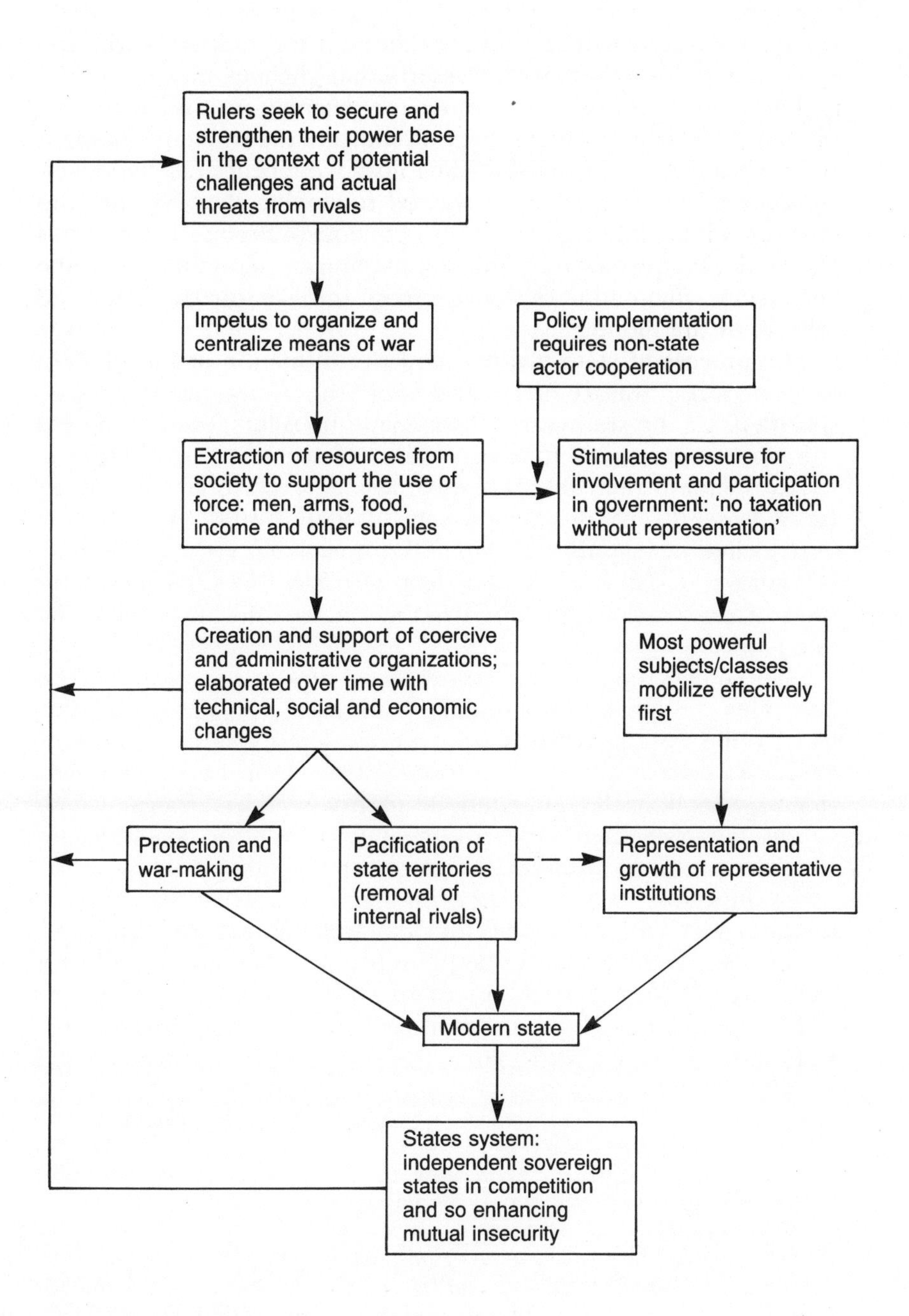

FIGURE 3.1 War and the modern state

p. 279). 'Peace' itself became the continuation of war by proxy (see Kim, 1984, p. 185; and see § 5.3).

The ability to wage war was dependent on a successful process of *extraction*; that is, on a state's capacity to extract resources – whether men, weapons, foodstuffs, taxes or income substitutes – in support of its endeavours. In the long run, however, subjects were unwilling to sacrifice their resources or lives without a struggle for some kind of return or recognition, and conflicts and rebellions against economic and political demands were rife. In response, state rulers built state structures – administrative, bureaucratic and coercive – in order to aid the coordination and control of their subject populations. Direct connections can be traced between a growth in the requirement for the means of waging war, an expansion in processes of extraction, and a concomitant formation of state executive and administrative offices to organize and control these changes. The development of some of the key organizations of the modern state emerged at the intersection of warfare and the attempt to pay for it (Tilly, 1975, p. 42, and 1990, p. 15; and see Anderson, P., 1974b, pp. 236ff).

Over time it was the increasing scale of war, and particularly its growing reliance on technological change and specialization, which gave the centralized nation-state its distinctive edge over other state forms. States that could mobilize and maintain standing armies and/or navies gained a war-making advantage. Those states, in particular, able to draw upon the resources of a large population, a relatively robust commercial economy and a tradition of technological innovation became the dominant political forces, laying down the rules of the political game for others. They specified the forms of war, the nature and limits of diplomatic interchange and, in the end, the type of state organization which would prevail – the unified, centrally governed nation-state itself.

The creation of new regulatory political bodies, however, did not simply eradicate conflict over novel forms of taxation and other means of extraction, especially in Europe and the United States. The relationship between warfare and state-building was mediated by mechanisms of representation and consultation, that is, the relationship set out on the right-hand side of figure 3.1. In fact, it has been argued that the more military superiority has depended on the ability of a state to mobilize large numbers of soldiers, particularly large numbers of lightly armed foot soldiers, the greater have been the prospects for representative or popular government (Dahl, 1989, p. 245; Andreski, 1968). The subject-soldier has often become, and struggled to become, a citizen-soldier (Janowitz, 1978, pp. 178–9). As Dahl put it:

> to see oneself as a member of a nation, a privilege for which one was expected to make sacrifices, could also justify one in making a more expansive claim, including a right to a fair share in governing . . . or at any rate [as] entitled to the franchise. Countries with mass armies . . . ushered in the Age of Democratic Revolutions. It was under these historical conditions in which military organisation and technology were more favourable to democratisation than they had been for many centuries that . . . the institutions of polyarchy [liberal democracy as defined on p. 51] took root in one country after another. (1989, p. 247)

The more costly and demanding war became, the more rulers had to bargain with and win the support of their subjects. For the increase in such demands increased the dependence of rulers on cooperative forms of social relations (Giddens, 1985, pp. 14–15 and 198ff). As a result, greater reciprocity was created between governors and governed, and the more reciprocity that was established, the greater were the opportunities for subordinate groups to influence their rulers. Moreover, the more people were drawn into preparations for war and war-making, the more they became aware of their membership in a political community and of the rights and obligations such membership might confer. While the nature of this emergent identity was often initially vague, it grew more definite and precise over time. The conditions for the development of citizenship varied across countries and regions (see Therborn, 1977; Turner, 1986; Mann, 1987). But the expansion of citizenship was undoubtedly bound up with the military and administrative requirements of the modern state and the 'politicization' of social relations and day-to-day activities which followed in its wake. It has been argued that the democratization of the modern nation-state was largely 'a martial accomplishment' (Therborn, 1977) and, irrespective of whether or not this statement is fully justified, it usefully highlights the impetus received by the institutions of representative democracy from the conditions of mass mobilization and the political demands created by the modern state. It would be misleading, however, to suggest that war created any one single pattern of causation in the building of democratic institutions, and while some democracies were stimulated by processes of mass mobilization (Britain, Canada and the Netherlands), others became democracies by defeat or imposition (Austria, Germany, Italy and Japan).

There is not scope here to focus in any detail on nationalism as such, but it is important to add that nationalism was a critical force in the development of the democratic nation-state (see § 6.1). The conditions involved in the creation of nationalism were also often the conditions which generated the modern state. Nationalism has been closely linked to the administrative unification of the state. For the process by which national identities were formed was often the result of both a struggle for membership in the new political communities, and a struggle by elites and governments to create a new identity to legitimize the actions of the state. In other words, the construction of national identity has been part of an attempt to bind people together within the framework of a delimited territory in order to gain or enhance state power. The requirements of political action have led to the deployment of national identity as a means of ensuring the coordination of policy, mobilization and legitimacy (see Breuilly, 1982, pp. 365ff).

Nevertheless, even where the establishment of a national identity was an explicit political project pursued by elites, it was rarely ever their complete invention. That nationalist elites actively sought to generate a sense of nationality and a commitment to the nation – a 'national community of fate' – is well chronicled. But 'it does not follow', as one scholar has aptly observed, that such elites 'invented nations where none existed' (Smith, A. D., 1990, pp. 180–1; see Gellner, 1964, ch. 7, and 1983). For those seeking to establish a national identity, the 'nation-to-be' was not any large, social or cultural entity; rather, it was a 'community of history and culture', occupying a particular territory, and often laying claim to a distinctive tradition of common rights and duties for its members. Accordingly, many nations were 'built up on the basis of premodern "ethnic cores" whose myths and memories, values and symbols shaped the culture and boundaries of the nation that modern elites managed to forge' (Smith, A. D., 1990, p. 180; and see Smith, A. D., 1986). The identity that nationalists strove to uphold depended, in significant part, on uncovering and exploiting a community's 'ethno-history' and on the latter's distinctiveness in the world of political and cultural values (cf. Hall, S., 1992). But the conditions of 'state-making' and of nationalism or nation-building never fully overlapped – and nationalism itself, especially in the late nineteenth and twentieth centuries, became a force frequently deployed to challenge existing nation-state boundaries (for instance in Northern Ireland) (see § 6.1; and Poggi, 1990, pp. 26–7).

It is a paradoxical result of the waging of war that it stimulated the formation of representative and democratic institutions. But to note this is not to claim that such institutions are fully accounted for by the pursuit of war. The historical conditions surrounding the rise of national democracies have been complex and varied. It is one thing to suggest that there is a direct connection in certain countries between, for example, the extension of the universal franchise and the emergence of modern infantry armies, but it is quite another to argue that democracy is thereby wholly explained. Furthermore, if war gave democracy an impetus within particular nation-states, the rights and principles of democracy were often explicitly denied to those who were conquered, colonized and exploited by powerful nation-states. While the expansion of Europe became the basis of the political unification of the world into a system of nation-states, the main purpose of this expansion was to further European commerce and trade; the rights of colonial subjects were a secondary matter, if a matter of concern at all.

3.2 States and capitalism

In the interpretation that has been offered so far of the development of the modern state, little has been said about the economic motives or economic interests of political and social actors, and about the economic conditions and limits of state action, other than to examine the issue of the extraction of men, arms, income and so on. The main emphasis has been on the non-economic features of the modern state. How does consideration of economic relations, and of the impact of the development of capitalism especially, affect the view set out so far of states as, above all, competing geopolitical entities under pressure to extend the process of representation to all those called upon to serve them? Did the modern states system shape and constrain the modern capitalist economy as the latter developed after AD 1500? Or was the formation of the capitalist economy on a progressively more international basis a, if not the, prime determinant of the scope or limits of the modern state? As state boundaries became more fixed, did the state's formal rulers 'rule the roost', or was the 'roost' impinged upon more and more by the rising economic classes? In short, what was the effect upon state organizations and representative institutions of the development of the modern economic system? It is useful to take several steps back in time before seeking to discriminate among, and weigh up, the multifarious factors which were at play.

At about AD 1000 the nearest approximation to a world-wide order of politics and trade was the Muslim world. Its position, however, was slowly challenged: faced with Mongol invasions in the thirteenth and fourteenth centuries, and later outflanked by European naval expeditions, the vitality of the Islamic world declined (Modelski, 1972; Hourani, 1992). Europe was to burst outward across the world. The growth of interconnections between states and societies – that is, of globalization – became progressively shaped by the expansion of Europe. Globalization initially meant 'European globalization'. Key features of the modern states system – the centralization of political power, the expansion of administrative rule, the legitimation of power through claims to representation, the emergence of massed standing armies – which existed in Europe in embryo in the sixteenth century were to become prevalent features of the entire global system. The chief vehicle for this was, to begin with, the European states' capacity for overseas operations by means of military and naval forces capable of long-range navigation.[4]

Among the early leaders in exploration were the Spanish and Portuguese. If the Iberian monarchies led the first two centuries of European expansion, their position was eroded in the seventeenth century by the Dutch and then by the British and French. British and French influence was markedly in the ascendant in the eighteenth century, although it was Britain which was quite dominant in the nineteenth.[5] British naval and military power conjoined with the centrality of London in terms of world trade and finance. However, until this moment no one single power was dominant; at least two powerful states were always contending for hegemony

[4] European states were not the first to have this capacity: the Chinese enjoyed it, although they did not exploit it systematically. See Kennedy, 1988, p. 7.

[5] 'Perhaps because it was so largely built round Britain', as Hobsbawm put it, 'the world economy of nineteenth-century capitalism developed as a single system of free flows, in which the international transfers of capital and commodities passed largely through British hands and institutions, in British ships between the continents, and were calculated in terms of the pound sterling' (1969, p. 14; cf. p. 314).

in Europe, and the expansion of world commerce drew in non-state actors as well (Tilly, 1990, p. 189). In addition, European rivalries were constantly fought out in colonial territories (although few of these developed into open conflict). The colonies became the 'jewels in the crown' of the new empires; hence the 'scramble' for Africa and the 'forward movement' into Southeast Asia (see Furnivall, 1948; Fieldhouse, 1966). Through the imposition of trade monopolies and special commercial arrangements, each empire tried to secure exclusive control of the flow of trade and resources for its own enrichment. The enhancement of national prestige as a result of successful conquest was also, of course, a motivating factor.

The expansion of Europe across the globe enhanced the demand, as one observer has noted, 'for organizations that would be capable of operating on such a scale. All the basic types of organization of modern society – the modern state, modern corporate enterprise, modern science – were shaped by it and benefited greatly from it' (Modelski, 1972, p. 37). In particular, European expansion became a major source of development of state activity and efficiency. While it was essential to equip, plan and finance overseas exploration, and manage newly acquired posts and territories, governments reaped some of the fruits of the 'discovery' and exploitation of non-European lands. In turn, executive powers and state bureaucracies were better resourced and this enhanced their autonomy in the face of local assemblies and parliaments. Once again, those states which were able to call upon an administrative infrastructure, a substantial population and a wide tax base, alongside arms and shipbuilding industries, gained an advantage. In the seventeenth and eighteenth centuries this advantage was enjoyed by absolutist and constitutional governments; in the nineteenth century by the emergent leading nation-states.

If the consolidation of the modern European state was aided by expansion, this process involved great social costs: the progressive erosion of non-European civilizations, among them the Muslim, Indian and Chinese; the destruction of the American Indians; the disorganizing effects of Western rule on a large number of small societies; and the interlinked degradation of the non-European and European worlds caused by the slave trade. The benefits and costs were not, however, just the result of the expansion of the European states system: the picture was more complicated.

The diffusion of European power occurred mainly through the medium of sea-going military and commercial endeavours; and in the process Europe became connected to a global system of trade and production relationships.[6] At the centre of the latter were newly expanding capitalistic economic mechanisms which had their origins in the sixteenth century, or in what is sometimes called the 'long sixteenth century' running from about 1450 to 1640 (Braudel, 1973). Capitalism was from the beginning an international affair; capital never allowed its aspirations to be determined by national boundaries alone (Wallerstein, 1979, p. 19). Consequently, the emergence of capitalism ushered in a quite fundamental change in the world order: it made possible, for the first time, genuinely global interconnections among states and societies; it penetrated the distant corners of the world and brought far-reaching changes to the dynamics and nature of political rule.

The development of the world capitalist economy initially took the form of the expansion of market relations, driven by a growing need for specie metals to lubricate economic transactions, and for raw materials and other factors of production. Capitalism stimulated this drive and was stimulated by it. It is useful to make a distinction between the expansion of capitalist market relations based on the desire to buy, sell and accumulate mobile resources or capital, and the formation of industrial capitalism involving highly distinctive class relations – based on those who own and control the means of production and those who have only their labouring capacity to sell (see Brenner, 1977). 'Capitalists', under the latter conditions, own factories and technology, while wage-labourers, or 'wage-workers', are without ownership in the means of production. It is only with the development of capitalism in Europe after 1500, and in particular with the formation of the capitalist organization of production from the middle of the eighteenth century, that the activities of capitalists and the capitalist system began to converge (Tilly, 1990, pp. 17 and 189; Giddens, 1985, pp. 122–47).

The development of capitalism itself can be partly explained as the result of changes in 'European' agriculture which stemmed from the twelfth century: changes resulting in part from the drain-

[6] The successful diffusion of European power may not have owed as much to the superiority of European military technology, social organization and skills as is often claimed. Some argue that European conquest and trading dominance owed more to the invasive power of the micro-organisms carried in European bodies. For particularly important accounts along these lines, see Crosby, 1986; McNeil, 1977; and cf. Cronon, 1983.

age and utilization of wet soils, which increased agricultural yields and created a sustainable surplus for trade in the long term. Linked to this was the establishment of long-distance trade routes in which the northern shores of the Mediterranean were initially prominent (Mann, 1986, p. 504). Economic networks created 'north–south corridors' across the European land mass, with those networks in the north-west becoming progressively more dynamic over time. It was a combination of agricultural and navigational opportunities which helped stimulate the European economic dynamic, as well as the continuous competition for resources, territory and trade. Accordingly, the objectives of war gradually became economic objectives: military endeavour and conquest became connected to the pursuit of economic advantage (see Kennedy, 1988). By the seventeenth century, the success of military conquest and the successful pursuit of economic interest became more directly linked than they had been in earlier epochs. For an intensive period, the globalization of political relations and that of economic relations converged on a similar track.[7]

The state slowly became more embroiled with the interests of civil society in part 'for its own sake' (see Offe, 1984). If state rulers and personnel wished to pursue and implement policy of their own choosing then they would require the financial wherewithal to do so; and the more successful the economic activity in their territories, the more – through customs, taxes, investments and other revenue-generating activity – they could sustain their own strategies and interests. Throughout the seventeenth and eighteenth centuries absolutist and constitutional states were drawn steadily into a coordinating role with respect to the activities of civil society. The trigger for this growing responsibility almost always emanated from military commitments. But beneath this lay a general and growing requirement to regulate the developing

[7] It is important to distinguish the form of globalization represented by empires like the British, which stretched across vast territories and sought to organize them politically and economically, from the dense networks of more contemporary global flows marked, for instance, by advanced capitalist countries making substantial investments in each other through multinational corporations (involved in extraction industries, manufactures and services), and by very high levels of short-term capital movements. The latter are discussed in chapter 6. The contrast between empires and the nature of recent types of globalization is drawn in detail in Goldblatt et al. (forthcoming).

capitalist economy, the spread of competing claims to property rights and the demands of subaltern groups, if the economic basis of the state itself was to be properly protected (Mann, 1986, p. 512). The other side of this process was, of course, the growing enmeshment of civil society with the state; for the latter's capacity in principle to stabilize and enforce law, contracts and currencies – to provide a coordinating framework for the new, emerging, capitalist economy – made it a growing object of attention for the powerful groups and classes of civil society who hoped to shape state action to suit their own interests.

What was the relationship between state organizations, representative institutions and classes in the era of the formation of the modern state? Any full answer to this question is likely to be controversial, and would have to be qualified in important details from one country to another. However, having said this, certain patterns can be detected. In the first instance, state development was filtered through the social structure of particular societies – that is, the particular constellation of social classes and groups, organized around different kinds of resource base, which were either cooperative with or resistant to state-makers (Tilly, 1990, pp. 15, 27–8, 57 and 117ff). For example, in 'capital-intensive' regions (areas of marked commerce, where market and exchange relations prevailed), merchants and capitalist entrepreneurs favoured, and sometimes achieved (as they did in the Dutch Republic and Britain), state structures which extended representation to include their interests. By contrast, in 'coercion-intensive' areas (areas of agricultural predominance, where direct coercion played a major role in sustaining order), landlords gained greater control of the state and were able to hinder the development of representative councils or assemblies. In fact, where an economically significant class of landlords, dependent on a supply of cheap labour, had control of or a significant influence on the state apparatus (as they did in the Russian Empire, for instance), particularly fierce resistance was generated to the extension of any form of representative or democratic rights (see Rueschemeyer, Stephens and Stephens, 1992, pp. 270–1 and 288–91).

Second, within capital-intensive areas themselves, a particular pattern, noted initially by Weber, can be uncovered between political rulers and the rising capitalist classes. Weber spoke of an 'alliance' between modern capitalism and the emergent modern state (Weber, 1923). Analysing the nature of this alliance further, Poggi has usefully drawn a distinction between two autonomous forces whose interests converged for a distinctive period (Poggi, 1990, pp. 95–7). The forces consisted, on the one hand, of political rulers seeking to centralize political power and fiscal arrangements by disrupting and eradicating vestiges of power held by the nobility, the church and various estate bodies, and, on the other hand, of the rising bourgeois classes seeking to remove impediments to the expansion of market relations based upon the trading arrangements established by powerful social networks, both country (aristocratic and landed power bases) and urban (the craft and guild systems). An account of how this 'alliance' changed and crystallized over time into different constellations of class and state power is beyond the scope of this volume, as is an account of how descendants of the *ancien régime* managed, to different degrees in different countries, to resist or incorporate the new pressures (see Mann, 1993). Nevertheless, it can be noted that the alliance appears to have endured up to and during the first phase of the industrial revolution, aiding both the expansion of commerce and the industrialization of the economy.

If there was an effective alliance between the interests of powerful political and economic groupings during the formative phase of the modern state it was not without conflicts. For the new capitalist classes sought to struggle not only against the remnants of feudal privilege, but also to ensure the progressive separation of the economy from the state so that the economy was free from any risk of arbitrary political interference.[8] It is at this juncture that the emerging economic classes often became the reforming classes of the eighteenth and nineteenth centuries, seeking to conjoin the struggle for an independent economic sphere with the struggle for representative government. The chief connecting mechanism was the attempt to establish civil and political rights (see below). For what was at issue in the establishment of these rights was the attempt to uphold 'freedom of choice' in areas as diverse as personal, family, business and political affairs. The pursuit of civil and political rights over time reconstituted the nature of both the state and the economy – driving the former towards a liberal democratic polity and the latter towards the capitalist market system.

[8] Of course, elements of the emergent capitalist classes were content to buy their way into the state, purchasing monopolies and trading privileges. But such strategies were ultimately vulnerable to campaigns to ensure both a free market and limited government.

But the meaning of membership in the modern state, that is, of citizenship, remained contested – by political rulers, anxious to preserve their traditional privileges, by powerful social groups and classes, hoping to inscribe their interests into the polity, and by many of those who remained excluded from political participation until well into the twentieth century: the working classes, women and many minority groups. Moreover, as the coordinating role of the state expanded, and it became more involved in determining the conditions of civil society, the state became more intensely contested. The risk of unwanted political interference in economic affairs, and the requirement for a regulatory framework for trade and business, gave the emerging classes of capitalist society a double incentive for involvement in setting the direction of state action.[9]

3.3 Liberal democracy and citizenship

Citizenship is a status which, in principle, bestows upon individuals equal rights and duties, liberties and constraints, powers and responsibilities (Marshall, 1973, p. 84). From the ancient world to the contemporary era, all forms of citizenship have had certain common attributes. Citizenship has meant a certain reciprocity of rights against, and duties towards, the political community. Citizenship had involved membership of the community in which one lives one's life; and membership has invariably involved degrees of participation. The analysis of citizenship involves examining the ways in which different groups, classes and movements have struggled to gain degrees of autonomy and control over their lives in the face of various forms of stratification, hierarchy and political obstacle (see Held, 1989, ch. 7).

[9] It has been argued that the impetus to the consolidation of representative government derived far less from the capitalist classes' interest in reform (although it is acknowledged that they were far more open to democracy than the landed classes), and more from the nature of capitalist development itself. For the latter weakened the position of the landed upper classes, and eventually strengthened the position of the subordinate classes by bringing them together in factories and cities, and by improving the means of communication, thus facilitating working-class organization. For a detailed comparative analysis of this argument, see Rueschemeyer, Stephens and Stephens, 1992, pp. 269–91; cf. Przeworski, 1985.

Throughout the formative phase of the modern state, the struggle for membership in the political community has largely been synonymous with the attempt to establish a form of popular sovereignty through the entrenchment of civil and political rights.[10] By 'civil rights' is meant those rights which are necessary for the establishment of individual autonomy, including liberty of the person, freedom of speech, thought and faith, the right to own property and to enter into contracts, and the right to be treated equally with others before the law. The eighteenth century was the main developmental phase for civil rights in Britain and the United States, when the rights of the liberty of the individual, and full and equal justice before the law, became established. Civil rights created new freedoms, freedoms which, in the first instance, gradually allowed the male citizen liberty from subservience to the place in which he was born and release from the restrictions on occupation created typically by custom or statute.[11] While such freedoms threatened many traditional forms of power and inequality, they did not strain the new forms of inequalities created by the emergence of the competitive capitalist market; on the contrary, they were essential to it (Marshall, 1973, p. 87). The fundamental reason for this is that the new rights allowed each person who enjoyed these rights the power to engage as an independent agent in economic competition; they created individuals who were 'free and equal in status', a status which was the foundation of modern contract (cf. Pateman, 1988).

The establishment of civil rights in Britain, the United States and elsewhere was a prerequisite to the secure establishment of the liberty of the subject. It was a significant step, moreover, in the development of political rights; for when the individual agent was recognized as an autonomous person – that is, as a person able to reflect upon and take decisions about the basic conditions of life – it was easier to think of that person as, in principle, capable of political responsibility. 'Political rights' refer to those elements

[10] While the argument below draws on Marshall's account of the development of citizenship (1973), particularly his notion of different types of citizenship rights, I do not accept his account of the origin of these rights, his tendency to regard rights clusters through an evolutionary lens of 'irrevisible stages', and his formulation of a 'contradiction' between capitalism and welfare (see Held, 1989, ch. 7).

[11] The slave population in the United States was, of course, excluded from these rights.

of rights which create the possibility of participation in the exercise of political power as a member of a political association, or as an elector of the members of such an association. Although political rights emerged in the late eighteenth century in some countries and ahead of the establishment of a full panoply of civil rights in others (for instance, in Sweden (see Koblick, 1975)), their entrenchment belongs, above all, to the nineteenth and early twentieth centuries. Entrenchment during this period reflects a growing interest in equality as a principle which could be applied to a range of spheres, and a growing appreciation of a tension between, on the one hand, the formal recognition of a person as 'free and equal' in civil matters and, on the other hand, the actual liberty of that person to pursue interests free of political impediment. Political rights were gradually recognized as indispensable to guaranteeing individual freedom on the ground, among others, that, since there is no good reason for believing that those who govern will act ultimately in anything other than a self-interested manner (just like those who are governed), government must, to avoid abuse, be directly accountable to an electorate called upon regularly to decide whether its objectives have been met (see chapter 1, pp. 9–12).

The establishment of 'political liberty' involved a process whereby the political rights which had previously been the monopoly of the privileged few were extended to the adult population as a whole. The rise of the trade-union movement and of the labour movement more generally, in alliance with sectors of the middle classes, was a critical factor in the development of political citizenship, alongside the struggles for women's suffrage (see Rueschemeyer, Stephens and Stephens, 1992, especially ch. 7). If citizenship was an entitlement, it had to be an entitlement to full membership of political society. Thus, the search for citizenship became the search for the conditions under which individuals could enjoy equal worth and equal opportunity. The scene was set for the struggle not only over the enactment of political rights but over 'social rights' as well.

With the achievement of the universal franchise in some countries, the organized working class was able to use its political strength to help combat social inequalities and to consolidate some social or welfare gains *as rights* (see Turner, 1990). However, this strength was rarely sufficient to push through the decisive, structural reforms which created welfare institutions. In fact, many welfare institutions were propelled primarily by ambitious politicians and 'visionary civil servants', as a means in part to promote national solidarity (Ashford, 1986, p. 6; see also de Swaan, 1988, pp. 5–11; and Esping-Andersen, 1990, pp. 40, 53, 112 and 133–5). It was not until the late nineteenth and twentieth centuries that social rights in their modern form were entrenched; that is, in the form of redistributive welfare measures – including measures introducing social security, public health provision and new forms of progressive taxation.[12] These rights remained fragile achievements, a fragility that became particularly plain to see in the light of efforts in the late 1970s and 1980s to 'roll back the state' and to restrict radically the scope of the state's action (see Held, 1989, chs 4–5; and see chapter 11 of this volume).

How was it that citizenship crystallized in many Western polities in the form of civil and political rights above all else, and how was it that liberal democracy triumphed over alternative forms of governance? Clues to these matters can be found in the convergence of at least three critical factors. The first lies in what can be called the 'reciprocity of power', which came to be recognized through the growing dependence of national systems of regulation on the cooperation of subject populations, a dependence which, as previously noted, became especially apparent during periods of national emergency, especially wars. The second lies in the crisis of political legitimacy faced by developing state powers in the context of the exhaustion of traditional forms of legitimation, particularly those based on religion and property rights. What was new from the late eighteenth century was not so much the widespread positive appeal of the ideas of self-determination and citizen self-rule, but more, as Dunn has written, 'the relative fragility' of the traditional systems of subjugation (1992, p. 246). The legitimacy promised by systems of representative democracy was based on a recognition of a reciprocal relationship between governors and governed, in which, on the one hand, the latter had a duty to respect the law and the authority of the state and, on the other hand, the former had a duty to act fairly in accordance with the broad mandate of 'the people'. The third factor which helps explain the victory of liberal representative democracy is that it did not threaten the forces (and growing autonomy) of economic

[12] The net redistributive effects of the welfare state were in some part quite limited because they became a vehicle for helping to consolidate the interests of a rising and expanding middle class (see Giddens, 1994, ch. 5).

civil society. The creation of a market-place for labour power and capital involved the separation of the 'economic' from the 'political'. The rights of the citizen to stand as a representative were not extended to work and, accordingly, the sphere of politics was not directly extended to industry; industrial capitalism could flourish side by side with the entrenchment of representative government (see Turner, 1986, pp. 37–44).[13] Representative democracy, accordingly, is democracy 'made safe' for the modern world and, particularly, for the modern capitalist economy (Dunn, 1992, pp. 248 and 250).

And yet representative democracy has remained a contested terrain, a terrain often charged by a gulf between democratic promise and actuality. From the pursuit of 'no taxation without representation' in seventeenth-century England to the diverse struggles to achieve a genuinely universal franchise in the nineteenth and twentieth centuries, advocates of greater accountability in government have sought to establish satisfactory means for choosing, authorizing and controlling political decisions. In the Central and East European revolutions of 1989–90, the principle of self-determination and the principle of consent to government action have once again challenged the principle of 'single-person' or, in this particular case, 'single-party' rule. Democracy has been conceived as a way of containing the powers of the state and of mediating among competing political projects; for it holds out the possibility of the entrenchment of a principle of legitimacy based, on the one hand, on the political involvement of each and all and, on the other, on a process of decision-making which can mediate differences and distil (by virtue of its adherence to this process) acceptable outcomes.

Struggles for citizenship and democracy have been guided by

[13] While the institutionalized separation of the economic from the political creates a basis for the development and expansion of capital, this separation also creates a significant space for the realization of political rights and freedoms. The relative separation of the political and economic means that there is a realm in which the citizen can enjoy rights unavailable to those in societies where this separation has not been established. While one consequence of the differentiation of the economic and political is to give the economy relative freedom and, thereby, to produce and reproduce systematic asymmetries in income, wealth and power, another is to create a space for the enjoyment of civil and political rights. The significance of this will be explored further below (see chs 7–9).

the anticipation of a political order which does not arbitrarily shape and constrain choices for individuals and groups. The urge to obtain this order is an urge towards a fuller measure of autonomy, the enrichment of the stuff of which citizenship is made and an increase in the number of those upon whom the status of autonomy can be bestowed (cf. Marshall, 1973, p. 84). This is an urge to realize what I call 'the principle of autonomy' – a principle that recognizes the indispensability of 'equal autonomy' for all citizens (see chapter 7). If people's equal interest in democracy is to be protected, they require an equal capacity to act across key political institutions and sites of power.

The anticipation of autonomy for each and all constitutes a regulative idea – an idea which has guided conflicts over the institutionalization of democracy. It is an idea, moreover, which has provided a normative standard which could be turned against existing institutions, as it has been by working-class, feminist, anti-racist and anti-colonial activists, to reveal the extent to which the principles and aspirations of equal liberty and equal political participation remain unfulfilled. And it is an idea which could be drawn upon to interrogate the degree to which democracy 'made safe' for the modern world has failed to address the problems of accountability created by sites of power beyond the state, such as those generated by leading economic organizations, which can thwart and limit the successful entrenchment of democracy itself (see chapter 8).

The triumph of the modern state

It remains in this chapter to draw together the grounds of why it was that the modern state came to be a national or nation-state. Briefly put, it has been argued that nation-states became supreme because they triumphed in war, were (relatively) successful economically, and achieved a significant degree of legitimacy in the eyes of their populations and other states.

They triumphed in war because, as warfare became more extended in scale and cost, it was larger national states which were best able to organize and fund military power; and as these states expanded overseas this ability increased (Tilly, 1990, pp. 65–6 and 190). They were economically successful because the rapid growth of their markets from the late sixteenth century, and particularly after the mid-eighteenth century, sustained the process of capital accumulation: as the economic basis of the centralized state expanded, it significantly reduced the war-making ability of smaller states (often with fragmented power structures) and traditional empires (which depended above all on coercive power for their success). And they gained in legitimacy because, as they extended their military, organizational and coordinating activities, they came to depend more and more on the active cooperation, collaboration and support of other collectivities, especially well-organized civil groups. In the wake of the erosion of the authority of the church and that of other erstwhile prominent institutions, the legitimacy of claims to political power came to depend on the view that such claims were justified and appropriate if popular or democratic. Calls for democratic government or democratic legitimacy became irresistible in the face of the expansion of state administrative power and the growth of new political identities – nationalism, citizenship and the 'public' persona.

Of course, the conditions under which national democracies developed have varied considerably. Several 'enabling factors' have been mentioned as central to the successful consolidation of national democracies, including a crisis of traditional forms of legitimacy creating new spaces for conceptual and institutional innovation; the development of a secular notion of political power and of law; the concentration of the means of violence in the hands of the state along with the emergence of a professional, standing army; the presence of strong, independent and reform-minded social groups and classes in civil society; and the impact of particular international conditions and crises (cf. Hall, J., 1993). While each of these factors has often had a mutually supporting and interlinked role in the development of democracy, they did not alone lead to its successful entrenchment; for a great deal has also depended, as it always does, on contingent circumstances and on the exercise of skilled political judgement (see Held, 1993c, part IV).

4

The Inter-State System

This chapter explores further why for most of the nineteenth and twentieth centuries democracy *in* nation-states has not been accompanied by democratic relations *among* states and societies. It endeavours to show that the heart or 'deep structure' of the modern system of nation-states can be characterized by a striking tension between the entrenchment of accountability and democratic legitimacy inside state boundaries and the pursuit of power politics outside such boundaries. The origins of this tension can be traced to the earliest stages of the states system, that is, to the entrenchment of territorial sovereignty by European powers seeking to consolidate national domains. This process of entrenchment set the structure of the states system, shaping the form and dynamics of inter-state relations well into the twentieth century. The grafting onto this structure of the United Nations in the aftermath of the Second World War, moreover, did not fundamentally alter its core features. In fact, the UN Charter enhanced the role of the 'great powers', further legitimating their claim to leadership in international politics.

However, an argument can be made that the growing involvement of states in regional and global networks, particularly in the second half of the twentieth century, has altered the extent and scope of their authority. The intensification of regional interconnectedness and the spread of global relations raise questions, on the one hand, about the ability of states (however powerful) to deal effectively with demands placed upon them by transnational forces and, on the other hand, about the accountability of states to many of those who are deeply affected by them. Sections 4.1 and 4.2 explore the nature and structure of the inter-state system while section 4.3 tentatively examines the issues which arise from the enmeshment of the states system in complex webs of economic, social and cultural activity.

4.1 Sovereignty and the Westphalian order

The history of the modern inter-state system, and of international relations more generally, has borne little relation to any democratic principle of organization. In fact, in the arena of world politics, Hobbes's way of thinking about power and power relations has often been regarded as the most insightful account of the meaning of the state at the global level (see, for example, Aron, 1966). It is said that Hobbes drew a comparison between international relations and the state of nature, describing the international system of states as being in a continuous 'posture of war'. As Hobbes wrote:

> in all times, Kings, and Persons of Soveraigne authority, because of their Independency, are in continuall jealousies, and in the state and posture of Gladiators; having their weapons pointing, and their eyes fixed on one another; that is, their Forts, Garrisons, and Guns upon the Frontiers of their Kingdomes; and continuall Spyes upon their neighbours. (1968, pp. 187–8)

A war of 'all against all' is taken as a constant threat, since each state is at liberty to act to secure its own interests unimpeded by any higher religious or moral strictures.

> [I]n States, and Common-wealths not dependent on one another, every Common-wealth (not every man) has an absolute Libertie to doe what it shall judge (that is to say, what that Man, or Assemblie that representeth it, shall judge) most conducing to their benefit. (1968, p. 266)

In the study of international affairs, Hobbes's account has become associated with the 'realist' theory of international politics, outlined earlier (see § 1.3; cf. Walker, 1993; Williams, 1994). Realism posits that the system of sovereign states is inescapably anarchic in character; and that this anarchy forces all states, in the inevitable absence of any supreme arbiter to enforce moral behaviour and agreed international codes, to pursue power politics in order to attain their vital interests. This *realpolitik* view of states has had a significant influence on both the analysis and practice of international relations, as it offers a convincing prima facie explanation of the chaos and disorder of world affairs (see Morgenthau, 1948; Wight, 1986; Smith, S., 1987). In this account, the modern system of nation-states is a 'limiting factor' which will always thwart any attempt to conduct international relations in a manner which transcends the politics of the sovereign state.

A concomitant of each and every modern state's claim to supreme authority is a recognition that such a claim gives other states an equal entitlement to autonomy and respect within their own borders. In the context of the rapid erosion of 'international Christian society' from the late sixteenth century, the development of sovereignty can be interpreted, as indicated in § 2.1, as part of a process of mutual recognition whereby states granted each other rights of jurisdiction in their respective territories and communities. Accordingly, sovereignty involved the assertion by the state of independence; that is, of its possession of sole rights to jurisdiction over a particular people and territory. And in the world of relations among states, the principle of the sovereign equality of all states gradually became adopted as the paramount principle governing the formal conduct of states towards one another, however representative or unrepresentative were their particular regimes.

The states order gradually superseded the organizing principles of medieval Europe and international Christian society, and became embedded in a complex of rules which evolved, from the seventeenth century, to secure the concept of the states system as a society – an international society – of sovereign nation-states (see Bull, 1977, pp. 127–61). At least three complexes of rules have played a part in the definition and maintenance of this order. The first complex constitutes the fundamental principle of world politics in the era of emerging nation-states: it identifies the 'idea of a society of states' – as opposed to such alternatives as that of an empire or a system of divided authority – as 'the supreme normative principle of the political organisation' of humankind (Bull, 1977, pp. 67–8). While this principle became entrenched in international law, it was an axiom of, and prior to, this law in the sense that it was presupposed in a whole complex of rules – legal, moral, customary and operational – as it developed over time. The principle is contained in several basic rules of international law, notably, those which have defined states as the only or the principal bearer of rights and duties in international law; as the sole and rightful agent for the use of force; and as the source of order and constraint in the international system.

The idea of a society of states was also given forceful expression by a second cluster of rules: the rules of so-called 'coexistence'. These rules specify the minimum conditions for states to organize their mutual affairs in the international order. They include rules about the legitimate use of force by sovereign states (and deny such legitimacy to other actors); about the nature of agreements, *pacta sunt servanda* (which connotes that agreements between states should be upheld if their terms are met); and about the state's proper jurisdiction. The latter concerns, above all, each state's duty to respect the sovereignty of every other state over its territory and people on the condition that this recognition is fully reciprocated. The further requirement of non-interference in the internal affairs of another country follows from this central stipulation.

A third cluster of rules shapes the form of cooperation among states, if relations are sustainable beyond mere coexistence. It includes rules that facilitate not merely political and strategic cooperation, but also social and economic affairs. The growth in the twentieth century of legal rules concerned with cooperation between and across states in economic, social, communications and environmental matters exemplifies the growing significance of rules organizing the dense networks of interaction within these domains. The result has been the rapid development of a multiplicity of organizations and regimes to guide and help stabilize transactions among state and non-state actors (see Murphy, 1994; and § 4.2 below).

The absence of a supranational authority – a 'higher coordinating body' – which might mediate and resolve disputes among states, does not entail that the international order of states has been without any common values or means of regulation (see Hinsley, 1963, 1986). Most states at some time have paid respect to the above complexes of rules in order to give form and substance to their collaborative endeavours, endeavours which serve their interests. For the *raison d'être* of these rules is to secure the existence of states and their mutual advantage. In the same way 'most states at most times', as Bull has observed, 'take part in the working of common institutions: the form and procedures of international law, the system of diplomatic representation, . . . and universal international organisations such as the functional organisations that grew up in the nineteenth century' (1977, p. 42). What marks out the regulative order of the states system from previous international systems is that it is, in principle, a *self-regulating* order.

However, while the states system is self-regulating in principle, it has also in practice been marked by the deployment of power and the systematic pursuit of the national interest. Nothing exemplifies this better than the rapid carving out of colonies by leading European countries in the nineteenth century. The earth, sea and air were all regarded as resources legitimately falling under the sovereign authority of states on the single condition that whoever possessed a territory and exercised actual control over it successfully secured a legal title (cf. Tully, 1994, especially pp. 86–8). In cases of *terrae nullius*, areas allegedly subject to no one, the principle 'first come first served' was not regarded as a sufficient basis for such a claim; an 'actual display of sovereignty' coupled with 'the intent to wield authority' were needed (see Cassese, 1986, pp. 376–7). The division of resources and space among states was essentially achieved by those powers that had the means to acquire and hold a portion of land; thereafter, international law legitimized the claim to sovereign rights over such territories. The partition of the world was a matter of power politics, the results of which were, ultimately, sanctioned by law. While there was one major exception to this basis of dividing the world – the high seas, which were regarded as a 'thing belonging to everybody'[1] – the principle of state sovereignty was successively extended across the globe.

The conception of international order which clarifies the nature of the inter-state system can be referred to as the 'Westphalian' model, after the Peace of Westphalia of 1648 which brought to an end the German phase of the Thirty Years War and which entrenched, for the first time, the principle of territorial sovereignty in inter-state affairs.[2] The model covers a period from 1648 to

[1] The exclusion of the high seas is not inconsistent with the underlying principles of this mode of appropriation; for it was not possible for any one state simply to lay claim to these seas. If there had been one state strong enough to appropriate the high seas, then the principle of state sovereignty, with its fully exclusive mechanisms, would probably have become entrenched even here. In the absence of such a power, the high seas were recognized by necessity as common property, as a *res communis omnium*.

[2] While the emergence of this principle can be linked directly to the Peace of Westphalia, the basic conception of territorial sovereignty was outlined well before this settlement, although it was not widely accepted until Westphalia (see Baldwin, 1992).

1945, although many of the assumptions underpinning it are still operative in international relations today.[3] It depicts the development of a world community consisting of sovereign states which settle their differences privately and often by force (or the threat of force); which engage in diplomatic relations but otherwise pursue minimal cooperation; which seek to place their own national interest above all others; and which accept the logic of the principle of effectiveness, that is, the principle that might eventually makes right in the international world – that appropriation becomes legitimation (Cassese, 1991, p. 256). The model of Westphalia is summarized in table 4.1 (adapting points from Falk, 1969, 1975b, ch. 2; and Cassese, 1986, pp. 396–9).

TABLE 4.1 The model of Westphalia

1. The world consists of, and is divided by, sovereign states which recognize no superior authority.
2. The processes of law-making, the settlement of disputes and law enforcement are largely in the hands of individual states.
3. International law is orientated to the establishment of minimal rules of coexistence; the creation of enduring relationships among states and peoples is an aim, but only to the extent that it allows national political objectives to be met.
4. Responsibility for cross-border wrongful acts is a 'private matter' concerning only those affected.
5. All states are regarded as equal before the law: legal rules do not take account of asymmetries of power.
6. Differences among states are ultimately settled by force; the principle of effective power holds sway. Virtually no legal fetters exist to curb the resort to force; international legal standards afford minimal protection.
7. The minimization of impediments to state freedom is the 'collective' priority.

This framework of international affairs had a lasting and paradoxical quality rich in implications: an increasingly developed and interlinked states system endorsed the right of each state to autonomous and independent action. As one commentator has aptly

[3] By a 'model' I mean a theoretical construction designed to reveal and explain the main features of a political order and its underlying structure of relations. Models in this context are 'networks' of concepts and generalizations about aspects of the political, economic and social spheres.

noted, the upshot of this was that states were 'not subject to international moral requirements because they represent separate and discrete political orders' (Beitz, 1979, p. 25). In this situation, the world consists of separate political powers, pursuing their own interests, backed ultimately by their organization of coercive power. Moreover, the resort to coercion or armed force by non-state actors is also, arguably, an almost inevitable outcome (although it is strictly illegal in Westphalian terms). For communities contesting established territorial boundaries have 'little alternative but to resort to arms in order to establish "effective control" over the area they seek as their territory, and in that way make their case for international recognition' (see Baldwin, 1992, pp. 224–5).

The principles and rules of the Westphalian system did not simply translate into one conception of international order, for there was always a gulf between the recognition of states as, in principle, equal before the law and enjoying an equality of status, and the actual asymmetries of power which pervaded the states system. This gulf gave rise to a number of efforts to construct alliances and agreements among powers, seeking to mould the international order to their own advantage (cf. Hall, J., 1996). The search for peace by Europe's great powers after the Napoleonic wars, for example, issued in an attempt to create a system of security that would ultimately embrace the whole of Europe. This 'Concert system', devised after intense negotiation by Tsar Alexander, Prince von Metternich and Viscount Castlereagh in Paris and Vienna, sought to establish an 'equilibrium of power' through the redistribution of territories and peoples: 'strategic rather than ethnic considerations dominated the planning' (Holsti, 1991, pp. 115 and 169). The norms of this settlement included respect for the new territorial balance of power and an emphasis on self-restraint and mutual consultation in the event of possible conflict.[4] While the Concert system was at some distance from a conception

[4] What distinguished the Concert system from the diplomatic procedures of other periods of international history can be summarized, according to Hinsley, by its commitment to three underlying principles:

> that the Great Powers had a common responsibility for maintaining the territorial *status quo* of the treaties of 1815 and for solving the international problems which arose in Europe; that, when the *status quo* had to be modified or a problem had to be settled, changes should not be made unilaterally and gains should not be made without their formal and common consent; that, since

of the international order as a war of 'all against all', it was not at a distance from a conception of the international order as 'anarchic', if by the latter is understood specifically self-regulation in the interests of coexistence and mutual advantage (see pp. 76–7).

The balance of power enshrined in the Concert system sought to maintain a network of great states and empires; and it was relatively effective in this matter for over forty years. The great powers, as one observer noted, 'determined the fate of the lesser states on no principle other than their own convenience' (Clark, 1989, p. 218). Concert diplomacy and the balance of power principle did not, therefore, 'dramatically improve the tenor of international politics' (Holsti, 1991, pp. 139 and 143). Areas such as the Balkans suffered from chronic crisis and war, and nationalist movements striving for states of their own became a source of greater and greater conflict. Against this background, the balance of military power became a preoccupation of European state leaders, particularly in the latter half of the nineteenth century, as the enterprise of state creation was pursued intensively, ultimately weakening the position of two of the key pillars of the post-Napoleonic peace, the Austro-Hungarian and Ottoman Empires. Thus, although the emphasis between 'concert' and 'balance' in the European order changed, and changed a number of times, this did not lead to a fundamental transformation in the nature and role of political power in the inter-state system: the distribution of power altered, but the Westphalian principle of effective power remained intact alongside the stratification of the international order (see Clark, 1989, pp. 217ff; cf. Kegley and Raymond, 1994, ch. 6).

The consolidation of the modern system of nation-states has not by any means, of course, been a uniform process, affecting each region and country in a similar way. From the outset this process has involved, as noted in the previous chapter, great costs for the

---

> the consent of all was needed, decisions were not to be reached by votes. (1963, p. 225).

The means for entrenching these principles were to be regular meetings of the great powers themselves. As such, the Concert system can be regarded as a pioneering institutional mechanism for conflict management and avoidance. The point of the system was not to abolish war itself: war was still regarded as a legitimate means to settle differences among states. Rather, the system aimed to prevent the development of a new hegemonic power in Europe and to prevent the erosion of the great powers' interests (see Kegley and Raymond, 1994).

autonomy and independence of many, especially in smaller states and extra-European civilizations (cf. Kiernan, 1982). In fact, the spread of the modern states system has been consistently characterized by both 'hierarchy' and 'unevenness' (see Falk, 1990, pp. 2–12). Hierarchy denotes the structure of political and economic globalization: its domination by a constellation of nation-states concentrated in the West and North. While there may be uncertainty about the precise distribution of influence at the centre of this constellation, the hierarchical structure of processes of globalization has firmly placed the leading Western and Northern economic powers in central positions (see § 3.2).[5]

The other side of hierarchy is unevenness. This refers to the asymmetrical effects of political and economic globalization upon the life-chances and wellbeing of peoples, classes, ethnic groupings, movements and the sexes. The contours of these processes of 'unevenness' are not difficult to discern, although they will not be documented here (see chapter 8). They are broadly correlated with geography, race and gender and, accordingly, with the clusters of poverty and deprivation found among the countries of the South, among non-whites and among women. However, the persistence of significant poverty and hardship in the North (in Europe and the US), the existence of unemployment in the most industrial countries (even during periods of marked growth), and the fate of many indigenous peoples indicate how approximate it is to conceive of unevenness in these terms alone. Unevenness is a phenomenon of both international and national development. The categories of social and political stratification must, therefore, be thought of as denoting systematic divisions within and across territories and regions (see Cox, 1987, ch. 9).

The effective power which sovereignty bestows on a state is, to a significant degree, connected to the resources at the disposal of that state. Clearly, the resources a polity can mobilize will vary according to its position in the hierarchy of states, its position in the global structure of economic relations, its place in the international division of labour, and the support it can muster from regional

[5] Although the decline of Europe's empires in the twentieth century has brought about a diminution in the direct political influence of European powers, their position has been partly protected by processes of economic globalization which have arguably become more significant than ever as the determinants of hierarchy and of the front line of geopolitics (see § 6.2).

networks. The growing awareness in many Western countries today that their sovereignty is under pressure from a variety of forces places before them (often for the first time) issues that have been apparent to other countries for a long time. The struggle for sovereignty and autonomy in many 'Third World' countries was closely related to the struggle for freedom from colonial domination. *De jure* sovereignty has been of the utmost importance to those countries that had previously been denied it; but *de jure* sovereignty is not of course the same thing as *de facto* or practical sovereignty. The often weak and debt-ridden economies of many developing countries leave them vulnerable and dependent on economic forces and relations over which they have little, if any, control. Although the internationalization of production and finance places many instruments of economic control beyond even the most powerful countries, the position of those at the lower end of the globalization hierarchy, experiencing the strongest effects of unevenness, is substantially worse.

Despite the diplomatic momentum and the international legal initiatives which followed the Second World War, and which aimed to transform the Westphalian system in fundamental respects (see below), the political independence which was achieved by former colonies often provided at best only a brief respite from the processes of marginalization in the world order. In countries such as those of the sub-Sahara, where the boundaries of the nation-state (with two small exceptions) do not correspond to the boundaries of any states that existed before colonization, where there has been no 'established habit' of exercising central authority and accepting its role, and where some of the most elementary human securities have often been absent, independence has been fraught with many types of difficulty (see Hawthorn, 1993; cf. Jackson and Rosberg, 1982). It has been handicapped by vulnerability to the international economy, by a fragile resource base which is threatening to the autonomy of political organizations, and by social groups often deeply divided by extreme poverty, hardship and ill-health as well as by ethnic, cultural and other divisions. But it has, in addition, been handicapped by the very *structure* of the international political system which leaves individual states, locked into the competitive pursuit of their own security and interests, without systematic means to pursue the accountability and regulation of some of the most powerful forces ordering national and international affairs (cf. Potter, 1993; Bromley, 1993). It is political and economic might which ultimately determines the effective deployment of rules and resources in a world constituted by Westphalian principles – a state of affairs which was, in certain respects, to remain remarkably constant in the face of attempts to rethink international relations in the era of the United Nations.

4.2 The international order and the United Nations system

The titanic struggles of the First and Second World Wars led to a growing acknowledgement that the nature and process of international governance would have to change if the most extreme forms of violence against humanity were to be outlawed, and the growing interconnectedness and interdependence of nations recognized. Slowly, the subject, scope and very sources of the Westphalian conception of international regulation, particularly its conception of international law, were all called into question (see Bull, 1977, ch. 6, for an overview).

First and foremost, opinion moved against the doctrine that international law, as Oppenheim put it, is a 'law between states only and exclusively' (see Oppenheim, 1905, ch. 1). Single persons and groups became recognized as subjects of international law. It is generally accepted, for example, that persons as individuals are subjects of international law on the basis of such documents as the Charters of the Nuremberg and Tokyo War Crimes Tribunals, the Universal Declaration of Human Rights (1948), the Covenant on Civil and Political Rights (1966), and the European Convention on Human Rights (1950).

Opinion has also moved against the doctrine that international law is primarily about political and strategic (state) affairs. According to this position, international law is concerned progressively with orchestrating and regulating economic, social and environmental matters. Linked to substantial increases in the number of 'actors' in world politics – for example, the United Nations (UN), the UN Economic and Social Council, the World Bank, the International Monetary Fund, the International Whaling Commission, the Food and Agricultural Organization and the World Health Organization[6] – there have been many pressures to increase the scope of inter-

[6] For an account of the development of these international organizations, which links them to changes in industrial technology, particularly to changes in new communication technologies, see Murphy (1994). Murphy's

national law. Faced with this development, there are those who characterize the changing reach of international law as being ever less concerned with the freedom or liberty of states, and ever more with the general welfare of all those in the global system who are able to make their voices count (cf., for example, Röling, 1960; Friedmann, 1964; Cassese, 1986, esp. chs 7–9).

Finally, the influential legal doctrine that the only true source of international law is the consent of states – either their expressed consent, or their implied consent – has been fundamentally challenged. Today, a number of sources of international law jostle for recognition. These include the traditional sources such as international conventions or treaties (general or particular) which are recognized by states; international custom or practice which provides evidence of an accepted rule or set of rules; and the underlying principles of law recognized by 'civilized nations'. They also include the 'will of the international community', which can assume the 'status of law' or which can become the 'basis of international legal obligation' under certain circumstances (cf. Bull, 1977, pp. 147–58; Jenks, 1963, ch. 5; Falk, 1970, ch. 5). The last represents a break in principle with the requirement of individual state consent in the making of international rules and responsibilities.[7]

Although the Westphalian model of international law had its critics throughout the modern era, particularly during the ill-fated efforts of the League of Nations, it was not until after the Second World War that a new model of international law and accountability was widely advocated and accepted, culminating in the adoption of the UN Charter. The image of international regulation projected by the Charter (and related documents) was one of 'states still jealously "sovereign" ', but linked together in a 'myriad of relations'; under pressure to resolve disagreements by peaceful

key thesis is that global IGOs (intergovernmental organizations) have played a role in the growth of 'industrial society' for over a century, providing significant 'modes of regulation' during economic and geopolitical crisis (1994, p. 9). Cf. § 5.2 below.

[7] It is interesting to note that the tradition of natural law thinking, which informed early-modern international law in particular, recognized a tension between the requirement of governmental consent and the pre-existence of certain international rights and duties. This notion is being both rekindled and recast in some contemporary international legal developments, which are explored further in § 5.1.

means and according to legal criteria; subject in principle to tight restrictions on the resort to force; and constrained to observe 'certain standards' with regard to the treatment of all persons on their territory, including their own citizens (Cassese, 1991, p. 256). Of course, how restrictive the provisions of the Charter have been to states, and to what extent they have been actually operationalized, are important issues. Before addressing them, however, leading elements of the Charter model (adapted from Cassese, 1986, pp. 398–400) should be sketched: see table 4.2 (p. 86).

The shift in the structure of international regulation from the Westphalian to the UN Charter model raised fundamental questions about the nature and form of international law, questions which point to the possibility of a significant disjuncture between the law of nation-states – of the states system – and of the wider international community. At the heart of this shift lies a conflict between claims made on behalf of individual states and those made on behalf of an alternative organizing principle of world affairs: ultimately, a democratic community of states, with equal voting rights in the General Assembly of nation-states, openly and collectively regulating international life while constrained to observe the UN Charter and a battery of human rights conventions. However, this conflict has not been settled, and it would be quite misleading to conclude that the era of the UN Charter model simply displaced the Westphalian logic of international governance. The essential reason for this is that the Charter framework represents, in many respects, an extension of the inter-state system.

The organizations and procedures of the UN were designed partly to overcome weaknesses in the League of Nations. The League, established by a multilateral treaty at the end of the First World War (Part 1 of the Treaty of Versailles), was founded in order to preserve peace and security and to promote economic and social cooperation among its members. Ultimately, sixty-three countries accepted membership, although the US Senate – despite Woodrow Wilson's leading role in creating the League – refused to ratify the initiative. Setting itself against the secret practices of traditional European statecraft, the League represented an aspiration for 'a new and more wholesome diplomacy' (Wilson). Building on the nineteenth-century Concert system's conception of regular conferences, it proposed a permanent apparatus for these, a system of conciliation and arbitration involving a judicial body (the Permanent Court of International Justice) and a system of guarantees linked to the *status quo post bellum* (Clark, 1989, pp. 150–2; cf.

TABLE 4.2 The UN Charter model

1 The world community consists of sovereign states, connected through a dense network of relations, both *ad hoc* and institutionalized. Individuals and groups are regarded as legitimate actors in international relations (albeit with limited roles).
2 Certain peoples oppressed by colonial powers, racist regimes or foreign occupants are assigned rights of recognition and a determinate role in articulating their future and interests.
3 There is a gradual acceptance of standards and values which call into question the principle of effective power; accordingly, major violations of given international rules are not in theory to be regarded as legitimate. Restrictions are placed on the resort to force, including the unwarranted use of economic force.
4 New rules, procedures and institutions designed to aid law-making and law enforcement in international affairs are created.
5 Legal principles delimiting the form and scope of the conduct of all members of the international community, and providing a set of guidelines for the structuring of international rules, are adopted.
6 Fundamental concern is expressed for the rights of individuals, and a corpus of international rules is created seeking to constrain states to observe certain standards in the treatment of all, including their own citizens.
7 The preservation of peace, the advancement of human rights and the establishment of greater social justice are the stated collective priorities; 'public affairs' include the whole of the international community. With respect to certain values – peace, the prohibition of genocide – international rules now provide in principle for the personal responsibility of state officials and the attribution of criminal acts to states.
8 Systematic inequalities among peoples and states are recognized and new rules – including the concept of 'the common heritage of mankind'[8] – are established to create ways of governing the distribution, appropriation and exploitation of territory, property and natural resources.

[8] First propounded in the late 1960s, the concept of 'the common heritage of mankind' was proposed as a device to exclude a state or private right of appropriation over certain resources and to permit the development of those resources, where appropriate, for the benefit of all, with due regard paid to environmental protection. See § 5.1.

Zimmern, 1936; Osiander, 1994, ch. 5). Underpinning these innovations was a desire to establish 'a community of like minded nations', cooperating fully with one another and 'settling their differences like reasonable men, enjoying peace under a law... which if need be they would pool their resources to enforce' (Howard, 1981, p. 91). Although the League fostered an infrastructure of international organizations which were to be of enduring significance, its aspirations were dashed, and its fate sealed, in the view of many commentators, by the growing international tensions of the 1930s and the eventual outbreak of the Second World War (see, for example, Carr, 1946; Hinsley, 1963). There certainly seems an abundance of evidence to suggest that few states, particularly among the most powerful, were willing to surrender one of the most integral elements of the idea of sovereignty: the freedom to define friend or foe and to pursue the most suitable policies towards them. The League's systems of discussion, arbitration and guarantees were at too great a distance from the realities of power politics.

The 'architecture' of the UN, therefore, was drawn up to accommodate the international power structure as it was understood in 1945.[9] The division of the globe into powerful nation-states, with distinctive sets of geopolitical interests, was built into the Charter conception. As a result, the UN was virtually immobilized as an autonomous actor on many pressing issues (see Falk, 1975a, pp. 169–96, 1975b, pp. 69–72; Cassese, 1986, pp. 142–3, 200–1, 213–14 and 246–50). One of the most obvious manifestations of this was the special veto power accorded to the Permanent Members of the UN Security Council. This privileged political status added authority and legitimacy to the position of each of the major powers; for although they were barred in principle from the use of force on terms contrary to the Charter, they were protected against censure and sanctions in the event of unilateral action in the form of their veto. Moreover, the Charter gave renewed credence (through Article 51) to unilateral strategic state initiatives if they were necessary in 'self-defence', since there was no clear delimitation of the meaning of this phrase. In addition, while the Charter

[9] As one commentator put it, 'the failure of the League persuaded the framers of its successor organization that international security was best to be attained, not by a rejection of the hierarchical ordering of states, but by due recognition of the need for such hierarchy in any security system' (Clark, 1989, p. 166).

placed new obligations on states to settle disputes peacefully, and laid down certain procedures for passing judgement on alleged acts of self-defence, these procedures have rarely been used and there has been no insistence on compliance with them. The possibility of mobilizing the collective coercive measures envisaged in the Charter itself against illegitimate state action has, furthermore, never materialized, and even the UN's peace-keeping missions have been restricted (a key exception being the case of Somalia in 1992–4) to areas in which the consent of the territorial state in question has first been given.

The UN's susceptibility to the agendas of the most powerful states has been reinforced by its dependence on finance provided by its members.[10] This position of vulnerability to state politics is underscored by the absence of any mechanism to confer some kind of direct UN status on regional and transnational functional or cultural forces (agencies, groups or movements) who often might have a significant perspective on international questions. In sum, the UN Charter model, despite its good intentions, failed effectively to generate a new principle of organization in the international order – a principle which might break fundamentally with the logic of Westphalia and generate new democratic mechanisms of political coordination and change.

Nonetheless, it would be wrong simply to leave the argument about the UN order here. Some of the deficiencies attributed to the UN can be better placed at the door of the states system itself, with its deep structural embeddedness in the global capitalist economy (see § 6.2). Further, the UN Charter system has been distinctively innovative and influential in a number of respects. It has provided an international forum in which all states are in certain respects equal, a forum of particular value to developing countries and to those seeking a basis for 'consensus' solutions to international problems. It has provided a framework for decolonization, and for the pursuit of the reform of international institutions. Moreover, it has provided a vision, valuable in spite of all its limitations, of a new world order based upon a meeting of

[10] The regular budget of the UN, excluding emergency costs, is some $8 billion a year. This sum is approximately what was spent last Christmas on Western children, or approximately what US citizens spend each year on cut flowers and potted plants (see Childers, 1993). The cost of UN humanitarian relief operations and peace-keeping currently amounts to about only half this sum.

governments and, under appropriate circumstances, of a supranational presence in world affairs championing human rights. Indeed, this vision, if carried to its logical extreme, challenges the whole principle that humankind should be organized as a society of sovereign states above all else. For if the rights of each person can be asserted on the world political stage over and against the claims of a person's state, and if each person's duties can be proclaimed irrespective of his or her position as a subject or citizen of a state, then, as Bull has so clearly stated, 'the position of the state as a body sovereign over its citizens, and entitled to command their obedience, has been subject to challenge, and the structure of the society of sovereign states has been placed in jeopardy.' Likewise, in circumstances in which international or supranational organizations are subjects of international law, the seeds of subversion are laid 'of the society of sovereign states in favour of an organising principle in which an international or supranational body, or a series of such bodies, has displaced sovereign states as the chief repositories of rights and duties' (Bull, 1977, pp. 152–3). Developments in international law and institutions portend a new possibility in which the nation-state becomes but one type of political actor, without exclusive privileges, in the international legal order. These developments need assessment.

4.3 The states system vs. global politics?

While the nation-state manifests continuing vitality, this does not mean that the sovereign structure of individual nation-states has remained unaffected by changes at the intersection of national and international forces and relations: rather, it signals, in all probability, shifting patterns of powers and constraints. The significance of this possibility can be explored by examination of an argument found in the literature on globalization – earlier referred to as the 'transformationalist' or 'modernist' view (p. 25) – which offers an account of the way growing global interconnectedness can lead to a decline or 'crisis' of state authority, and the requirement of nation-states to collaborate ever more intensively with one another (see Keohane and Nye, 1972; Morse, 1976; Mansbach, Ferguson and Lampert, 1976; Rosenau, 1980; Soroos, 1986). In setting out the argument, it is *not* my intention to endorse it, but rather to sketch issues and concerns with which the following chapters will engage. For the sake of brevity, the argument is set out in schematic form.

1 The traditional conception in international politics of the relation between 'state' and 'society', in which the former is posited as the fundamental unit of order in the world, presupposes the relative homogeneity of the state and other key types of actor, that is, that they are entities with singular purposes (Young, 1972, p. 36). But the growth of international and transnational organizations and collectivities, from the UN and its organizations to special lobby groups and social movements, has altered the form and dynamics of both state and society. The intensification of processes of regional and global interconnectedness, and the proliferation of international agreements and forms of intergovernmental cooperation to regulate the unprecedented growth of these phenomena, in the post-Second World War period especially, have eroded the distinction between external and internal affairs, between international and domestic policy. The state has become a fragmented policy-making arena, permeated by international groups (governmental and non-governmental) as well as by domestic agencies and forces. Likewise, the extensive penetration of civil society by transnational actors has altered its form and dynamics.

2 With the increase in global interconnectedness, the number of political instruments available to individual governments and the effectiveness of particular instruments show a marked tendency to decline (see Keohane and Nye, 1972, pp. 392–5; Cooper, 1986, pp. 1–22). This tendency occurs, in the first instance, because of the loss of a wide range of border controls – whether formal or informal – which formerly served to restrict transactions in goods and services, production factors and technology, ideas and cultural interchange (see Morse, 1976, chs 2–3). The result is a shift in the costs and benefits of deploying different policy options and a decrease in the efficacy of those policy instruments which enable the state to control activities within and across its borders.

3 States can experience a further diminution in options because of the expansion in transnational forces and interactions which reduce and restrict the influence particular governments can exercise over the activities of their citizens. The impact, for example, of the flow of private capital across borders can threaten reflation measures, exchange rates, taxation levels and other government policies.

4 In the context of a highly interconnected global order, many

of the traditional domains of state activity and responsibility (defence, economic management, communications, administrative and legal systems) cannot be fulfilled without resort to international forms of collaboration. As demands on the state have increased in the post-war years, the state has been faced with a whole series of policy problems which cannot be adequately resolved without cooperating with other states and non-state actors (cf. Keohane, 1984a; McGrew, 1992a). Individual states are no longer the only appropriate political units for either resolving key policy problems or managing a broad range of public functions.[11]

5 Accordingly, states have had to increase the level of their political integration with other states (for example, in regional networks such as the European Union and the Organization of American States) and/or increase multilateral negotiations, arrangements and institutions to control the destabilizing effects that accompany interconnectedness (for example, through the International Monetary Fund and the World Bank, which, along with other international agencies, generated an organizational environment for economic management and intergovernmental consultation after the Second World War).

6 The result has been a vast growth of institutions, organizations and regimes which have laid a basis for the orderly management of global affairs, that is, global governance. (Of course, to say this is by no means to confuse such developments with the emergence of an integrated world government. There is a crucial difference between an international society which contains the possibility of political cooperation and order, and a supranational state which has a monopoly of coercive and legislative power.) The new global politics – involving, among other things, multibureaucratic decision-making within and between governmental and international bureaucracies, politics triggered by transnational forces and agencies and new forms of multinational integration between states – has created

[11] The issues raised by point (4) constitute one of the main fault lines dividing neo-realists and 'transformationalists'. The former interpret the rapid growth in forms of international collaboration, such as regimes, in a manner which is broadly consistent with realist assumptions, while the latter understand these as evidence that world politics can no longer be grasped by assuming that states, as unitary, sovereign structures, are the fundamental unit of such politics.

a framework in and through which the rights and obligations, powers and capacities of states have been redefined (Kaiser, 1972, pp. 358–60). The state's capacities have been both curtailed and expanded, allowing it to continue to perform a range of functions which cannot be sustained any longer in isolation from global or regional relations and processes. The steps in these arguments are shown in figure 4.1.

What these arguments suggest is that the meaning of national decision-making institutions today has to be explored in the context of a complex international society, and a huge range of actual and nascent regional and global organizations which transcend and mediate national boundaries. Moreover, the nature of these organizations and entities, the nature of their political dynamics and the nature of their accountability (if any) are pressing matters.

From the perspective of this transformationalist account, the modern state is increasingly trapped within webs of global interconnectedness permeated by quasi-supranational, intergovernmental and transnational forces, and unable to determine its own fate. Globalization is portrayed as a homogenizing force, eroding political 'difference' and the capacity of nation-states to act independently in the articulation and pursuit of domestic and international policy objectives: the territorial nation-state seems to face decline or crisis (see, in particular, Morse, 1976; Brown, 1988). Yet, while there has been rapid expansion of intergovernmental and transnational links, the age of the nation-state is by no means exhausted. If the territorial nation-state has suffered decline, this is a distinctively uneven process, particularly restricted to the power and reach of dominant Western and Eastern nation-states. European global society reached a pinnacle of influence at the close of the nineteenth century and the beginning of the twentieth, and American hegemony was a particular feature of the immediate decades following the Second World War. The decline of these power systems should not be taken to indicate the decline of the states system as such. Further, the recent transformation of the political regimes of Eastern Europe has generated a cluster of states, all asserting their independence and autonomy. While the 'classical empires' such as the British, French and Dutch are now largely eradicated, the 'new empires' created in the aftermath of the Second World War have undergone fundamental transformation.

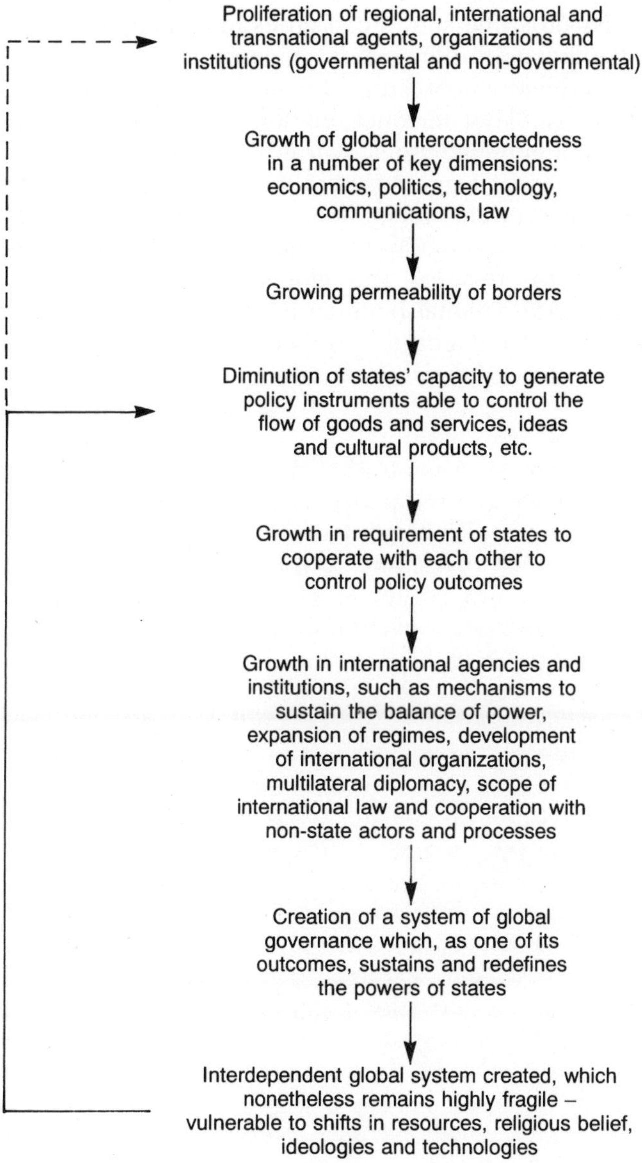

Proliferation of regional, international and transnational agents, organizations and institutions (governmental and non-governmental)

↓

Growth of global interconnectedness in a number of key dimensions: economics, politics, technology, communications, law

↓

Growing permeability of borders

↓

Diminution of states' capacity to generate policy instruments able to control the flow of goods and services, ideas and cultural products, etc.

↓

Growth in requirement of states to cooperate with each other to control policy outcomes

↓

Growth in international agencies and institutions, such as mechanisms to sustain the balance of power, expansion of regimes, development of international organizations, multilateral diplomacy, scope of international law and cooperation with non-state actors and processes

↓

Creation of a system of global governance which, as one of its outcomes, sustains and redefines the powers of states

↓

Interdependent global system created, which nonetheless remains highly fragile – vulnerable to shifts in resources, religious belief, ideologies and technologies

FIGURE 4.1 States, borders and international cooperation

The 'nationalization' of global politics is a process which has by no means fully run its course (cf. Modelski, 1972; Herz, 1976; Gilpin, 1981). The importance of the nation-state and nationalism, territorial independence and the desire to establish or regain or maintain 'sovereignty' does not seem to have diminished in recent times. Further, some of the world's most seemingly intractable regional crises do not escape the pull of sovereignty. The problems of the West Bank and the Gaza Strip and of the territories of the former Yugoslavia, for instance, can scarcely be thought through without reference to the idea of sovereign autonomy (Krasner, 1988, p. 40). Certainly, Bosnia is the rock on which many internationalist aspirations have foundered.

Moreover, the 'nuclear stalemate' or 'balance' achieved by the great powers created a paradoxical situation for them which can be referred to as the 'unavailability of force'; that is, new spaces offering opportunities for non-nuclear powers and peoples to assert themselves in the knowledge that the great powers' nuclear option is barely feasible and the cost of conventional military intervention makes it a colossal political, military and economic gamble (Herz, 1976, pp. 234ff). Vietnam (1964–75) and Afghanistan (1978–89) are obvious cases in point. Of course, miscalculations can be made about the likelihood of great power intervention, as they were in Argentina in 1982 and in Iraq in 1991; if 'overwhelming force' can be used against a smaller power (especially without resort to weapons of mass destruction), it clearly remains an option. Nevertheless, the intensity of nationalist politics, in the context of the deployment of nuclear weaponry and the high costs of military 'solutions', constitutes powerful pressures in the direction of a 'multipolar world' and a fragmented international order.

In addition, globalization in the domains of communication and information, far from creating a sense of common human purpose, interest and value, has arguably served to reinforce the sense of the significance of identity and difference, further stimulating the 'nationalization' of politics. As one commentator has aptly noted: 'awareness of other societies, even where it is "perfect", does not merely help to remove imagined conflicts of interest or ideology that do not exist; it also reveals conflicts of interest and ideology that do exist' (Bull, 1977, p. 280).

One consequence of this is the elevation in many international forums of non-Western views of rights, authority and legitimacy (see Bozeman, 1984). The meaning of some of the core concepts of the international system are subject to the deepest conflicts of interpretation, as illustrated at the UN World Conference on Human Rights in Vienna (June 1993). Despite the enshrinement of rights in a battery of international and regional treaties, the attempts to enact human rights in and through the operation of the global system have achieved at best limited success (see Vincent, 1986). Human rights discourse may indicate aspirations for the entrenchment of certain liberties and entitlements across the globe but it by no means reflects common agreement on rights questions. If the global system is marked by significant change, this is perhaps best conceived less as an end of the era of the nation-state and more as a challenge to the era of 'hegemonic states' – a challenge which is as yet far from complete.

Another clear testimony of the durability of the states system is the reluctance of states, on the whole, to submit their disputes with other states to arbitration by a 'superior authority', be it the UN or any other international body. At the heart of this 'great refusal' is the protection of the right of states to go to war (Hinsley, 1986, pp. 229–35).[12] The modern state is still able in principle to determine the most fundamental aspect of people's life-chances – the question of life and death. Moreover, although the course of a state's foreign policy can be contested by another state at the International Court of Justice (whose role is specified in Articles 92–6 of the UN Charter), this possibility is only rarely available and often involves both great costs and uncertain benefits (see Rosenne, 1985; Falk, 1986). For instance, when the Sandinista government of Nicaragua (taking advantage of its acceptance of compulsory jurisdiction before the Court) initiated proceedings against the United States for mining its harbours and lending assistance to insurgents in 1984, the United States attempted to

[12] While the Iraqi invasion of Kuwait in 1991 is clearly consistent with this refusal, the United States' subsequent organization of an alliance against Iraq through the UN might be said to be inconsistent with it. But it would be hard to make the latter case convincingly; for the organization of the alliance against Iraq was not a case of submitting a dispute to an independent arbitration procedure, but a case of organizing an acceptable international basis for a US-led war to restore the sovereignty of Kuwait and, at one and the same time, to uphold Western oil and energy policy (see Bromley, 1991, pp. 245ff). The US initiative is best represented as one of protecting its leadership role through multilateral means. See President Clinton's remarks to this effect quoted in the *Guardian* (1993), and in note 1, p. 269.

withdraw the dispute from the Court's competence and, having failed to achieve this result, defied the Court's ruling. There is little, if anything, the Court could achieve in the face of such defiance. At present a member of the UN is automatically a party to the Statute of the Court, but it is not obliged to accept the Court's jurisdiction unless it makes a separate commitment to do so; at the present time, few major states have made such a commitment.

Those who herald the end of the state all too often assume the erosion of state power in the face of globalizing pressures and fail to recognize the enduring capacity of the state apparatus to shape the direction of domestic and international politics. The degree to which the modern state enjoys 'autonomy' under various conditions is underexplored and, therefore, a key basis for a systematic and rigorous account of the form and limits of modern polities is too hastily put aside. The impact of global process is clearly likely to vary under different international and national conditions – for instance, a nation-state's location in the international division of labour, its place in particular power blocs, its position with respect to the international legal system, its relation to major international organizations. Not all states, for example, are equally integrated into the world economy; thus, while national political outcomes will be heavily influenced by global processes in some countries, in others regional or national forces might well remain supreme.

Further, it needs to be emphasized that processes of globalization themselves do not necessarily lead to growing global integration, that is, to a world order marked by the development of a homogeneous or unified society and politics. Local transformation is as much an element of globalization as the lateral extension of social relations across space and time (Giddens, 1990, p. 64). New demands can be unleashed for regional and local autonomy as groups find themselves buffeted by global forces and by inappropriate or ineffective political regimes. These circumstances carry the risk of an intensification of sectarian politics. In addition, by creating new patterns of transformation and change, globalization can weaken old political and economic structures without necessarily leading to the establishment of new systems of regulation. Political fragmentation or disintegrative trends are a clear possibility.

In sum

A number of points can usefully be drawn together from this and the previous two chapters. These can be put briefly:

1 The modern state became the supreme form of the state because it most successfully marshalled the means of waging war, economic resources and claims to legitimacy. Modern states mobilized effectively for war, for the enhancement of economic activity (capitalist expansion) and for their own legitimation. It is at the intersection of these particular formative processes that the distinctive organization and form of the modern state emerged.
2 The establishment of the universal franchise, among other liberal democratic institutions, can be related to the state's search for loyalty and resources when it has been most pressed (before, during and after wars), and to its claim to a distinct form of legitimacy. At the centre of the self-image of the modern state lies its claim to be an 'independent authority' or 'circumscribed impartial power', accountable only to its citizen body. To the extent that this claim has been redeemed, the modern state has been able to enjoy an advantage over rival political forces in the battle for legitimacy in the modern world. However, the nature and meaning of this claim have been contested from the outset of the modern state to the present day.
3 The inter-state system developed in the context of two key processes: the assertion of the state to sovereignty and the spread of new economic relationships on a global basis via capitalist economic mechanisms. States faced both inwards towards their populations and outwards towards the states order created and maintained by the states themselves. The Westphalian model of state sovereignty granted each state an entitlement to rule in its own territories while endorsing ultimately the principle of effective power; thereafter, the 'security dilemma' of the state locked all states into a process of actual or potential conflict with each other.
4 The development of the United Nations system did not fundamentally alter the logic and structure of the Westphalian order. Powerful states had their authority enhanced through the granting of special powers. Nevertheless, the UN system

contains within it legal and political developments which point to the possibility of a new organizational principle in world affairs. This vision, however, is in marked tension with the form and dynamics of the states system itself.

5 Globalization, a process reaching back to the earliest stages of the formation of the modern state and economy, continues to shape and reshape politics, economics and social life, albeit unevenly with differential impacts on individual countries. The stretching of social relations across space and time, via a variety of institutional dimensions (technological, organizational, legal and cultural), and their intensification within these institutional domains create new problems for and challenges to the power of the state and the inter-state system. Against this background, the effectiveness and viability of the sovereign, territorially bounded nation-state seems to be in question. How far exactly it is so remains to be explored, especially since the nation-state continues to command loyalty, both as an idea and as an institution.

5

DEMOCRACY, THE NATION-STATE AND THE GLOBAL ORDER I

The contemporary nature and scope of the sovereign authority of nation-states can be mapped by looking at a number of 'internal' and 'external' disjunctures between, on the one hand, the formal domain of political authority they claim for themselves and, on the other, the actual practices and structures of the state and economic system at the national, regional and global levels. The powers of political parties, bureaucratic organizations, corporations and networks of corporatist influence are among a variety of forces which put pressure on the range of decisions that can be made within a nation-state. At the international level, there are disjunctures between the idea of the state as in principle capable of determining its own future, and the world economy, international organizations, regional and global institutions, international law and military alliances which operate to shape and constrain the options of individual nation-states. In the discussion that follows the focus will be on such 'external' disjunctures. The enumeration of external disjunctures, it should be stressed, is largely illustrative; it is intended to indicate the different ways in which globalization can be said to constitute constraints or limits on political agency in a number of key domains; and to what extent the possibility of a democratic polity has been transformed and altered.

When assessing the impact of disjunctures, it is important to bear in mind that sovereignty is eroded only when it is displaced by forms of 'higher' and/or independent authority which curtail the rightful basis of decision-making within a national framework. For I take sovereignty to mean the political authority within a community which has the acknowledged right to exercise the powers of the state and to determine the rules, regulations and policies within a given territory. The doctrine of sovereignty has, as previously indicated, two distinct dimensions: the first concerned with the 'internal' aspect of sovereignty; the second concerned with the 'external' (see §§ 2.2 and 4.1). The former involves the belief that a political body established as sovereign rightly exercises the 'supreme command' over a particular society. Government – however defined – must enjoy the 'final and absolute authority' within that terrain (see Hinsley, 1986, pp. 1 and 26). The latter, external, dimension involves the claim that there is no final and absolute authority above and beyond the sovereign state. In the international context, the theory of sovereignty has implied that states should be regarded as independent in all matters of internal politics, and should in principle be free to determine their own fate within this framework. External sovereignty is an attribute which political societies possess in relationship to one another; it is associated with the aspiration of a political community to determine its own direction and policies, without undue interference from other powers.

Sovereignty should be distinguished from state 'autonomy', or the capacity of state managers and agencies to pursue their policy preferences without resort to forms of international collaboration or cooperation (see Held and McGrew, 1993; and, for an elaboration, Goldblatt et al., forthcoming). State autonomy can be differentiated with respect to its 'scope' and the 'domains' within which it can be exercised. By 'scope' is meant the level or intensity of constraints on state representatives and personnel, constraints which disrupt the possibility of the translation of national policy preferences into effective policy outcomes. 'Domains' refers to the policy spaces or issue-areas over which such constraints operate. In short, sovereignty refers to the entitlement of a state to rule over a bounded territory, while autonomy denotes the actual power a nation-state possesses to articulate and achieve policy goals independently. Bearing these distinctions in mind, it can be shown that external disjunctures map a series of conditions and processes which alter the range and nature of the decisions open to political decision-makers within a delimited terrain. The central questions to pose are: has sovereignty remained intact while the autonomy of the state has diminished? Has the modern state actually faced a loss of sovereignty? Has the efficacy of national democracies changed? And is the idea of democratic legitimacy compromised in the face of networks of regional and global relations? In addressing these questions, the focus will continue to be on processes and relations which impinge most directly on the states of Europe. It is the fate of the states of Europe which will be uppermost, although wider issues will be explored and comparisons drawn between Europe and other regions.

5.1 Disjuncture 1: international law

The development of international law has placed individuals, governments and non-governmental organizations under new systems of legal regulation. International law has recognized powers and constraints, and rights and duties, which transcend the claims of nation-states and which, while they may not be backed by institutions with coercive powers of enforcement, nonetheless have far-reaching consequences.

Throughout the nineteenth century, international law was conceived, as noted earlier, as a law between states; states were its subjects and individuals its objects. The exclusion of the individual from the provisions of international law has been challenged and undermined in the twentieth century. From the minorities treaties, associated with the establishment of the League of Nations after the First World War, to the UN's Universal Declaration of Human Rights (1948) and subsequent Covenants on Rights (1966), it has been recognized that individuals have rights and obligations over and above those set down in their own judicial and authority systems (see Vincent, 1992, pp. 269–92). Not only have some states conceded that individuals may legitimately refuse to serve in national armies (for instance, by recognizing legally the status of conscientious objection), but they have also accepted that there are clear occasions when an individual has a moral obligation beyond that of his or her obligation as a citizen of a state – opening up a gap between the rights and duties bestowed by citizenship, and the creation in international law of new forms of liberties and obligations.

This gap is exemplified by the results of the International Tribunal at Nuremberg (and the parallel Tribunal in Tokyo). The Tribunal laid down, for the first time in history, that when *international rules* that protect basic humanitarian values are in conflict with *state laws*, every individual must transgress the state laws (except where there is no room for 'moral choice') (Cassese, 1988,

p. 132). The legal framework of the Nuremberg Tribunal marked a highly significant change in the legal direction of the modern state, for the new rules challenged the principle of military discipline and subverted national sovereignty at one of its most sensitive points: the hierarchical relations within the military. Contemporary international law has generally endorsed the position taken by the Tribunal, and has affirmed its rejection of the defence of obedience to superior orders in matters of responsibility for crimes against peace and humanity.[1]

Of all the international declarations of rights which were made in the post-war years, the European Convention for the Protection of Human Rights and Fundamental Freedoms (1950) is especially noteworthy. In marked contrast to the Universal Declaration of Human Rights and the subsequent UN Covenants of Rights, the European Convention was concerned, as its preamble indicates, 'to take the first steps for the *collective enforcement* of certain of the rights stated in the Universal Declaration' (emphasis added). The European initiative was committed to a most remarkable and radical legal innovation: an innovation which in principle would allow individual citizens to initiate proceedings against their own governments. European countries have now accepted an (optional) clause of the Convention which permits citizens to petition directly the European Commission on Human Rights, which can take cases to the Committee of Ministers of the Council of Europe and then (given a two-thirds majority on the Council) to the European Court of Human Rights. While the system is far from straightforward and is problematic in many respects, it has been claimed that, alongside the other legal changes introduced by the European Community, it no longer leaves the state 'free to treat its own citizens as it thinks fit' (Capotorti, 1983, p. 977; cf. Coote, 1992). It is interesting, in addition, to note that the Treaty of European Union (the Maastricht Treaty) makes provision, in principle, for the establishment of a European Union citizenship and an ombudsman to whom citizens may directly appeal.

Human rights have also been promoted in other regions of the

[1] However, moves to apply the Nuremberg principles consistently and impartially across diverse geopolitical circumstances have been unsuccessful, although there remains some support for the development of an International Criminal Court with legal competence to apprehend and try those who initiate and perpetrate 'crimes of state', even when the accused are *in absentia* (see pp. 103–4).

world, partly in response to United Nations encouragement that such rights should be entrenched in institutions at regional levels. Notable developments have occurred in America and Africa. The American Convention on Human Rights, which came into force in 1978, has both a commission and a court, although they are as yet far less well-used than their West European counterparts. The Organization of African Unity adopted the African (Banjul) Charter of Human and People's Rights in 1981; it too has a commission concerned to promote human rights. While citizens in many African countries have established organizations to seek compliance with this agreement, many of its leading provisions remain substantially unenforced. Nonetheless, what all these charters highlight is further evidence of a gradual shift from the principle that state sovereignty must be safeguarded irrespective of its consequences for individuals, groups and organizations. Respect for the autonomy of the subject, and for an extensive range of human rights, creates a new set of ordering principles in political affairs which, where effectively entrenched, can delimit and curtail the principle of state sovereignty itself.

There are two legal rules which, since the very beginnings of the international community, have been taken to uphold national sovereignty: 'immunity from jurisdiction' and 'immunity of state agencies'. The former prescribes that 'no state can be sued in the courts of another state for acts performed in its sovereign capacity'; and the latter stipulates that 'should an individual break the law of another state while acting as an agent for his country of origin and be brought before that state's courts, he is not held "guilty" because he did not act as a private individual but as the representative of the state' (Cassese, 1988, pp. 150–1). The underlying purpose of these rules is to protect a government's autonomy in all matters of foreign policy and to prevent domestic courts from ruling on the behaviour of foreign states (on the understanding that all domestic courts everywhere will be so prevented). And the upshot has traditionally been that governments have been left free to pursue their interests subject only to the constraints of the 'art of politics'.

It is notable, however, that these internationally recognized legal mainstays of sovereignty have been progressively questioned by Western courts. Efforts have been made, for instance, to increase the accountability of political leaders for wrongdoing while in office. A recent step in this direction has been the attempt to make leaders of foreign states vulnerable to civil claims in relation to acts of law-breaking by them. A well-known case involves claims for compensation against Imelda Marcos and the estate of Ferdinand Marcos, pursued in the US by the estates of two young labour leaders, murdered in Seattle some years ago, in what was allegedly a covert operation by a Philippines intelligence unit (Falk, 1991a, p. 17). Although national sovereignty has most often protected foreign leaders against charges of wrongdoing, civil or criminal, the tension between national sovereignty and international law is now marked – in the Marcoses' case, $15 million was awarded to the plaintiffs – and it is by no means clear how it will be resolved.

There is a further tendency in contemporary international law no longer to regard a state as legitimate simply by virtue of the effectiveness of its claim to public power; that is to say, there is a tendency to reject a principle of legitimacy which is indifferent to the nature, form and operation of political power. Entrenched in certain legal instruments is the view that a legitimate state must be a democratic state that upholds certain common values.[2] The full status of this tendency is ambiguous, but it is noteworthy. For instance, the Universal Declaration of Human Rights asserts the democratic principle along with enumerated rights as a 'common standard of achievement for all peoples and nations' in Article 21 (see United Nations, 1988, pp. 2 and 5). However, the word 'democracy' does not itself appear in the Declaration and the adjective 'democratic' appears only once (in Article 29). The UN International Covenant on Civil and Political Rights (1966) (which came into force in 1976), by contrast, elaborates this principle in Article 25 as a legal obligation, although it only loosely specifies its meaning (see United Nations, 1988, p. 28).

The European Convention on Human Rights is explicit in its connection of democracy and state legitimacy, as is the statute of the Council of Europe which makes a commitment to democracy a condition of membership. But one of the most significant indicators of the erosion of an unqualified endorsement of state sovereignty in international law comes from the challenge to the principle and practice of non-interference in the internal affairs of a state. The clearest statement of this challenge in recent times can be found in the 1992 declaration of the Helsinki Conference on Security and Cooperation in Europe (CSCE), involving over fifty states including the US and Canada. In the declaration the

[2] I would like to thank Kevin Boyle for drawing my attention to this cluster of issues. For a thorough treatment see James Crawford (1994).

states recognize their accountability to each other and underline the rights of citizens to demand from their governments respect for democratic values and standards:

> We emphasise that the commitments undertaken in the field of the human dimension of the CSCE [that is, human rights] are matters of direct and legitimate concern to all participating States and do not belong exclusively to the internal affairs of the State concerned. The protection and promotion of human rights and fundamental freedoms and the strengthening of democratic institutions continue to be a vital basis for our comprehensive security. (CSCE 1992, para. 8, p. 2)

While these commitments remain fragile and far from universal, they signal the beginnings of a new approach to the concept of legitimate political power in international law.

The decline in the efficacy of state sovereignty is evidenced further in recent questioning of the traditional principles regulating the appropriation of territory and resources. At the heart of classical international law (the Westphalian model), the earth, sea and air were recognized as phenomena legitimately falling under the sovereign authority of states on the condition that 'whoever possessed a territory and exercised actual control over it successfully secured a legal title' (see § 4.1). While the principle of state sovereignty has been extended in recent times to cover the control of resources in a variety of domains, including the continental shelf and 'economic zones' (areas which stretch up to 200 nautical miles from coastal states), a new concept was propounded in 1967 as a potential vehicle for rethinking the legal basis of the appropriation and exploitation of resources: the 'common heritage of mankind' (see p. 86). Although the principle was subject to intensive discussion in the United Nations and elsewhere, it was eventually enshrined in two important treaties, the Convention on the Moon and Other Celestial Bodies (1979) and the Convention on the Law of the Sea (1982). First introduced as a way of thinking about the impact of new technologies, which opened up the possibility of the exploitation of resources (on the sea-bed or on stars and other planets) which were beyond national jurisdiction, its early champions saw it as a basis for arguing that the vast domains of hitherto untapped resources should be developed for the benefit of all, particularly the poor and the developing nations. There are five elements to the concept of the common heritage, namely, '(1) the exclusion of a right of appropriation; (2) the duty to exploit . . . resources in the interest of mankind . . . ; (3) the duty to explore and exploit for peaceful purposes only; (4) the duty to pay due regard to scientific research; and (5) the duty duly to protect the environment' (Cassese, 1986, p. 390).

The introduction of the concept of the common heritage points to the possibility of a legal order based on equity and cooperation. Although there is still a great deal of argument as to exactly where and how this principle should be applied, and how the benefits which accrue from the exploitation of new resources should be distributed, the introduction of the concept was a turning point in international legal thinking. Furthermore, it has been taken up in debates about the environment and, in particular, in discussions about the management of the 'global commons' and their shared ecosystems (see World Commission on Environment and Development, 1987, pp. 18–19). Moreover, elements of the concept can be traced in the Rio Declaration on Environment and Development and in Agenda 21, both adopted at the Earth Summit in Brazil in 1992.

The Rio Declaration takes as its primary goal the creation of 'a new and equitable global partnership through the creation of new levels of cooperation among states, key sectors of societies and people' (United Nations, 1993, vol. 1, p. 3). Principle 7 of the Declaration demands that 'states shall cooperate in a spirit of global partnership to conserve, protect and restore the health and integrity of the Earth's ecosystem'; and Principle 12 calls for 'environmental measures addressing transboundary or global environmental problems' which should, 'as far as possible, be based on an international consensus' (ibid., pp. 4 and 5). Setting out what this new global partnership might mean, Agenda 21 specifies that

> This partnership commits all States to engage in a continuous and constructive dialogue, inspired by the need to achieve a more efficient and equitable world economy, keeping in view the increasing interdependence of the community of nations and that sustainable development should become a priority item on the agenda of the international community. It is recognized that, for the success of this new partnership, it is important to overcome confrontation and to foster a climate of genuine cooperation and solidarity. (ibid., p. 14; and see pp. 111 and 238)[3]

[3] The Rio Declaration and Agenda 21 also embody remarkable tensions between the declared (and reaffirmed) 'sovereign rights of states'

International law is a vast and changing corpus of rules, quasi-rules and precedents which set out the basis of coexistence and cooperation in the international order. Traditionally, international law has identified and upheld the idea of a society of sovereign states as 'the supreme normative principle' of the political organization of humankind (Bull, 1977, pp. 140ff). In recent decades, the subject, scope and source of international law have all been contested; and opinion has shifted against the doctrine that international law is and should be a 'law between states only and exclusively' (see Oppenheim, 1905, ch. 1). At the heart of this shift lies a conflict between claims made on behalf of the states system and those made on behalf of alternative organizing principles of world order. While the recent political resurgence of Islam, and the renewed intensity of many nationalist struggles, indicate that this conflict is far from settled, new directions in international law are clearly discernible.

5.2 Disjuncture 2: internationalization of political decision-making

A second major area of disjuncture between the theory of the sovereign state and the contemporary global system lies in the vast array of international regimes and organizations that have been established, in principle, to manage whole areas of transnational activity (trade, the oceans, space and so on) and collective policy problems. The growth in the number of these new forms of political association reflects the rapid expansion of transnational links, the growing interpenetration of foreign and domestic policy, and the corresponding desire by most states for some form of international governance and regulation to deal with collective policy problems (see Luard, 1977; Krasner, 1983).

---

and the prerogatives of the new global partnership, although even in those sections affirming the former there is a concern to ensure that activities which fall within the jurisdiction or control of particular states do not cause damage to the environment of other states or to areas beyond the limits of national jurisdiction (see Principle 2, ibid., p. 3). On principles of accountability and enforcement, however, there is little precision.

The development of international regimes[4] and international organizations has led to important changes in the decision-making structure of world politics. New forms of multilateral and multinational politics have been established and with them distinctive styles of collective decision-making involving governments, IGOs and a wide variety of transnational pressure groups and international non-governmental organizations (INGOs). In 1909 there were 37 IGOs and 176 INGOs, while in 1989 there were nearly 300 IGOs and 4624 INGOs. In the middle of the nineteenth century there were two or three conferences or congresses per annum sponsored by IGOs; today the number totals close to 4000 annually (Zacher, 1993). Against this background, the range and diversity of the participants at the Earth Summit in Rio de Janeiro in June 1992 – including delegates from over 120 governments and from hundreds of national and transnational environmental pressure groups – may not seem quite as remarkable as the occasion initially suggested.

[4] Regimes can be defined as 'implicit or explicit principles, norms, rules, and decision-making procedures around which actor expectations converge in a given issue area of international relations' (Krasner, 1983, p. 2). Regimes are not merely temporary or *ad hoc* agreements; rather, they can be thought of as 'intervening variables' between the basic power and economic characteristics of the international system, and definite outcomes. The failure, for example, of markets to regulate the supply and distribution of goods and services, or to resolve pressing transnational problems, may provide incentives for states to create regimes. Regimes can provide a framework of legal liability, improve available information and reduce the transaction costs of arriving at individual policy decisions. Keohane has sought to show that there is considerable scope in the international order for the expansion of cooperative ventures among states even assuming that they are egoistic rational actors (1984a). He argues that what explains the massive increase in state cooperation in the post-war years is the perceived recognition of international regimes as methods of reducing costs to states of 'going it alone' in resolving pressing issues; reducing the costs of coordination among states by providing a common framework of information; creating rules for public bureaucracies to aid their operations; and reducing the general sense of uncertainty in an era in which many important political problems escape the control of individual polities. International regimes are an expression of the necessity to find new modes of cooperation and regulation. However, while this may be helpful as an account of the origin and persistence of 'negotiated' regimes, it is not an account of all forms of regime, some of which are an expression of powerful states' abilities to impose them (see below; cf. Young, 1989).

Among the spectrum of international agencies and organizations are those whose primary concerns have been technical: the Universal Postal Union, the International Telecommunications Union, the World Meteorological Organization and a host of other bodies. These agencies have tended to work effectively and uncontroversially – providing, in most cases, extensions to the services offered by individual nation-states (Burnheim, 1986, p. 222). To the extent that their tasks have been sharply delimited, they have been politically unexceptionable. At the opposite pole lie organizations like the World Bank, the IMF, the UN Educational, Scientific and Cultural Organization (UNESCO) and, of course, the UN itself. Preoccupied with more central questions of the management and allocation of rules and resources, these bodies have been highly controversial and politicized. Unlike the smaller, technically based agencies, these organizations are at the centre of continual conflict over the control of regional and global policy (Burnheim, 1986, pp. 220ff). While the mode of operation of these agencies tends to vary, as do their requirements for the approval of decisions (unanimity, weighted voting, among other devices), they have all benefited over the years from a certain 'entrenchment of authority' which has bestowed on some decisive powers of intervention. In addition to these agencies, there also exists a range of more informal global networks of political coordination which have considerable influence on global affairs. Among the latter are the economic summits of the leading industrial countries, the so-called 'Group of 7' (G7). The G7 operates as a kind of 'global directorate'; and in the context of the end of the Cold War, it is not inconceivable that it will come to wield increasing political and economic influence (see Lewis, R., 1991; and, for an example of such influence, see p. 129).

The operations of the IMF and the World Bank provide interesting illustrations of some of the more contentious issues raised by international organizations. While the IMF was founded in 1944 at the Bretton Woods Conference to oversee global rules governing money and currency relations, its primary purpose in recent times has been to provide technical advice, economic direction and financial loans to hard-pressed economies, predominantly in the developing world (see Babai, 1993a). Access to financial assistance has, beyond a minimum threshold, been tied by the IMF to specific conditions, commonly referred to as the principle of 'conditionality'. The IMF may insist that a government restrict credit expansion, cut public expenditure, limit public-sector wages and employment, devalue its currency and reduce subsidized welfare programmes if it is to secure financial support. In a developing country, for instance, this may trigger intense social conflict and perhaps the fall of a government, or it may contribute directly to the imposition of martial law (see Girvan, 1980). Tough conditionality lending has often been tantamount to 'shock treatment' for a country, fundamentally unsettling its institutions and customs. It has to be borne in mind that IMF intervention takes place routinely at the request of governmental authorities or of particular political factions within a state, and is often the result of the recognition that there is minimal scope for independent national economic policies; it cannot be interpreted, therefore, as a simple threat to sovereignty. Nonetheless, a striking tension has emerged between the idea of the state – centred on national politics and national institutions – and the nature of decision-making at the international level. While *de jure* sovereignty may not be directly infringed, the decision-making process of the IMF raises serious questions about the conditions under which a political community is able to determine its own policies and directions. The IMF has tended in recent times to take 'structural adjustment' to the international economy as a fixed point of orientation, downplaying both the external origins of a country's difficulties and the structural pressures and rigidities of the world economy itself. In current circumstances, there is little a developing country can do to resist this.

The political questions posed by the level and scope of IMF conditionality have also been raised in connection with the World Bank. As the leading international development institution, the World Bank has been embroiled in debates about development policy. Although its lending policy has gone through a number of phases, it became associated in the 1980s directly with 'structural' and 'sector adjustment' loans, requiring of borrowers exacting standards of monetary and fiscal rectitude, increased leeway for the private sector, the steady removal of domestic protections from the forces of the international economy, and greater reliance on market solutions to production and distribution questions (see Babai, 1993b; cf. Mosley, Toye and Harrigan, 1991). More recently, conditionality has been extended to embrace the requirements of 'good governance', comprising respect for human rights, liberal democratic mechanisms of political accountability and effective public administration. These prescriptions for developmental assistance have been insisted upon by the 'dominant coalition' of advanced industrial countries which effectively control World Bank policy (see Leftwich, 1993a, 1994). As in the IMF, the voting rights of Bank members on policy are distributed largely in relation to their individual financial contributions. Geo-economic strength is integrated into decision-making procedures. Not surprisingly, therefore, the World Bank has become involved in intense disputes about whether its policy reflects sound economic judgement or whether it amounts to a strategy of 'recolonization' (see, for example, Tandon, 1994). Those who take the latter position insist that the sovereign rights of countries are violated by World Bank policy directives which undermine the political space for national self-determination. The World Bank, accordingly, is seen to impose its own economic and political standards – the standards, that is, of the North as a whole – on the struggling nations, without regard for a proper consideration of local circumstances and interests (cf. Leftwich, 1993b). Irrespective of how much of this view one accepts, and as with the IMF it is a view complicated by the 'invited' status of World Bank assistance packages (thus making it more of a threat to autonomy than to sovereignty), it throws into sharp relief the contested role of some international organizations and, in particular, their processes of policy formation, policy enforcement and (limited) mechanisms of accountability.[5]

The European Community (EC), or the European Union (EU) as it is now called, provides an important additional illustration of the issues posed by international organizations. However, its significance reaches further than that of any other kind of international organization by virtue of its right to make laws which can be imposed on member states; more than any other international body, it justifies the label 'supranational'. Within Union institutions, the Council of Ministers has a unique position, for it has at its disposal powerful legal instruments (above all, 'regulations' and 'directives') which allow it to formulate and enact policy with a minimum of national democratic accountability. Of all these instruments 'regulations' are the most notable because they have the status of law independently of any further negotiation or action

[5] The World Bank has recently announced sweeping changes in its approach to Africa's economic problems, declaring that 'the bank would no longer dictate development plans to African countries and would stop "imposing" foreign expertise on reluctant governments' (Hultman, 1993, p. 11). What difference these changes will make, and the extent to which they help build the region's capacity to help itself, remain to be seen.

on the part of member states. Disputes about national interpretations and applications of regulations and directives can be heard at the European Court of Justice; and the Court has taken on a major role in the harmonization of law within the Union.

With the passing of the Single European Act in 1986, unanimity within the Council of Ministers has been replaced by 'qualified majority voting' for a significant number of issue-areas (see Noel, 1989). While there are certain safeguards to national sovereignty built into this change (decisions about which issues can be decided by majority voting must themselves be based on unanimity), policies can be adopted which are opposed by individual governments. The place of national sovereignty is, thus, no longer guaranteed. The Treaty on European Union, agreed at the Maastricht Summit of December 1991, seeks, moreover, not only to extend the scope of economic and monetary union, but also to extend the framework of cooperation to security policy. If the Treaty is fully implemented, the member states will have taken several major steps towards becoming a highly integrated, if not federal, association (see Pinder, 1992; Ross, 1995).

The member states of the European Union are no longer the sole centres of power within their own borders. As the EU's Court of Justice noted, 'by creating a Community of unlimited duration, having its own institutions, its own personality . . . and, more particularly, real powers stemming from a limitation of sovereignty or a transfer of powers from the States to the Community, the member States have limited their sovereign rights' (Mancini, 1990, p. 180). On the other hand, it is important to bear in mind that the Union's powers were gained by the 'willing surrender' of aspects of sovereignty by individual states – a 'surrender' which, arguably, has actually helped the survival of the European nation-state faced with the dominance of the US in the first three decades after the Second World War and the rise of the Japanese economic challenge (see Wallace, W., 1994). In brief, like many other international organizations, the European Union provides distinctive opportunities and restraints. The member states of the Union retain the final and most general power in many areas of their affairs – and the Union itself seems to have strengthened their options in some of these domains. In addition, the entrenchment of the notion of 'subsidiarity' within the EU legal framework after Maastricht may enhance policy choices in certain spheres (see Neunreither, 1993). However, within the Union sovereignty is now also clearly divided: any conception of sovereignty which assumes that it is an indivisible, illimitable, exclusive and perpetual form of public power – embodied within an individual state – is defunct.

Although the challenge to national sovereignty has perhaps been more clearly debated within the countries of the European Union than in any other region of the world, sovereignty and autonomy are under severe pressure in many places. They are under pressure from a confluence of constraints imposed, on the one hand, by the structure of the international system, particularly by the organization of the global economy (see § 6.2) and, on the other hand, by the policies and activities of leading agencies and organizations, both regional and international. This combination of factors has particular poignancy in countries such as those in sub-Saharan Africa, where recognition of the limits of their powers is combined with widespread acknowledgement of the near bankruptcy of many of their economies (see Hawthorn, 1993). Here the balance of opportunities and restraints is a frequent source of sustained concern. For countries such as Zimbabwe, it has been suggested that, in the context of the end of the Cold War and the end of Soviet support, international assistance programmes have left its people with less control over their destiny than they had twenty years ago (see Tandon, 1994). Even if it could be argued that their entitlement to govern has remained broadly intact, their autonomy – or practical sovereignty – is severely restricted, markedly curtailing policy options.

5.3 Disjuncture 3: hegemonic powers and international security structures

There is an additional disjuncture involving the idea of the state as an autonomous strategic, military actor and the development of the global system of states, characterized by the existence of great powers and power blocs, which sometimes operates to undercut a state's authority and integrity. The insertion of an individual state into the global power hierarchy imposes constraints upon the kinds of defence and foreign policy which governments, particularly democratically elected governments, may pursue.

From the period following the Second World War until 1989, the nature of national security was shaped decisively by the 'Great Contest' between the United States and the Soviet Union. The dominance of the US and USSR as world powers, and the operation of alliances like NATO and the Warsaw Pact Treaty (WTO), constrained decision-making for many states in the post-war years. A state's capacity to initiate particular foreign policies, pursue certain strategic concerns, choose between alternative military technologies and control certain weapon systems located on its own territory was limited by its place in the international system of power relations (see Herz, 1976; Kaldor and Falk, 1987).

At one end of the spectrum of constraint lay direct military participation in the affairs of another country. In 1987, the US had 492,500 troops abroad while the Soviet Union had 730,090. Of these the US had 250,000 troops in West Germany, 54,000 in Japan and 43,000 in South Korea; the Soviet Union deployed 380,000 in East Germany, 110,000 in Afghanistan, 65,000 in Hungary, and 60,000 in Czechoslovakia (Tilly, 1990, p. 208). While the purposes served by these troops was by no means always the same, the troops certainly operated to forestall regime change and alterations in the balance of international power. Less intrusive forms of constraint include the sharing of weapon systems with allies, which, like the deployment of land-based cruise missiles in the United Kingdom in the mid-1980s, remain effectively controlled by the dominant power; in the latter case, by the United States (see Thomson, 1983; Campbell, 1984).

European security was dependent for most of the post-war period upon the operation of NATO and the WTO. These alliance systems provided measures of collective security although they were distinctive in respect of their decision-making structures and levels of military integration. Clear evidence of what can be referred to as 'internationalization of security' can be found in NATO's joint and integrated military command structure. Ever since NATO was established in the late 1940s, its concern with collective security has trodden a fine line between, on the one hand, maintaining an organization of sovereign states (which permits, in principle, an individual member state not to act if it judges this appropriate) and, on the other, developing an international organization which *de facto*, if not *de jure*, operates according to its own logic and decision-making procedures. The existence of an integrated supranational command structure – headed by the Supreme Allied Commander in Europe, who has always been an American general appointed by the US president – ensures that, in a situation of war, NATO's 'national armies' would operate within the framework of NATO's strategies and decisions (Smith,

D., 1984). The sovereignty of a national state is decisively qualified once its armed forces are committed to a NATO conflict.

Even without such a conflict, state autonomy as well as sovereignty can be limited and checked, for the routine conduct of NATO affairs involves the integration of national defence bureaucracies into international defence organizations; these, in turn, create transgovernmental decision-making systems which can escape the control of any single member state. Such systems can lead, moreover, to the establishment of informal but nonetheless powerful, transgovernmental personnel networks or coalitions which are difficult to monitor by national mechanisms of accountability and control (cf. Kaiser, 1972; Richelson and Ball, 1986).

Membership of NATO does not annul sovereignty or autonomy; rather, in creating new decision-making structures for collective security during periods of war and peace, it qualifies them for each member state in different ways. But no account of NATO would be satisfactory without emphasizing that its members are also rivals competing for scarce resources, arms contracts, international prestige and other means of national enhancement. Accordingly, aspects of state sovereignty and autonomy are negotiated and renegotiated through the NATO alliance.

The WTO was created in 1955, after the accession of West Germany to NATO. While all the members of the WTO were in principle equal, the Soviet Union held the dominant position until the end of 1989, shortly before the Treaty's dissolution in 1991 (see Garthoff, 1993). The WTO established a joint command over the armed forces of its members and coordinated joint military exercises for nearly thirty years. Around this command structure crystallized a plethora of military and political bodies to integrate Warsaw Pact strategy. The formal rationale of the WTO was to provide a force capable of countering NATO and of defending communism whenever this was necessary; but it also provided a justification for Soviet military presence on the territory of several of the Treaty's members, and for forestalling or reversing regime change in these countries (cf. Remington, 1971; Holloway and Sharp, 1984). In 1956, as is well known, Hungary was prevented from leaving the WTO by Soviet military intervention. Although the WTO did not formally take part in the invasion of Czechoslovakia in 1968, several of its members did, spearheaded by the Soviet army, enforcing what came to be known as the 'Brezhnev Doctrine' (that is, the policy of protecting the 'achievements of socialism' in Central and Eastern Europe by force if necessary).

The political significance of the Brezhnev Doctrine in containing and policing Central and Eastern Europe can be gauged by the dramatic results which followed from its abandonment. While the roots of the dramatic transformation of the state socialist system in 1989–90 were complex and many, it was shifts in strategic thinking in the Kremlin that were probably the proximate cause of the success of the revolutions (see Lewis, P., 1990). Of particular significance was the Soviet decision to replace the Brezhnev Doctrine with the 'Sinatra Doctrine'. The policy of tolerating nationally chosen paths to progress and prosperity – 'do it your way' – had decisive consequences, intended and otherwise, for the capacity of state socialist regimes to survive. By removing the threat of Red Army or Warsaw Pact intervention, and by refusing to sanction the use of force to crush mass demonstrations, the 'Sinatra Doctrine' effectively pulled the carpet from under East European communism (see Held, 1993a).[6]

In the post-Cold War world of the 1990s the constraints upon state security policy have not been eradicated but have been reconfigured.[7] Instead of bipolarity, the global system now exhibits more of the characteristics of a multipolar distribution of political and economic power. Within this more complex structure the strategic and foreign policy options confronting an individual state are still defined by its location in the global power hierarchy; it remains the case that global power relations exert a profound constraint upon state action. For instance, NATO continues to operate as the main international forum within which Western security matters are debated and defence policies coordinated. Indeed, following the collapse of the WTO, NATO took new initiatives establish-

[6] The developments in East Germany were a notable case in point. When Hungary opened its border with Austria, and triggered the massive emigration of East Germans to the West, pressures within East Germany rapidly intensified and demonstrations, held in Leipzig and nearby cities, escalated. Without the routine recourse to force, the East German authorities sought to placate their rebellious citizenry by sanctioning access to the West via new openings in the Berlin Wall. The result is well known: the authorities lost control of an already demanding situation, and within a short time both their legitimacy and effectiveness were undermined.

[7] I have drawn material for the following two paragraphs from my joint paper with Anthony McGrew (1993, pp. 267–8).

ing the North Atlantic Cooperation Council (NACC) and the Partnership for Peace. NACC brings together the governing bodies of the Alliance and military and diplomatic representatives from the newly established East European and ex-Soviet states to discuss and rethink European-wide security and military matters, while the Partnership for Peace seeks to encourage, among others, the states of the former WTO to establish greater transparency and cooperative arrangements in international security (see Gallis, 1994).

In addition, military matters are being examined by the Western European Union (WEU) and by the CSCE, both of which have been given new responsibilities and functions involving the establishment of distinctive mechanisms of multilateral consultation and coordination.[8] Europe, in effect, is witnessing the emergence of new structures of collective security – a new 'Concert of Europe' – which invite a stronger international integration of military and security affairs. Moreover, given increasing budgetary constraints and the escalating costs of defence hardware, it is likely that, now or in the not too distant future, 'no European country will be able to mount a unilateral conventional military campaign that can defeat any adversary able to conduct modern military operations' (see Zelikow, 1992, pp. 12–30). One implication of this is to intensify the pressure, especially in the context of the renewed instabilities in Europe (the fragmentation of the Soviet Union, the break-up of Yugoslavia, among other notable developments) for stronger collective organization of defence functions. For many European states the new 'Concert of Europe' implies a recognition of the limits of state autonomy and sovereignty, and a potential willingness to renegotiate key elements of both.

Irrespective of the exact form of collective security arrangements and alliance structures, the questions posed for state sovereignty and autonomy by the modern state's organization of security and defence do not end here. For some of the most corrosive consequences of this organization are generated by the very dynamics of states themselves; that is, by the 'interactive effects' which the security establishments of states have upon one another. State security is still often conceptualized in a manner that creates – even guarantees – insecurity. At the root of this lies the 'security

[8] The WEU is a collective defence organization of nine West European states formed in 1948. It is developing a significant military and political role, linking EU and NATO structures.

dilemma' of the modern state, referred to earlier (see § 3.1). Since the inception of the modern states system, 'security' has remained the predominant concern of individual states in the international order. Yet the perennial search for security seems to have brought only chronic insecurity. As one observer aptly noted: 'all the principles of historical and contemporary international systems – the balance of power principle, the concert or collective security principle, the deterrence principle – are based implicitly or explicitly on the notion that security is a function of managing (or balancing) military power between the contending actors in the international system' (Kim, 1984, p. 185).

The interconnectedness of states and societies means that one country's national security policy has direct consequences for that of another; and the dynamics of the security system of the global order as a whole has consequences for each and every nation. In making national security decisions, a government not only governs for itself but governs for others. If a country feels threatened, it might increase its ability to threaten others, which will in turn have security implications for those beyond the immediate parties involved. Furthermore, in an age in which modern weapons systems can inflict devastating consequences on the environment – through, for example, radioactive fall-out, climate change, or the massive destruction of populations – the actions of each and every state are deeply interlocked with the future and destiny of every other political entity. In addition, where nuclear and non-nuclear weapons of mass destruction may be deployed at any moment by many different nations, 'no country can maintain its own security while ignoring or even inadvertently increasing the insecurity of other societies' (Johansen, 1991, p. 213). In short, the proliferation of weapon systems of mass destruction radically increases the prospect of political instability and the insecurity of all.

Against this background, it can be seen that the existing system of national security undermines simple-minded distinctions between 'enemy' and 'friend'. These distinctions made some sense in the age of massed battles, where battlegrounds themselves were relatively contained. But under the conditions of modern technological warfare, the impact of a war can be as devastating for 'a friend' as it can be for 'an enemy'. In fact, the very meaning of these categories breaks down as the possibility of modern nuclear (or chemical or biological) technology creates the nightmare of fundamental and irreversible damage to the human environment.

In this context, it may make very little difference whether one is a 'friend' or an 'enemy'.

The logic of statist security has profound consequences for national systems of accountability, and for democracy more generally (see Johansen, 1991, pp. 209–42). First, it denies democracy internationally by reinforcing the sense of the separateness of sovereign states and of their ultimate responsibility for their own defence and security. Accordingly, states accept, at best, minimum responsibility for people in other countries. Second, it erodes democracy within nation-states by legitimizing institutions which are hierarchical, which thrive on secrecy and which, in an age of weapons of mass destruction, give a tiny group of people power over the future of life itself. While the end of the Cold War has changed the immediate security equation for Europe, the United States and many other countries, the underlying structure of self-perpetuating insecurity remains intact. As Johansen has written:

> contemporary security policies continue to reinforce adversarial military relations among national sovereignties, not serious diplomatic programmes to include the adversary within a system of universal rules and a form of transnational governance that would deliberately induce a nation-state to give up its own national war-making function of sovereignty in return for other governments throughout the world doing the same. (1993a, p. 228)

The bipolar world created in the aftermath of the Second World War led to an intensive struggle for the allegiance of Third World states. This struggle locked most of the states of Africa, the Middle East and Asia into an arms race and security posture which mimicked the great powers, especially the United States and the Soviet Union (see Tilly, 1990, pp. 197–224). Resources drained away from possible civilian usage to programmes of extensive militarization; the East–West conflict massively exacerbated the momentum and logic of statist security across the Third World. The contemporary heritage of this situation includes the risk not only that a war in developing countries will involve nuclear weapons, but also that other types of weapon of mass destruction might be used. The post-Cold War era has done little as yet to reduce such a risk. While contemporary security policy is premised on the overriding importance of national war-making ability, it is hard to see how this state of affairs will fundamentally alter. The logic of state security has created a cycle of violence and preparation for violence in the international system which hinders the development of policy for a durable peace – whether national, regional or global.

6

Democracy, the Nation-state and the Global Order II

The intensification of regionalization and globalization, particularly in the post-Second World War era, has contributed simultaneously to an expansion of the liberal democratic state's functional responsibilities and to an erosion of its capacity to deal effectively alone with many of the demands placed upon it. Goods, capital, people, knowledge, images, communications and weapons, as well as crime, culture, pollutants, drugs, fashions and beliefs, readily flow across territorial boundaries. Transnational networks, social movements and relationships extend through virtually all areas of human activity. The existence of global systems of trade, finance and production binds together the prosperity and fate of households, communities and nations across the world. Territorial boundaries are therefore arguably increasingly insignificant in so far as social activity and relations no longer stop – if they ever did – at the 'water's edge'. In the sections which follow (§§ 6.1 and 6.2), two further disjunctures will be explored: those associated with cultural identity and changing economic circumstances. In the conclusion to the chapter (§ 6.3), the implications of the analysis of disjunctures for political thought and democratic politics will be drawn out.

6.1 Disjuncture 4: national identity and the globalization of culture

The consolidation of state sovereignty in the eighteenth and nineteenth centuries helped foster the identity of people as political subjects – as citizens (see § 3.1). It meant that those subject to a state's authority were slowly made aware of their membership in a community and of the rights and obligations such membership might confer. While the nature of this identity was often initially vague, it grew more definite and precise over time. The formation of national identities was often the result both of a struggle for membership in the new political communities, and of a struggle by political elites and governments to create a new identity to legitimize the modern state itself.

Since the introduction of mechanical printing into Europe in the second half of the fifteenth century, mechanized technologies of communication have influenced the formation of political identities (see Anderson, B., 1983). They have extended the range and scope of individual reflexivity and have contributed to the creation of collective pools of information – in the spheres of economics, culture and politics – upon which people could draw despite being spatially separated from one another. Indeed, they formed an essential element of the forces which eroded reliance upon oral culture and which weakened fundamentally the reproductive mechanisms of traditional societies (see Giddens, 1990, pp. 36ff; and Thompson, 1990, ch. 4).

The globalizing impact of the modern communications media – often referred to as part of a process of 'cultural globalization' – has been commented upon by many writers, especially since the period of the early growth of mass circulation newspapers in the nineteenth century. Thus, in 1892 one observer noted that an inhabitant of a village who reads a paper 'interests himself simultaneously in the issue of a revolution in Chile, a bush-war in East Africa, a massacre in North China, a famine in Russia' and is, accordingly, likely to be better informed about the world 'than the Prime Minister of a hundred years before' (Nordau, 1968, p. 39). People are not only more aware of regional and global developments than in previous generations, but they also have access to a resource through which they can, in principle, consistently extend their understanding both of their own and of other societies. This 'expansion of horizons' would have been impossible without the pooling and dissemination of knowledge which constitutes the basis of all 'news' and forms a core component of contemporary communication (see Giddens, 1990, p. 77).

The 'stretching' of social, political and economic activity across the globe, and the intensification of interaction within each of these domains, has been heavily dependent on the invention and diffusion of the modern electronic media. It is remarkable to note that in 1946 the world had just one computer, built at the University of Pennsylvania, weighing 30 tons and covering 1500 square feet (Blumenthal, 1987/8, p. 532). Since then the revolution in microelectronics, in information technology and in computers has established virtually instantaneous world-wide electronic links which, when combined with the technologies of television, cable, satellite and jet transportation, have dramatically transformed the nature of communication.

The development of new communication systems creates a world in which the particularities of place and individuality are constantly mediated by regional and global communication networks. Cultural products, from soap operas to news documentaries, can be produced and dispersed across a variety of nominally separate territories. But the relevance of these networks goes far beyond the reach of such products; for the new communication systems are a vehicle, if not the vehicle, for the other processes of change documented in disjunctures 1–3 (chapter 5); that is to say, they are fundamental to the legal, organizational and military developments transforming modern political communities and the states system more generally. For instance, the extension of diplomatic relations and networks of military cooperation, the development and monitoring of international law, and the continued recognition of the UN as an important forum – as a centre for deliberation and discussion about common interests and values despite discord in the world – all received an impetus from the new communication systems and all depend on them as a means to further their projects.

The new global communication systems offer access to social and physical settings which may never have been encountered by individuals or groups; they enable individuals and groups to 'overcome' geographical boundaries which once might have prevented contact; and they create access to a range of social and cultural experiences with which the individual or group may never have had an opportunity to engage (see Giddens, 1991, pp. 84–5). These systems transform relations between physical locales and social circumstances, and alter the 'situational geography' of political and social life: 'more and more [the] media make us "direct" audiences to performances that happen in other places and give us access to audiences that are not physically present' (Meyrowitz, 1985, p. 7). In these circumstances, the traditional link between 'physical setting' and 'social situation' is broken; the new communication systems create new experiences, new commonalities and new frames of meaning independently of direct contact between people. As such, they can serve to detach, or disembed, identities from particular times, places and traditions, and can have a 'pluralizing impact' on identity formation, producing a variety of options which are 'less fixed or unified' (Hall, S., 1992, pp. 303 and 309). Moreover, these systems operate in large measure independently of state control and are, accordingly, not easily amenable to direct political regulation.

National cultures and identities are deeply rooted in ethnohistories, as previously noted, and are, thus, quite unlikely to be stamped out by the imprint of global mass culture (see § 3.1). Nonetheless, the growth of global commnunications, above all of television, video and film, gives people new ways of 'seeing and participating' in global developments. In principle, this opens up the possibility of new mechanisms of identification. For example, it was possible for people to read about Poland in 1968 and to read about Chile in 1973; but countless millions saw what was happening in China in Tiananmen Square in 1989, and in Russia in Red Square in 1991 (see Boden, 1992). The fact that television cameras recorded these events as they were unfolding created access to, and potential involvement with, events which, although they were in distant localities, came to impinge immediately and directly on everyday life in many parts of the world. While everyone has a local life, 'phenomenal worlds' are now increasingly interpenetrated by developments and processes from diverse settings. This alteration in the range of everyday awareness is reinforced by changes in the structures of economic life which stretch beyond national boundaries, by alterations in environmental circumstances which bring home sharply the interconnectedness of peoples, and by the transformations in military technology which underscore the global risks of 'local' confrontations. These developments have been interpreted as creating a sense of global belonging and vulnerability which transcends loyalties to the nation-state; that is, to 'my country right or wrong' (see, for instance, Falk, 1991a).

The warrant for this latter claim can be found, it has been argued, in a number of processes and forces, including the development of transnational grass-roots movements with clear regional or global objectives, such as the protection of natural resources and the environment, and the alleviation of disease, ill-health and poverty (cf. Ekins, 1992). Groups like Greenpeace have derived some of their success precisely from their ability to show the interconnectedness of the problems they seek to tackle across nations and regions. In addition, the considerable assemblage of actors, agencies and institutions – from regional political organizations to the UN – which are structured in relation to international and transnational issues is cited as further evidence of a growing global political orientation. Finally, a commitment to human rights as indispensable to the dignity and integrity of all peoples – rights entrenched in international law and championed by transnational groups such as Amnesty International – is held as additional support of a new 'global perspective'. These factors, it is also maintained, are the integral elements of an emerging 'global civil society' (Falk, 1991a). Such claims, however, seem somewhat premature.

While the new communication systems create access to other peoples and nations, and the possibility of new avenues of political cooperation and development, they also generate an awareness of difference – of diversity in life styles and value orientations (see Gilroy, 1987; Robins, 1991; Massey, 1991). While this awareness may enhance understanding, it may also lead to an accentuation of what is different, further fragmenting cultural life. Awareness of 'the other' by no means guarantees intersubjective agreement, as the Salman Rushdie affair has only too clearly illustrated (see Parekh, 1989). In addition, while the new communication technologies may encourage a language of their own, they confront a multiplicity of languages and discourses in and through which people interpret their lives and cultures (Thompson, 1990, pp. 313ff). There is no common global pool of memories; no common global way of thinking; and no 'universal history' in and through which people can unite. There is only a manifold set of political systems through which any new global awareness must struggle for survival (see Bozeman, 1984). Given the deep roots of ethno-histories, and the many ways they are often remade, this can hardly be a surprise. The evidence points sharply towards the persistence of a plurality of frames of political meaning and reference – not a universal political history in the making.

The new networks of communication and information technology, thus, both stimulate new forms of cultural identity and rekindle and intensify old forms. Any attempt to limit their reach to national boundaries alone is doomed to failure; these networks are already forming a dense web of relations linking particular cultures to one another, and transforming the latter's nature and scope. On the other hand, these same communication networks, as has been aptly noted, 'make possible a denser, more intense interaction between members of communities who share common cultural characteristics, notably language; and this fact enables us to understand why in recent years we have been witnessing the re-emergence of submerged ethnic communities and their nationalisms' (Smith, A. D., 1990, p. 175).

The globalization of the media involves a complicated set of processes which have implications for the reordering of political identities at many levels. The city of Los Angeles is an interesting illustration of this, since it is the city not only of Hollywood but also of a complex web of ethnic radio and television.[1] Local changes in identity are as much part of 'the new cultural processes' as any lateral extension of organizations and societies across space and time. These processes can weaken the cultural hegemony of nation-states and restimulate the ethnic and cultural groups which compose them. And as nation-states are weakened, a growing pressure for local and regional autonomy cannot be ruled out: thus, old political-cultural identities may well be challenged across the world both from above and from below. However, while a growing disjuncture can be noted between the pull of national identities and the diverse orientations of contemporary cultural and communication systems, it is far from clear what the exact outcome of this heterogeneous set of pressures will be. It is improbable either that a global culture will emerge or that national identities will persist unaltered by their enmeshment in wider communication structures. The result is indeterminate; but, by the same token, so too is the future cultural position of the nation-state in this ever more complex web. Certainly, the outcome itself is beyond the immediate control of individual nation-states and of their infrastructural reach. The cultural space of nation-states is being rearticulated by forces over which states have, at best, only limited leverage.

The political leverage that may exist, like the possibilities of democratic control in the areas of activity discussed in disjunctures 1–3 (chapter 5), is shaped decisively by the resources which are available to initiate and sustain self-chosen directions in cultural life. Access to, and control over, the new communication systems is very unevenly distributed around the globe, between regions and between different groups of the population within regions and nation-states (see Massey, 1991). There are unequal relations of power at the heart of cultural and communication flows which

[1] I am indebted to Tony McGrew for this example.

profoundly affect what is produced and received by whom. In addition, many of these flows have been, in essence, the result of the exporting of a particular culture. It is still, as Stuart Hall has observed, 'the images, artefacts and identities of Western modernity, produced by the cultural industries of "Western" societies (including Japan), which dominate the global networks' (1992, p. 305). Patterns of unequal cultural exchange persist. But the resurgence of ethnic and national identities in recent times – within and beyond the West – testifies to the still ambiguous outcomes of the massive global flows which wash the shores of particular national cultures. The momentous movements of people from 'the peripheries' to 'the centre' in the last few decades have exacerbated this ambiguity (see Hall, S., 1992; King, R., 1995). Nonetheless, the nature of the control over and accountability of these cultural and communication flows remains a pressing matter. To what extent and how people are able to determine their own identity, culture and values in the face of the international and transnational media networks are crucial issues at the end of the twentieth century.

Developments in transnational media networks are directly linked, of course, to the globalization of economic activity which has challenged local, national and regional ways of life in many parts of the world. Gray has referred to the 'destructive radicalism of market institutions' which uproots traditional communities and turns cities into Hobbesian states of nature, all in the name of international free trade (1993). How far economic forces are internationalized or globalized, and how far they are beyond the control of political communities, is the subject of the following section.

6.2 Disjuncture 5: the world economy

There is a clear disjuncture between the formal authority of the state and the spatial reach of contemporary systems of production, distribution and exchange which often function to limit the competence and effectiveness of national political authorities.[2] Two aspects of international economic processes are central: the internationalization of production and the internationalization of financial transactions, organized in part by multinational companies

[2] See Gourevitch, 1986; Keohane and Nye, 1989; Frieden, 1991; Webb, 1991; Garrett and Lange, 1991; O'Brien, 1992.

(MNCs).[3] Most MNCs organize their production, marketing and distribution on a regional or global basis. Even when MNCs have a clear national base, their activities are predominantly geared to maximizing their international competitive position and profitability such that individual (national) subsidiaries operate in the context of an overall corporate strategy. Investment and production decisions, therefore, may not always reflect local or national conditions. Financial organizations such as banks are also progressively more global in scale and orientation; they are able to monitor and respond to developments, be they in London, Tokyo or New York, almost instantaneously. New information technology has radically increased the mobility of economic units – currencies, stocks, shares, 'futures' and so on – for financial and commercial organizations of all kinds.

There is considerable evidence to support the claim that technological advances in information technology, communication and transportation are eroding the boundaries between hitherto separate markets – boundaries which were a necessary condition for independent national economic policies (Keohane and Nye, 1972, pp. 392–5). World production and financial systems are being reshaped by technological change. The impact of the new technologies appears twofold. It radically increases the scope of economic interconnectedness, both regional and global; and it enables the rapid intensification of patterns of interconnectedness – in this case, of the volume and velocity of transactions. Companies can, in principle, coordinate, locate and manage their manufacturing units and economic interests with an eye to deriving maximum benefit from the different production and marketing conditions across the world economy.

If the impact of the new technologies on the productive process has been remarkable it has been even more so in the financial market-place. While productive resources and manufacturing plants can be coordinated and managed on a vastly larger terrain than hitherto, it is still the case that they require substantial investment which takes a fixed period to generate a return. Productive resources cannot be moved around the globe in an instantaneous

[3] While there are difficulties collecting reliable data on MNCs, recent figures indicate the importance of them to global economic processes: multinational corporations now account for an impressive 30 per cent of gross global output, 70 per cent of world trade, and 80 per cent of international investment (Myers, 1994).

manner, although for manufacturing units the tie to a specific location may now be no more than five years, the figure often cited as the time it takes for an investment in a microelectronics factory to generate a satisfactory profit (see Frieden, 1991, pp. 427–33). This connection to particular locales is in marked contrast to the operations of the financial sector. The financial sector generates returns not simply on the basis of sound long-term investments, but also on the basis of managing turnover in the financial marketplace itself. The more rapid the turnover, the larger the commissions that can be earned by key financial players (see Strange, 1986). New technologies have had a profound impact on the operations of these financial mechanisms. Their impact can be specified in at least four ways.

> First, information is now universally available, in real time . . . in every financial centre of the world. Second, technology has tied all the principal countries and world financial and banking centres together into one integrated network. Few countries or parts of the world can any longer remain insulated from financial shocks and changes, wherever they may occur. Third, technology has made possible the establishment of a new, comprehensive system and highly efficient world market to match lenders and borrowers, to pool resources and share risk on an international scale, without regard to national boundaries. Finally, technology has engendered a vast amount of innovation or new 'products', mostly to hedge against changes in interest rates or exchanges rates. (Blumenthal, 1987/8, pp. 537–8)

It is possible to speak of the emergence of a single global financial market with almost round-the-clock trading – a phenomenon which has even been referred to by one commentator as amounting to the 'end of geography' (O'Brien, 1992).

Markets, and societies, are becoming more sensitive to one another even when their distinctive identities are preserved: the October stockmarket crash of 1987 is one clear example of this.[4] The very possibility of successfully pursuing a national economic

[4] The crash of 1987 contrasts with that of 1929 in two noteworthy respects; first, the speed with which different markets around the world collapsed was much greater in 1987; and, second, the rapidity with which the international financial community, especially the finance ministries of the G7 countries, arranged a collaborative response was markedly different to the disorganized efforts of 1929.

policy – of a country acting alone, that is, in the furtherance of its economic objectives – is, accordingly, reduced. The monetary and fiscal policies of individual national governments are frequently dominated by movements in the international financial markets. As one observer noted, 'in April 1989, foreign exchange trading in the world's financial centres averaged about $650 billion a day, equivalent to nearly $500 million a minute and to forty times the amount of world trade a day' (Frieden, 1991, pp. 427–8).[5] The figure is especially noteworthy because it was twice the amount of the total foreign reserve holdings of the US, Japanese and UK central banks combined for the entire month (Webb, 1991, p. 320). This factor, combined with the dependency of levels of employment, investment and revenue within a country on the decisions of MNCs about the location of their facilities, suggest that a government's capacity to pursue independent macroeconomic strategies effectively is, at best, tightly circumscribed (see Garrett and Lange, 1991).

In the wake of these developments, national rules and national regulatory systems for the control and development of markets have, in some cases, lost their traditional meaning. One example is the control of monopolies or anti-trust legislation. Within the context of national markets, governments and citizens' groups have often been concerned to control the development of monopolies. But today, in the face of regional and global markets, the very meaning of a national monopoly has arguably changed. While the idea of a monopoly has a clear meaning within the framework of a nation-state, it makes less sense in the context of international economic competition: a national monopoly may by no means be of economic significance in the global market-place. In fact, corporations have grown rapidly in order to counter international competition. As one analyst observed, 'there has already been a . . . tentative, albeit reluctant, recognition that technology has made obsolete the traditional definition of the market and that some old restrictions no longer make sense . . . for example, allowing a group of strong US competitors in the information industry to pool their

[5] The most recent figures from the Bank of International Settlement indicate that foreign exchange trading now amounts to an approximate working daily total turnover of $1 trillion. The ratio of turnover to trade has mushroomed to 54 to 1. The vast majority of foreign exchange dealing has been speculative (see Goldblatt et al., forthcoming, for an analysis of the globalization of financial markets and multinational banking).

resources and collaborate on research would not have been acceptable in earlier days. But it makes sense under the [new] . . . conditions' (Blumenthal, 1987/8, p. 540). The dispersion of markets, the internationalization of production and finance, the rapid change in technology, have all combined to intensify product competition, to reduce the life-cycles of products, and to suggest that intercorporate expertise may have to be combined in order to survive the new competition (cf. Archibugi and Michie, 1995).

To a large extent (although exactly how large remains subject to controversy) it can be argued that many concepts of national economic policy formation are now of doubtful value. It is not that 'national rules and policies are obsolete or no longer needed'; rather, it is that they 'cannot work unless close attention is paid to what is being done elsewhere' (Blumenthal, 1987/8, p. 539). National controls and regulations have limited effectiveness if they are at odds with wider international conditions. In other words, the standards and rules of regional and global markets cannot be infringed in the long run. Or, to put the point somewhat differently, government economic policy must to a large degree be compatible with the regional and global movements of capital, unless a national government wishes to risk serious dislocation between its policy objectives and the flows of the wider international economy. A country needs to be extremely well protected economically and politically (enjoying the benefit of robust domestic coalitions) to risk such dislocation. For the price of such dislocation is invariably a run on its currency, the outflow of capital to safer havens and the loss of potential private investment.

The globalization of economic relationships has altered the possibility of deploying whole ranges of economic policy. Although there are many reasons why Keynesianism may no longer work today, one fundamental reason is that it is much harder for individual governments to intervene and manage their economies faced with a global division of labour, the absence of capital controls and the operations of the world financial markets. Keynesian demand management functioned well in the context of the system of 'embedded liberalism' which provided the political and economic foundations for both national and international economic regulation in the years following the Second World War (Keohane, 1984b). But with the breakdown of the post-war 'liberal consensus' in the wake of the 1973 oil crisis, the possibility of managing a national economy and of 'bucking' international economic trends became more difficult.[6] The forces and constraints of the international economy – including, for example, the mechanisms which transmitted inflation and recession, the changing terms of trade, and the challenging issues posed by the expansion of industrial capitalism at the so-called 'periphery' of the international economy (in South Korea, Taiwan and the other newly industrializing countries) – became more apparent. The increasing interconnectedness of the world's economies was, accordingly, more readily acknowledged, especially by those governments which sought to make much of the market as a, if not the, leading standard of rational decision-making.

The loss of control of national economic programmes is, of course, not uniform across economic sectors or societies more generally: some markets and some countries can isolate themselves from transnational economic networks by such measures as attempts to restore the boundaries or 'separateness' of markets, and/or to extend national laws to cover internationally mobile factors, and/or to adopt cooperative policies with other countries for the coordination of policy (Cooper, 1986, pp. 1–22; Gilpin, 1987, pp. 397ff; Webb, 1991). In addition, the regionalization of sections of the world economy, with economic activity clustering around a number of poles (among them the European market, the United States, Canada and Mexico, and the Pacific Basin and Japan), provides scope for some regulation of market trends (cf. Hine, 1992, p. 119). The particular tensions between political and economic structures are likely to be different in different spheres, and between them: West–West, North–South, East–West. It cannot, therefore, simply be said that the very idea of a national economy is superseded; distinctive national styles of economic management persist and governments continue to have policy options. Among

[6] Another way to put this point is to note that a government's capacity to reflate its economy at a time of its own choosing has become more problematic, although it retains deflationary options in order to bring its economy into line with wider market trends. 'In an international economic system that permits and fosters vast, instantaneous ... movements of short-term capital', as one observer has noted, 'an effective veto' is exercised 'on expansionary economic policies'; however, deflationary policy options remain but put at risk the 'social stability' of the trading system, since their social costs, measured by such phenomena as unemployment, are high (see Hutton, 1993, p. 1, and 1995).

these are to be counted a wide range of sector-and region (sub-national)-specific policies (see Frieden, 1991).

However, the internationalization of production, finance and other economic resources is unquestionably eroding the capacity of an individual state to control its own economic future. In addition, firms' responses to these changing circumstances – including strategies of adjustment to compete with low-cost producers and/or concentration on high-value-added goods tailored to specialized markets – are not particularly favourable to national strategies of regulation: in the former case, national regulatory strategies have either to assist the process of adjustment or to risk a declining tax base as production facilities move abroad; in the latter case, governments must, in the face of increasingly heterogeneous production requirements, find less macro and more micro or local regulatory regimes to guide and assist economic activity. The pace of technological and economic change implies, as has been aptly stated, 'that substantive "command and control" regulation increasingly risks immediate obsolescence' (Cohen, J. and Rogers, 1992, p. 453). Thus, at the very latest, it can be said that there appears to be a diminution of state autonomy in the sphere of economic policy, and a gap between the idea of a political community determining its own future and the dynamics of the contemporary world economy.[7] Of course, such factors are felt most acutely in the world's marginal and weaker economies (cf. Amin, 1990; Hawthorn, 1993).

These trends may seem somewhat ironic, if not paradoxical, in the context of the preceding account (chapter 3) of the formation of the modern state, the consolidation of political power and the extension of the state's 'policy reach', especially in the nineteenth and early twentieth centuries. In addition, the development of the welfare state and the attempt to impose forms of social regulation

[7] None of this, it should be emphasized, should be taken to imply that all forms of nationally based government intervention are moribund. A strategy to develop the production of high-value-added goods, for instance, can benefit substantially from policies aimed at generating a steady flow of skilled labour; the conditions for rapid adaptation by workers to new technical circumstances through social security and retraining systems; a buoyant basic science research system; nationally shaped systems of risk capital transfer; and so on. See chapter 11 for a discussion of new possible balances between 'macro' and 'micro' policies and for a consideration of the new possible meanings of these terms.

on market forces have been characterized by some as the period of 'organized capitalism' (a term first coined by Hilferding, 1981). According to this latter view, the concentration and centralization of capital from the late nineteenth century allowed large firms a significant degree of control over their markets while capital itself became more integrated with the state; the growth of large-scale enterprises was accompanied by the expansion of a rationalized bureaucratic form of management, with links across the private and public sectors. Central control was increased over a range of phenomena hitherto subject to direct market regulation, including innovation, output and prices as well as aspects of social welfare. Market-orientated industrial capitalism was slowly supplanted by organized or planned economic advance (see Schumpeter, 1976; cf. Held, 1987, ch. 5). But while it is important to acknowledge aspects of these developments, it is also important to recognize that any enhanced regulatory capacity established within the boundaries of leading nation-states, and within their territories overseas, was not easily extended to many of the transnational economic networks already in place. Furthermore, the intensification of economic globalization after the Second World War promoted the internationalization of capital on a scale which reduced such economic power as the nation-state possessed. For some observers, this alone justifies referring to the contemporary era as a new epoch – the epoch of 'disorganized capitalism' (Offe, 1985; Lash and Urry, 1987; cf. Callinicos, 1990, ch. 5).

Viewed historically, the characterization of the contemporary period as disorganized capitalism does not seem wholly accurate, since the regulatory power of the nation-state has always been limited in relation to the dynamics and development of the world economy. However, unquestionably, the demise of the European empires, the erosion of the US's economic position in recent times and the increase in the internationalization of productive capital and of finance, particularly in the last twenty years, have left even powerful nation-states with fewer options (and illusions) than heretofore about the range of economic policy at their disposal (cf. Keohane, 1984a; Kennedy, 1988). While this alone does not amount to a direct erosion of an individual state's entitlement to rule its roost – sovereignty – it leaves nation-states exposed and vulnerable to the networks of economic forces and relations which range in and through them, reconstituting their very form and capacities.

In sum: disjunctures 1–5

Taken together, the five major disjunctures identified in this and the previous chapter – law, polity, security, identity and economy – highlight shifting patterns of powers and constraints which are redefining the architecture of political power associated with the nation-state. While a complex pattern of global interconnections has been evident for a long time, there is little doubt that there has been recently a further 'internationalization' of domestic activities and an intensification of decision-making in international and transnational frameworks (cf. Kaiser, 1972, p. 370). The evidence that international and transnational relations have eroded the powers of the modern sovereign state is certainly strong. Global processes have moved politics a long way from activity which simply crystallizes first and foremost around state and inter-state concerns.

The 'disjunctures' reveal a set of forces which combine to restrict the freedom of action of governments and states by blurring the boundaries of domestic politics, transforming the conditions of political decision-making, changing the institutional and organizational context of national polities, altering the legal framework and administrative practices of governments and obscuring the lines of responsibility and accountability of national states themselves. These processes alone warrant the statement that *the operation of states in an ever more complex international system both limits their autonomy (in some spheres radically) and impinges increasingly upon their sovereignty.* Any conception of sovereignty which interprets it as an illimitable and indivisible form of public power – entrenched securely in individual nation-states – is undermined. Sovereignty itself has to be conceived today as already divided among a number of agencies – national, regional and international – and limited by the very nature of this plurality.

In a world of interconnected political authorities and power centres, how should democracy be understood? Can the idea of a democratic polity or state be sustained in the face of systematic challenges from above and below? And can the principle of democratic legitimacy be defended when the international order is structured by agencies, organizations, associations and companies over which citizens have minimum, if any, control, and in regard to which they have little basis to signal (dis)agreement; and when both routine and extraordinary decisions taken by representatives of nations and nation-states profoundly affect not only their citizens but also the citizens of other nation-states? In short, what is, and ought to be, the meaning of democracy in the context of the changing enmeshment of the local, national, regional and global?

6.3 The new context of political thought

Three elements of regionalization and globalization are essential to recognize: first, the way processes of economic, political, legal, military and cultural interconnectedness are changing the nature, scope and capacity of the modern state, as its 'regulatory' ability is challenged and reduced in some spheres; secondly, the way regional and global interconnectedness creates chains of interlocking political decisions and outcomes among states and their citizens, altering the nature and dynamics of national political systems themselves; and thirdly, the way cultural and political identities are being reshaped and rekindled by such processes, leading many local and regional groups, movements and nationalisms to question the nation-state as a representative and accountable power system. Democracy has to come to terms with all three of these developments and their implications for national and international power centres. If it fails to do so, it is likely to become ever less effective in determining the shape and limits of political activity. Accordingly, the international form and structure of politics and civil society has to be built into the foundations of democratic thought and practice.

While democratic theory can no longer be elaborated as a theory of the territorially delimited polity alone, nor can the nation-state be displaced as a central point of reference. Global processes should not be exaggerated to represent either a total eclipse of the states system or the simple emergence of an integrated world society (Ruggie, 1983). States have surrendered some rights and freedoms, but in the process they have gained and extended others (cf. § 5.2). Furthermore, it is clear that any general account of the impact of globalization has to be qualified in relation to different patterns of local and regional development. What is called for, in short, is not a theory of the modern state *per se*, or a theory of the international order *per se*, but a theory of the place of the state and democracy within the international order.

Does a system of interlocking authority structures, creating diverse and potentially conflicting demands, pose a threat to the very basis of the modern state as an impersonal and privileged legal or constitutional order – a circumscribed structure of power with supreme jurisdiction over a territory accountable to a determinate citizen body? It is not part of the argument presented here that national sovereignty, even in regions with overlapping and divided authority structures, has been wholly subverted. But it is part of the argument that political domains clearly exist with criss-crossing loyalties, conflicting interpretations of rights and duties, and interconnected authority structures which displace notions of sovereignty as an illimitable, indivisible and exclusive form of public power. While massive concentrations of power are formed and reformed within many states, these are frequently embedded in, and articulated with, fractured domains of political authority.

Extrapolating from current trends, and casting them in the form of an ideal type, it is not fanciful to imagine, as Bull once observed, the development of an international system which is a modern and secular counterpart to the kind of political organization that existed in Christian Europe in the Middle Ages, the essential characteristics of which were overlapping authority and divided loyalty (see § 2.1). As Bull explained:

> In Western Christendom in the Middle Ages . . . no ruler or state was sovereign in the sense of being supreme over a given territory and a given segment of the Christian population; each had to share authority with vassals beneath, and with the Pope and (in Germany and Italy) the Holy Roman Emperor above . . . If modern states were to come to share their authority over their citizens, and their ability to command their loyalties, on the one hand with regional and world authorities, and on the other hand with sub-state or sub-national authorities, to such an extent that the concept of sovereignty ceased to be applicable, then a neo-mediaeval form of universal political order might be said to have emerged. (1977, pp. 254–5)

Such a system, especially if it congealed into a form of universal political organization, might in principle lay claim to a number of advantages; notably, the provision of institutional mechanisms to bind large populations together peacefully while avoiding, on the one hand, the typical dangers and 'continuall jealousies' (Hobbes) of the states system and, on the other, the risk of huge concentrations of power which might accompany a system of 'world government'. But there is no guarantee that such a system would be any more orderly, secure, accountable and legitimate than previous forms of political organization – perhaps less so, in all these respects.

It might be less orderly and secure, for, it is important to recall, agreement to tolerate differences of belief and ideology was a founding principle of the modern states system. The modern states system developed in the context of the schisms and bitter conflicts which dominated Europe from the start of the Reformation. It was a system of overlapping authority structures and conflicting loyalties which was one of the critical background conditions of the rise of the modern state: the latter emerged in part as a conceptual and institutional resolution to the strife and turmoil created by the former. What basis would there be for thinking that a new secular medievalism could uphold and defend the principle of toleration? How – conceptually and institutionally – would a system of 'divided sovereignty' sustain order and provide a framework of rules and procedures to sustain tolerance? If the modern secular state was the conceptual and institutional solution to the conflicting claims, demands and interests of rulers and ruled, what, if anything, is its counterpart in a political system in which the territorial state has to share its 'exclusive authority' with other organizations and agencies?

Moreover, is there any reason for thinking that a system of overlapping authority structures, even where it already exists, could be more accountable than traditional models of democracy, could operate more effectively in this respect than existing mechanisms of accountability, that is, the institutions and practices of representative democracy and the states system? Representative democracy has been championed as the key institutional innovation to underpin both authority and liberty: the dilemma of how to secure the sovereign power of the state while ensuring strict limits upon that power can be resolved, liberal democrats have always argued, by recognizing the political equality of mature individuals and empowering them with a vote (see §§ 1.1 and 3.3). But what, if anything, would be the equivalent mechanism in a system of divided sovereignty? If the efficacy of the system of representative democracy is being strained and eroded in the face of regional and global interconnectedness, what mechanisms could ensure accountability in the new international order? The challenge to the idea and coherence of democracy, posed, on the one hand, by the national and international interconnectedness of political decisions and outcomes and, on the other, by the limits imposed on a nation's control of its fate by the web of emergent regional and global organizations, raises pressing questions about the nature of the organizations and forces which are mounting this challenge; that is, about the accountability of such diverse organizations and agencies as MNCs, the IMF and NATO. While mechanisms exist in principle to provide a measure of accountability in some of these organizations – to shareholders, in the case of MNCs, to representatives of member sovereign states, in the case of the IMF and NATO – the nature of their accountability, if any, to the ordinary citizens of the nation-states in which they operate, or to the diverse groups they affect beyond a given nation-state, remains an acute and pressing question.

In addition, if the democratic underpinning of the organizations and forces of the international order is open to doubt, so too is the basis of their legitimacy. The principle of consent, expressed through the principle of majority rule, has been, as previously noted, the underlying principle of legitimacy of modern democracy (see § 1.2). The argument in this volume suggests not only that both routine and extraordinary decisions taken by representatives of nations and nation-states profoundly affect citizens of other nation-states – who in all probability have had no opportunity to signal consent or lack of it – but also that the international order is structured by agencies and forces over which citizens have minimum, if any, control and in regard to which they have little basis to signal their (dis)agreement. Traditionally in Western democracies, legitimacy is closely related to democratic principles and procedures; the revolutions of 1989–90 drove home, if it ever needed driving home, the importance and closeness of this connection, politically and philosophically. But just as more and more people today are claiming the principle of democratic legitimacy for themselves – and asserting that they should control their destinies and that government must operate on their behalf if it is to be legitimate government – the very scope and relevance of this principle is being contested by processes of regional and global restructuring.

The international order is characterized both by the persistence of the sovereign states system and by the development of plural structures of power and authority, many of which have, at best, weak or obscure mechanisms of accountability. The objections to such a hybrid system are severe. It is open to question whether it offers any solutions to the fundamental preoccupations of modern political thought, among the most prominent of which have been the rationale and basis of order and toleration, of democracy and accountability, and of legitimate rule. But these objections can be met, and the dangers they signal coherently addressed, within a framework of constitutional and democratic thought. For the dangers may in principle be surmounted if a multiple system of authority is bound by fundamental ordering principles and rules. The potentially fragmentary and undemocratic nature of these developments can be overcome if they are part of a common order committed to close collaboration, similar principles and constitutional guidelines. The dangers posed by a threat of a 'new medievalism' can be addressed if its component parts entrench and enact the rules required for 'a common structure of political action'. International agencies, organizations, corporations and states could opt to become part of this structure if they chose a democratic political future. I refer to this possibility as the 'cosmopolitan model of democracy' or the 'cosmopolitan model of democratic autonomy' by which I mean, in the first instance, a system of democratic governance which arises from and is adapted to the diverse conditions and interconnections of different peoples and nations.

The problems involved in elaborating a new account of democracy are numerous. If one takes seriously the task of thinking beyond exogenous and endogenous frameworks of analysis in politics, several fundamental concepts at the heart of contemporary political thought have to be re-examined, and their relevance to the interwoven worlds of national and international life reconsidered. This task amounts, in short, to a reassessment of the conceptual and institutional bases of democracy. The chapters which follow provide, if they are compelling, an account of the form and limits of this new democratic project.

Part III

Reconstruction:
Foundations of Democracy

7
RETHINKING DEMOCRACY

The transformation of politics which has followed in the wake of the growing interconnectedness of states and societies and the increasing intensity of international networks requires a re-examination of political theory as fundamental in form and scope as the shift which brought about the conceptual and institutional innovations of the modern state itself. It has always been open to dispute how far the claims of the modern state to be 'independent' and 'impartial' were redeemed in practice. To the extent that the state has been locked into the maintenance and reproduction of systematic inequalities of power and resource, distorting decision outcomes in favour of particular interests, the basis of its claim to legitimacy and distinct allegiance has been open to question. Nonetheless, the idea of the modern state was a guiding political orientation with far-reaching consequences. How far this idea remains applicable to the contemporary era, faced with distinctive and novel forms of power and authority, is, however, another matter. Likewise, how far the concepts of political order, authority and the democratic good can be elaborated at the level of state institutions and practices alone is a pressing and contentious problem.

The chapters which comprise the following parts (III and IV) are focused on the reconstruction of political ideas. Reconstruction in this context connotes reflection upon the basic concepts and circumstances of modern politics with the aim of elucidating the conditions and possibility of democratic political community in the contemporary world. The chapters take as their background the empirical context outlined in part II, but, unlike part II, they offer an essentially theoretical discourse, motivated by the necessity to rethink the theory of democracy to take account of the changing nature of the polity both within pre-established borders and within the wider system of nation-states and global forces.

Part III aims to provide an analysis of the concepts and theoretical terms that are central to an understanding of modern democratic political communities. It addresses a set of questions that has to be posed about the forces and divisions of power and interest that exist within communities – issues that arise, for example, from disputes about the nature of political power, the public and the private realms and the social struggles over the extent and dimensions of citizenship which have buffeted the liberal democratic state since its inception. At root, part III is concerned with the fundamental conditions of a democratic polity and the limitations of existing accounts of democracy.

Accordingly, this chapter reflects further upon the idea of the modern state – the supreme modern political association. The tension between the ideas of the modern state and of democracy, an issue glossed over so far, will be the prime consideration. Chapter 8 extends the analysis by examining the concept of power, and several different dimensions of power which constitute political communities in significant ways, enhancing and restricting the possibility of democracy and autonomy. Understanding these dimensions enables reconsideration of the proper relation between power, authority, law and politics. The material that follows in chapter 9 seeks to consolidate the discussion by recasting the nature of the democratic good in the context of the complex interplay between the ideal of the democratic good and the everyday, practical demands of politics.

Part IV then assesses the nature of the democratic good in relation to the changing meaning of political community, and lays a basis for the advocacy of a new model of democracy. It confronts a set of questions which arises as a result of the forces and divisions which exist in some sense 'beyond' political communities but which cut across them as well; forces and divisions generated by the agencies, organizations, institutions and collective problems that form (as documented in chapters 4–6) the interconnected world of states and societies. Thus, the chapters in part IV (chapters 10–12) explore the application and proper scope of concepts such as political power, legitimate authority, self-determination, autonomy and the democratic process in the face of changes to the nation-state, to sovereignty, to the relations between domestic and international law, and so on.

Three ideas will be elaborated in parts III and IV which form the backbone of the constructive argument of the volume: the principle of autonomy, the notion of a democratic legal state, and the concept of cosmopolitan democracy. The principle of autonomy is at the core of the democratic project and has to be grasped if the *raison d'être* of democracy is to be understood. The notion of a democratic legal state is the basis for resolving tensions between the ideas of the modern state and of democracy. Cosmopolitan democracy is a conception of democratic legal relations suitably adapted to a world of nations enmeshed in regional and global processes. Several conceptual building blocks must be in place before the case for these three notions is fully developed, but by the end of the book these should all be present and, thereby, a new framework established for democratic theory. But, first, more needs to be said about the notions of the modern state and of democracy and, thus, about the principle of autonomy.

7.1 The principle of autonomy

The importance and appeal of the idea of the modern state lies in the notion of a circumscribed system of power which provides a regulatory mechanism and check on rulers and ruled alike. Governments are entrusted with the capacities of the state to the extent that they uphold the rule of law. The equal treatment of all before the law, and the protection of subjects from the arbitrary use of political authority and coercive power, are *sine qua non*. While the state is the burden individuals have to bear to secure their own ends, it is also the basis upon which it is possible to safeguard their claims to equal rights and liberties. The appeal of the state lies, in short, in the promise of a community which is governed by a fair framework – a framework which is, in principle, equally constraining and enabling for all its members.

The idea of democracy derives its power and significance, by contrast, from the idea of self-determination; that is, from the notion that members of a political community – citizens – should be able to choose freely the conditions of their own association, and that their choices should constitute the ultimate legitimation of the form and direction of their polity. A 'fair framework' for the regulation of a community is one that is freely chosen. If democracy means 'rule by the people', the determination of public decision-making by equally free members of the political community, then the basis of its justification lies in the promotion and enhancement of autonomy, both for individuals as citizens and for the collectivity. In this context, the concept of 'autonomy' connotes the capacity of human beings to reason self-consciously, to be self-reflective and to be self-determining. It involves the ability to deliberate, judge, choose and act (or not act as the case may be) upon different possible courses of action in private as well as public life, bearing the democratic good or, in Rousseau's terms, the 'common good' in mind (see § 2.2).[1]

The relation between 'the state' as a fair framework and 'the people' as deliberately determining agent(s) requires further specification. What is at issue is the relation between the state and democracy or, more precisely, the relation between the idea of the state as an independent corporation or basic structure of law and institutions, and the idea of democracy as the autonomous determination of the conditions of collective association. The nature of this relation is a highly contested terrain in political thought, to say the least. From the earlier section on the discourse of sovereignty (§ 2.2), it can be concluded that there are good grounds for being sceptical about the traditional formulation of this relation found in the leading doctrines of state sovereignty and popular sovereignty. While the former tended to place the state in an all-powerful position with respect to the community and failed to offer an adequate account of public right and the nature of accountability, the latter ultimately rendered the community all-powerful and failed to offer a coherent account of what is distinctive about the powers of the state. If in the first case the 'artificial person' is conceptualized without an adequate basis of accountability to all citizens, in the second case it is reduced to a commission of the people's will with no independent kernel of authority, for instance, to draw effective limits on the decisions of a majority pursuing anti-minority or anti-democratic objectives. Conceptions of sovereignty which fail to demarcate the limits or legitimate scope of political action need to be treated with the utmost caution.

Clues to an alternative position to the thesis of the sovereignty

[1] In the discussion which follows immediately below, I leave aside the nature of political 'choice' and the difference, in particular, between the statement of personal preferences and reflection on the common good. I return, however, to this important matter later (see §§ 9.4–9.5).

of the state and the sovereignty of the people can be found by reflecting on what I earlier referred to as the 'principle of autonomy' (see p. 71) – a principle that finds resonances in all those traditions of political thought and practice preoccupied with ascertaining the circumstances under which people can enjoy 'free and equal' relations. The principle of autonomy can be stated as follows:

> *persons should enjoy equal rights and, accordingly, equal obligations in the specification of the political framework which generates and limits the opportunities available to them; that is, they should be free and equal in the determination of the conditions of their own lives, so long as they do not deploy this framework to negate the rights of others.*[2]

The principle of autonomy expresses essentially two basic ideas: the idea that people should be self-determining and the idea that democratic government must be limited government – government that upholds a legally circumscribed structure of power. *Contra* state sovereignty it insists on 'the people' determining the conditions of their own association, and *contra* popular sovereignty it signals the importance of recognizing limits on the power of the people through a regulatory structure that is both constraining and enabling. I take these ideas to be fundamental to all those who have sought to defend the project of the modern nation-state, particularly in its liberal democratic guise. Moreover, I take these ideas to be at the root of the aspirations of most eighteenth- and nineteenth-century thinkers who have sought to clarify and balance the relation between the 'sovereign state' and the 'sovereign people'; that is, who have been preoccupied with embedding democracy within the framework of constitutional procedures and the rule of law (see Held, 1987, chs 2–9; cf. Elster and Slagstad, 1988). But before spelling out in more detail how the terms of the principle of autonomy should be understood, it is important to say something further about its standing and rationale.

The standing and rationale of the principle of autonomy are, to borrow a phrase from John Rawls, 'political not metaphysical'

[2] I have modified my earlier conception of this principle and its rationale, to be found in Held, 1987, pp. 270–1, and 1991a, pp. 228–30, although what follows seeks to build on the arguments contained in these earlier publications.

(1985).[3] By 'political' Rawls means that the basic ideas of a defensible political theory can be derived from 'intuitive ideas' that are embedded in public political culture – in an 'overlapping consensus' that includes opposing philosophical, moral and religious doctrines (see 1993, pp. 10 and 13–15). Reflecting critically on the core notions of this consensus, he believes it is possible to disclose principles which can be drawn upon to adjudicate contending traditions and to provide guidance for our major institutions. These principles form a 'deep structure' or framework of ideas which can be deployed to shape the constitution and reconstitution of public affairs. For Rawls the task of political theory is to explicate the basic intuitions and concepts implicit in our 'way of life' in order to examine possible 'bases of agreement'. A theory is political, therefore, if it represents an articulation of ideas latent in public political life and, in particular, if, against the background of Western democratic culture, it builds on the distinctive conception of the person as a citizen who is, in principle, 'free and equal' in a manner 'comprehensible' to everyone. A theory of this kind is a theory anchored in and worked out for a specific subject: 'the basic structure of a constitutional democratic regime' (see Rawls, 1993, pp. 11–15, 29–35 and 257ff).

I shall not dwell here on the complex ramifications of Rawls's arguments and the extensive controversies to which they have given rise (see Kukathas and Pettit, 1990; Mulhall and Swift, 1992). Rather, what I shall simply seek to do is to argue that the principle of autonomy can be understood as political in one specific Rawlsian sense; that is, in the sense that it is a principle embedded in the public political culture of a democratic society. 'Embedded' connotes in this context that the principle has developed as part of, and has been constructed upon, the conceptual and institutional resources of Western democratic culture (its political movements, key texts and sedimented institutions) in a manner that could, in

[3] In more recent writings, Rawls has rephrased this contrast as one between the 'political' and 'comprehensive'. Since the meaning of 'the political' is what primarily concerns me here, I shall leave aside Rawls's distinction between the 'metaphysical' and 'comprehensive'. At issue, basically, is a contrast between a political doctrine and a comprehensive moral doctrine or a religious or philosophical statement covering 'all recognized values and virtues' within one carefully articulated system. See Rawls (1993, pp. 8–14) and Mulhall and Swift (1992, ch. 5) for a discussion.

principle, be understood and fully acknowledged by all citizens (see § 8.1; cf. Rawls, 1993, pp. 13–14 and 66–71). However, the principle of autonomy can only be fully traced to one of the core traditions of Western democracy – the liberal democratic tradition. This is because democracy – as shown in chapters 1 and 3 – is a fundamentally contested terrain, and the liberal democratic tradition is only one of the democratic traditions which have claimed distinctive authority over time. The principle of autonomy is not a principle found at the heart of the radical democratic project of Rousseau, or of the Marxist tradition, or, in fact, at the heart of any of those models of participatory democracy which place the active citizen exclusively at their centre. For these models all tend to leave the complex relations among individual liberty, distributional matters and political processes to the ebb and flow of democratic decision. In making democracy at all levels the primary objective to be achieved, these models all overly rely upon a 'democratic reason' – a wise and good democratic will – for the determination of just and positive political outcomes. They do not ask systematically whether an essentially democratic *demos* can be depended upon; whether the 'democratic will' will be wise and good; and whether 'the general will of the majority' is a sufficient basis for non-arbitrary government – and, if not, what the legitimate limitations on public power might be (see §§ 1.1 and 2.2; Held, 1987, chs 3, 4 and 8).

The principle of autonomy is, however, at the core of the modern liberal democratic project – a project preoccupied with the capability of persons to determine and justify their own actions, with their ability to choose among alternative political programmes, and with the necessity of introducing guidelines to delimit the democratic process. This democratic tradition has upheld both of the ideas at the centre of the principle of autonomy – self-determination and limited government – ideas which can be traced directly to the political movements and intellectual traditions which have sought to embed liberal democratic governance in political communities.

The actual pursuit of equal membership in political communities reconstituted the shape of modern Western politics. It did so, because, as explored in chapters 2 and 3, the struggle for citizenship rights reformed earlier understandings of legitimate realms of independent action. If the early attempt to achieve rights involved struggles for autonomy from the locale in which one was born, and from prescribed occupations, later struggles involved such things as freedom of speech, expression, belief and association, freedom for women in and beyond marriage, free and fair voting in elections, and an inclusive suffrage. The autonomy of the citizen can be represented by that bundle of rights which people can enjoy as a result of their status as free and equal members of particular communities – as a result, that is, of the extent to which they have succeeded in entrenching the possibility of autonomy in their political associations and, thereby, recasting both the form and limits of their polities. The passage from absolutism to the liberal democratic nation-state marks out the terrain of this struggle.

While the political theorists of liberal democracy have frequently diverged in many of their emphases, all the main approaches to liberal democracy – mainstream and radical – have had certain elements in common. To the extent that they have been concerned to advocate free and equal relations among mature adults in public and private life, they have been concerned to secure certain outcomes. These include:[4]

1 Protection from the arbitrary use of political authority and coercive power (involving an assumption of respect for privacy in all matters which are not the basis of potential and demonstrable 'harm' to others).[5]
2 The involvement of citizens in the determination of the conditions of their association through the provision of their consent in the maintenance and legitimation of regulative institutions (involving an assumption of respect for the authentic and reasoned nature of individuals' judgements).
3 The creation of the best circumstances for citizens to develop their nature and express their diverse qualities (involving an assumption of respect for individuals' capacities, their ability to learn and enhance their potentialities).
4 The expansion of economic opportunity to maximize the availability of resources (involving an assumption that when individuals are free from the burdens of unmet physical need they are best able to realize their ends).

The idea of 'autonomy' links these various aspirations and helps

[4] The material in the following three paragraphs paraphrases material discussed in Held, 1987, esp. pp. 268–71.

[5] Some of the complex connotations of the 'harm' principle are explored in § 9.3 below.

explain why they have been shared so widely. 'Autonomy', as previously indicated, connotes the capacity of human beings to reason self-consciously, to be self-reflective and to be self-determining. It involves the ability to act, in principle, as the author or maker of one's own life, in public and private realms. Since Locke, liberalism has advanced the challenging view that individuals are capable of determining and justifying their own actions, and are capable of entering into self-chosen obligations (see pp. 42–4; cf. Pateman, 1985, ch. 8). The development of autonomous spheres of action, in religious, social, political and economic affairs, became a (if not *the*) central mark of what it was to enjoy freedom and equality. Although liberals have frequently failed to explore the actual circumstances in which individuals live – how people are integrally connected to one another through complex networks of relations and institutions – they have nonetheless generated the strong belief that a defensible political order must be one in which people are able to develop their nature and interests free from the arbitrary use of political power and coercive relations. And although many liberals stopped far short of proclaiming that for individuals to be 'free and equal' they must themselves be sovereign, their work has been preoccupied with, and has affirmed the overwhelming importance of, uncovering the conditions under which individuals can determine and regulate the structure of their association subject to constitutional arrangements protecting their position and placing limits on public power. That is to say, liberals have been committed to a version of the principle of autonomy.

Building on this heritage, liberal democrats have argued that it is only through the institutions of representative democratic government that the commitment to autonomy can be fully upheld. A typical figure here was John Stuart Mill. According to him, the only feasible model of democracy in the modern world is representative democracy, which alone can combine the possibility of political participation with limited government and skilled administration. The classical idea of the *polis* cannot be sustained in modern society; the notion of self-government or government by open meeting is pure folly for any community exceeding a single small town (1951, pp. 217–18). Apart from the vast problems posed by sheer numbers of people, there are obvious geographical and physical limits to when and where people can meet together: these limits are hard to overcome in a small community; they cannot be overcome in a large one. The problems posed by coordination and regulation in a densely populated country are insuperably complex for any system of classical or direct democracy (1951, pp. 175–6 and 179–80). Moreover, when government is government by all citizens there is the constant danger that a knowledgeable minority will be overshadowed by the lack of knowledge, skill and experience of the majority. The latter can be slowly countered by experience in public affairs (voting, jury service, extensive involvement in local government), but only to a limited extent. Hence, the 'ideally best polity' in modern conditions comprises a representative democratic system in which people 'exercise through deputies . . . the ultimate controlling power' and deputies, bound by a division of offices and a circumscribed system of authority, are 'periodically elected by all citizens' (1951, pp. 228, 241 and 246–7). Government can be popular, accountable and effective if it is limited.

To disclose the liberal democratic commitment to the principle of autonomy is not, it should be emphasized, to affirm any one model of liberal democracy as it stands. It is one thing to acknowledge the significance of the principle of autonomy, quite another to accept that it must be conceptualized and entrenched as prescribed in the main theories of liberal democracy. Advocates of liberal democracy, stretching back as far as Madison and Bentham, have tended to be concerned, above all else, with the proper principles and procedures of democratic government (see § 1.1). While this focus is quite understandable in these thinkers, writing at a time when the struggle for an independent, accountable polity was an urgent issue on the public agenda, it is a focus with high costs in democratic theory as a whole if it is taken to eclipse considerations which derive from other sites and factors of power. For a focus on 'government' alone tends to draw attention away from a thorough examination of the relation between formal rights and actual rights; between commitments to treat citizens as free and equal and practices which do neither sufficiently; between the concept of the state as, in principle, an independent authority, and state involvement in the reproduction of the inequalities of everyday life; between notions of political leadership and political parties as appropriate structures for bridging the gap between state and society, and the array of power centres which such structures cannot reach. To ignore these matters is to risk the establishment of 'democracy' in the context of a web of political, economic and social circumstances – from the power systems of leading social groups to the international organizations of the states system and the global flows of capital markets – which challenges the control and reach of democratic governance in its traditional cast (see chapters 5–6 and the discussion which follows in chapter 8). And it is to risk the creation of, at best, a very partial form of democratic politics – a form in which the involvement of some bears a direct relation to the limited participation or non-participation of others.

The implications of these points are, I believe, profound. While one cannot escape the necessity of recognizing the importance of a number of fundamental liberal tenets, concerning the centrality, in principle, of an 'impersonal' structure of public power, of a constitution to help guarantee and protect rights, and of mechanisms to promote competition and debate among alternative political platforms, for democracy to flourish it has to be fully entrenched in and among those sites of power which have unnecessarily restricted its form and efficacy. This theme is the focus of the remainder of part III. But before examining it directly, the principle of autonomy needs to be specified in more detail along with considerations about its conditions of enactment.

7.2 The terms of the principle of autonomy

In order to grasp the theoretical significance of the terrain marked out by the principle of autonomy – the ground on which a coherent account of the state and democracy can be developed – several notions embedded in the principle require to be sketched. Although their meaning will be specified further later, the following notions provide the initial terms of reference for subsequent analysis:

1. The principle of autonomy seeks to articulate the basis on which public power can be justified; it should be thought of as a principle of political legitimacy.
2. The notion that persons should enjoy equal rights and obligations in the political framework which shapes their lives and opportunities means that they should enjoy a *common structure of political action* in order that they may be able to pursue their projects – both individual and collective – as free and equal agents.[6] A common structure of political action is,

[6] Cf. Rawls (1985, pp. 254ff) for a discussion of the notion of a 'basic structure of society' as a limiting framework of action.

in principle, a 'neutral' basis of relations and institutions which can be regarded as impartial or even-handed with respect to personal ends, hopes and aspirations. Such a structure is inconsistent with, and, if it is applied systematically, would need to filter out, those ends and goods, whether public or private, which would erode or undermine the structure itself.[7]

3 The concept of 'rights' connotes, in the first instance, entitlements: entitlements to pursue action and activity without the risk of arbitrary or unjust interference. As explicated in § 3.3, rights define legitimate spheres of independent action (or inaction). Consistently with this, rights can be further defined as *entitlement capacities*, since unless entitlements translate into a capacity to act (or not act as the case may be), the efficacy of rights cannot be linked to an ability to make them count in practice. It is this ability to make rights count in practice which distinguishes a purely formal entitlement from a substantive practical gain.

While the benefits of rights are defined for particular persons (or groups or agencies), they are a public or social phenomenon because they circumscribe networks of relationships between the individual, or right-holder, and others, or the community and its representatives (see Dagger, 1989, pp. 304–5; cf. Hohfeld, 1964). Rights are entitlement capacities within the constraints of community, enabling – that is, creating spaces for action – and constraining – that is, specifying limits on independent action so that the latter does not curtail and infringe the liberty of others. Hence, rights have a structural dimension, bestowing both opportunities and duties. Further rights, if they are to specify the ability of people to enjoy a range of liberties not only in principle but also in practice, must be both formal and concrete. This entails the specification of a broad range of rights, with a 'cutting edge', in the realms of both state and civil society. As such, rights can be thought of as creating an equality of status with respect to the basic institutions of a community; that is, they are an entitlement to claim and be claimed upon (see Rawls, 1971, pp. 544–5; Barry, 1989, p. 200).

[7] As Miller succinctly put it, 'an institution or practice is neutral when, as far as can reasonably be foreseen, it does not favour any particular conception of the good at the expense of others' (1989, p. 77; see pp. 72–81; cf. Benhabib, 1992, pp. 40–6).

4 The particular rights and obligations entailed by the principle of autonomy are those necessary to protect each person's equal interest in the principle – an interest which follows from each person's status as a citizen with an equal entitlement to self-determination. The cluster of rights and obligations which allow the principle of autonomy to be effective – that is, which delimit and generate a common structure of political action – can be referred to as the set of 'empowering' or 'participatory' entitlement capacities. Taken together, these can be thought of as a structural system – a set of 'recursive relations' through which different types of entitlement capacity can be connected one to another through the specification of the means of participation. Such a system designates the rules and resources people must be able to draw upon in order to enjoy the opportunity to act as citizens (see Sen, 1981, pp. 1–8 and 45–51). Thus the principle of autonomy, entrenched in a system of empowering relations, can be regarded as both a foundation and a constraint upon public life – the constitutive basis of what will subsequently be called *democratic public law*.

5 The idea that people should be free and equal in the 'determination' of the conditions of their own lives means that they should be able to participate in a process of deliberation, open to all on a free and equal basis, about matters of public concern. A common structure of political action, articulated by the principle of autonomy and its related cluster of rights and obligations, specifies the framework of possible participation in and through which people may enter and take a position in the fray of public debate. Agreed judgement about policy and law should ideally follow from public debate and the 'force of the better argument' – not from the intrusive outcome of non-discursive elements and forces (see Habermas, 1973; Held, 1980, ch. 12). Further, a legitimate decision, within the arena of such debate, is not one that results necessarily from the 'will of all', but rather one that results from 'the deliberation of all' (Manin, 1987, p. 352). The process of deliberation is, accordingly, compatible with voting at the decisive stage of collective decision-making and with the procedures and mechanisms of majority rule.

6 The qualification stated in the principle – that a person's rights require explicit protection – represents a familiar call for constitutional government. The principle of autonomy

> specifies both that people must be 'free and equal' and that 'majorities' should not be able to impose themselves arbitrarily upon others. There must always be institutional arrangements to protect the individuals' or minorities' positions, that is, constitutional rules and safeguards. The principle of autonomy, and the set of 'empowering' rights and obligations, are the 'self-binding' mechanisms of democratic life, which allow its functioning and reproduction over time.

For persons to be free and equal in the determination of the conditions of their association requires, in brief, a common structure of political action which specifies the rights and obligations which are necessary to empower them as autonomous agents. The principle of autonomy, entrenched in democratic public law, ought to be regarded, therefore, not as an individualistic principle of self-determination, where 'the self' is the isolated individual acting alone in his or her interests, but, rather, as a structural principle of self-determination where 'the self' is part of the collectivity or 'the majority' enabled and constrained by the rules and procedures of democratic life. Autonomy, in this account, has to be understood in relation to a complex base of rules and resources – individuals are equally free when they can enjoy a common structure of political action. Hence, this form of autonomy can be referred to as 'democratic autonomy' – an entitlement to autonomy within the constraints of community. It can be clearly distinguished from an unbridled licence for the pursuit of individual interests in public affairs (see chapters 8 and 9).

7.3 The idea of a democratic legal state

It has been said that the principle of autonomy is a structural, not an individualistic, principle of self-determination. Accordingly, the scope and form of self-determination require elaboration if it is to be entrenched adequately in politics and in law; options for action must be created and foreclosed. Among those to be foreclosed is the option to abolish self-determination, which, once the principle of self-determination is accepted, would be a contradiction in terms. One cannot freely choose to renounce one's capacity to choose freely without defeating the very arguments or purpose which constituted the justification of the original choice in favour of self-determination. In other words, 'to preserve voluntariness,

voluntariness itself must be restricted' (Holmes, 1988, p. 239, and see his excellent discussion on pp. 238–40 of the same volume). The delimitation of political action, or the self-binding of democracy, is not only necessary but mandatory. In order for democracies to be sustained, the powers of decision-makers, of citizens and representatives alike, must be constrained.[8]

Rethinking the relationship between democracy, the state and constitutionality requires conceiving the power and authority which comprise the constitutive features of a public regulatory agent, whether a person or body of persons, as derivative of, and justified in relation to, a system of empowering rights and obligations, that is, democratic public law. State powers and institutions must be constituted and circumscribed by the requirement to enact this law, if the operation of democratic life is to be suitably restricted and framed. To the extent to which democratic public law is upheld, the basis is created for legitimate rule. Public power, in other words, can be conceived as legitimate to the degree to which it recognizes the principle of autonomy; that is, to the degree to which public agencies can be said to promote and enhance democratic autonomy. The form and scope of state powers and political authorities require justification in relation to this end. Within these terms, the proper form of the 'artificial person' can be said to be the democratic *Rechtstaat*, the democratic legal state – the state circumscribed by, and accounted for in relation to, democratic public law.[9]

If sovereignty is the rightful capacity to take political decisions and to enact the law within a given community with some degree of finality, it must be entrenched in certain rules and institutions from which it cannot free itself (King, P., 1987, pp. 492 and 495). Political authorities should be entrusted with the powers of the

[8] As Holmes wrote '[i]n general, a democracy choosing to destroy the framework in which non-violent disagreement and conflict-resolution can occur would be acting suicidally . . . [s]elf-binding becomes not only permissible but obligatory . . . The majority must limit its own powers to guarantee that it will remain a majority which can learn' (1988, pp. 239–40).

[9] Habermas has written a volume which presents, in some respects, a parallel conception (see 1996). Interesting elements of this are trailed in his 'Three models of democracy' (1994), where he argues that the self-organization of a democratic legal community should be conceived as embedded in rules and procedures which are 'not at the disposal of the citizens' will in any way' (p. 10).

democratic legal state in order to protect and enhance autonomy, and can enjoy legitimacy if these ends are embedded as the regulative or guiding ideals of public life. If these ends are systematically violated by such authorities, the latter can be said to be in conflict, or perhaps even at war, with segments of their own citizenry; conversely, if these ends are undermined by citizens, they too can become opponents of democratic autonomy. A democratic legal state is a condition for the flourishing of democracy; but it alone cannot guarantee this. A 'will to democracy' and a democratic culture are indispensable supporting conditions (see § 9.1).

8

SITES OF POWER, PROBLEMS OF DEMOCRACY

If a theory of democratic autonomy is to be compelling, it must be concerned with both theoretical and practical issues, with philosophical as well as organizational and institutional questions. Without this double focus, the meaning of political principles remains poorly specified and endless abstract debates about them are encouraged. An inquiry into the conditions of their realization is an indispensable component of a proper understanding of political principles. Accordingly, the meaning of the principle of autonomy must be further unfolded in the context of an examination of the conditions of its entrenchment. What might count as legitimate and illegitimate constraints on citizens' freedom of action? What arrangements have to be made, what policies pursued, in order to render citizens free and equal in the determination of the conditions of their association? And how can these be decided upon?

The principle of autonomy has both a normative and an empirical basis. If the empirical basis can be derived from unfolding the different ways in which people have struggled for membership of, and potentially full participation in, the modern political community, the normative basis can be derived from a reflection on the conditions under which autonomy is possible. This reflection can be developed by an attempt to elaborate a conception of autonomy based on a 'thought experiment' – an experiment into how people would interpret their capacities as citizens, and which rules, laws and institutions they would consider justified, if they had access to a fuller account of their position in the political system and of the conditions of possible participation (cf. Habermas, 1976, pp. 111–17, 1988, pp. 41–82). Such a thought experiment is guided by an interest in examining the ways in which the practices, institutions and structures of social and political life might be transformed to enable citizens more effectively to understand, shape and organize their lives; hence, it can be referred to as a 'democratic thought experiment'. The experiment reveals conditions of enactment of the principle of autonomy which have been largely unanticipated by the liberal democratic tradition, as well as by the political frameworks so long championed as the alternative to liberal and democratic thought: Marxism and state socialism.

8.1 Democratic thought experiment

A thought experiment of the kind proposed is a device of argument – a device which is designed to explore tensions between the principle of autonomy and its diverse possible conditions of enactment. It operates within, and takes its *raison d'être* from, the conceptual space provided by the dominant political tradition of the modern democratic state, while seeking to test the claims of this tradition to have entrenched its ideals adequately. It is, thus, a mechanism of immanent critique. Following the understanding of the rationale of the principle of autonomy as derived from the liberal democratic tradition, the democratic thought experiment seeks to model the idea of a democratic society in which citizens are conceived as free in equal measure. The democratic thought experiment cannot, as will be seen below, produce a wholly unambiguous result, but rather can lend weight to the direction of the argument so long as the premise of the experiment – a commitment to the principle of autonomy – is accepted. Of course, if one stands outside the liberal democratic tradition, then the acceptance of the premise, let alone the result, would be in doubt. The democratic thought experiment is a device of democratic argument and can, of course, be resisted by those who resist the language of autonomy and self-determination.[1]

[1] Thus, following Rawls's understanding of the 'original position' within the framework of the political, the democratic thought experiment can be thought of as 'a device of representation whose function is to dramatize and articulate a particular substantive conception of the person as citizen' and which 'forms part of an argument for the

At its core the democratic thought experiment is concerned to flesh out the conditions of an ideal autonomy, that is, the conditions, rights and obligations people would accept as necessary for their status to be met as equally free members of their political community. It is an inquiry which aims to abstract from existing power relations in order to disclose the fundamental enabling conditions for possible political participation and, therefore, for legitimate rule. It is, thus, an analytical mechanism which helps discriminate among forms of acceptance or compliance to political arrangements and outcomes.

There are many possible bases for obeying a command, complying with a rule, or agreeing or consenting to something. People may accept or comply with specific political circumstances because there is no choice in the matter (coercion or following orders); or, little or no thought has ever been given to such circumstances and people do as they have always done (tradition); or, they are unconcerned and indifferent (apathy); or, although they do not like a situation (it is not satisfactory and far from ideal), they cannot imagine things being really different and so they accept what seems like fate (pragmatic acquiescence); or, they are dissatisfied with things as they are but nevertheless go along with them in order to secure a particular end – they acquiesce because it is in the long run to their advantage (instrumental acceptance or conditional agreement); or, in the circumstances before them, and with the information available to them at that moment, they conclude it is 'right', 'correct', 'proper' for them as individuals or members of a collectivity: it is what they genuinely should do (practical normative agreement); or, finally, it is what in ideal circumstances – with, for instance, all the knowledge they would like, all the opportunity to discover the circumstances and requirements of others – they would have agreed to do (ideal normative agreement) (Held, 1987, pp. 182–3, 237–8 and 298–9).

These distinctions are analytical: in ordinary circumstances different types of agreement are often fused together. But only an exploration of what can be called an 'ideal normative agreement' or an 'ideal deliberative judgement' can disclose the possible conditions under which people would follow rules and laws because they think them right or correct, given a full range of information

---

development and maintenance of a type of society within which citizens accord a particular moral status to one another' (Mulhall and Swift, 1992, p. 210).

and choices. An ideal normative agreement is a hypothetically projected agreement about particular political arrangements, set out on the grounds that they are the arrangements people would have agreed to in ideal conditions (see below). It provides the *telos* of the thought experiment and enables one to ask not only what the circumstances would have to be like, but also how they might be altered, to enable people to follow rules, laws and policies they think right, justified or worthy of respect. It allows a distinction to be made between legitimacy as belief in existing law and political institutions, and legitimacy as 'rightness' or 'correctness' – the worthiness of a political order to be recognized because it is the order people would accept under ideal deliberative conditions as that which fully entrenches the principle of autonomy in public life. Accordingly, a democratic thought experiment can be conceived, not as an optional element of political understanding, but as a requirement of any attempt to grasp the different circumstances underpinning political support and legitimacy; for without this form of counterfactual reasoning, the distinction between legitimacy as 'belief' and legitimacy as 'rightness' could not be made (cf. Benhabib, 1994).

In order to investigate what people might agree to in the absence of coercive relations, and postulate a favourable environment for deliberation, the context of such reflection requires further specification. To begin with, it needs to be assumed that the constraints of everyday interaction are suspended; that is, that people can put aside their particular social positions, ends and interests for the purposes of the experiment. In addition, it needs to be assumed that the people who are attempting to justify their views and reach agreement are unable to coerce one another either by direct or by indirect means. There is only one compulsion possible, 'the force of the better argument', and only one acceptable motive, the cooperative search for agreement (see Habermas, 1973, pp. 239–40 and 358–9, 1990, pp. 43ff; Held, 1980, ch. 12; Barry, 1989, pp. 342–3). Moreover, it needs to be presupposed that deliberative agents can, in such conditions, reflexively monitor their circumstances, generate a coherent conception of their ends and come to an understanding of how alternative means would bear on the prospects of reaching those ends.[2]

[2] The conditions of this type of discourse can be specified formally in terms of an 'ideal deliberative situation'. Such a situation must ensure equal opportunity for discussion, free from all coercion and

A thought experiment that evokes the notions of an ideal deliberative situation and an ideal normative agreement will not produce a straightforward deductive proof of a set of principles or conditions necessary for an ideal autonomy. But this does not mean that such an approach is 'toothless'. There are two methods, outlined particularly clearly by Brian Barry, which can be adapted to derive the conditions necessary for such autonomy: the first, the philosophical *a priori*, asks whether there are political circumstances that 'nobody would reasonably accept' unless backed by power relations; and, the second, the empirical-analytic, examines the dynamics of power to illuminate systematic obstacles to an ideal deliberative situation (see Barry, 1989, pp. 347–8 and 345). These approaches do not generally enable one to claim that a particular practice or institution is the only one compatible with the principle of autonomy and its entrenchment, but they do enable the elimination of a distinct cluster of practices and institutions as incompatible with autonomy; that is, as incompatible with the terms of reference of the principle of autonomy.

It needs to be stressed that the proposed inquiry is *not* an exercise in search of an endless list of goods; rather, it is an exercise to disclose the constitutive basis of democratic public law – the political, economic and social circumstances consistent with equally free political participation. Furthermore, the goal is to elucidate those conditions of autonomy capable of defence on the ground that they are in principle equally acceptable to all parties or social groups (see Habermas, 1973, pp. 239–40; cf. Barry, 1989, p. 342).

---

domination, whether arising from conscious strategic behaviour and/or from unacknowledged conditions of action. At issue is a discursive situation in which there are equal chances to enter dialogue, recognition of the legitimacy of each party to participate in the dialogue as an equal partner, and the possibility of mutual understanding and agreement due simply to 'the better argument'. A judgement reached in these circumstances can be regarded as a justified or grounded judgement (see Habermas, 1973, 1976, pp. 111–17, 1984; Cohen, J., 1988, 1989, for the most rigorous statement of an 'ideal deliberative procedure').

In assuming that the parties to the democratic thought experiment can participate in a discourse of this type, it is also being assumed that differences in natural endowments will not in themselves be the basis of an agreement. In other words, it is assumed that all participants have sufficient natural talents and abilities to engage in the experiment and to weigh up contending positions (see § 9.2; cf. Rawls, 1993, p. 272).

As such, the objective is not in itself an actual agreement between possible participants in democratic life, but rather, in the first instance, a hypothetical stipulation of the conditions all parties or groups would consent to if they engaged in a similar thought experiment.

By a party or social group I mean a set of people who occupy a common social location; that is, who share a determinate pattern of life-chances and participative opportunities stemming from a category (or categories) of social relations, for instance, class, sex, race and ethnicity (see § 8.2).[3] A political position which no party 'could reasonably reject' can be said to meet the theoretical test of impartiality (cf. Barry, 1989, p. 370). In order to meet this standard a number of particular tests can be applied, including an assessment of whether all points of view have been taken into consideration; whether there are groups in a position to impose on others in such a manner as would be unacceptable to the latter, or to the originator of the action (or inaction) if the roles were reversed; and whether all parties would be equally prepared to accept the outcome as fair and reasonable irrespective of the social positions they might occupy now or in the future (see Barry, 1989, pp. 372 and 362–3).

The pursuit of the test of impartiality, the willingness, that is, to reason from the point of view of others, is not a solitary theoretical exercise; for in this context the efficacy of a judgement rests on the possibility, in principle, of coming to an understanding with other citizens. As Arendt has eloquently written:

> The power of judgement rests on a potential agreement with others, and the thinking process which is active in judging something is not . . . a dialogue between me and myself, but finds itself always and primarily, even if I am quite alone in making up my mind, in an anticipated communication with others with whom I know I must finally come to some agreement. . . . And this enlarged way of thinking . . . cannot function in strict isolation or solitude; it needs the presence of others 'in whose place' it must think, whose per-

[3] Barry has argued that arguments for inequality could only be accepted as justified if there were good grounds for believing that they would be equally acceptable to 'everyone' (1989, pp. 347–8). But this seems too strong a requirement, for it bestows upon individuals enormous veto power. 'Everyone' is a hostage to individual idiosyncrasies and desires.

spective it must take into consideration, and without whom it never has the opportunity to operate at all. (1961, pp. 220–1)[4]

The aim of a 'theoretical conversation' about political impartiality is an anticipated agreement with all those whose diverse circumstances affect the realization of people's equal interest in the principle of autonomy. Of course, as an 'anticipated agreement' it is a hypothetical ascription of an intersubjective or collective understanding. As such, the ultimate test of its validity must depend in contemporary life on the extension of the conversation to all those whom it seeks to encompass. Only under the latter circumstances can an analytically proposed interpretation become an actual understanding or agreement among others (cf. Habermas, 1988, p. 32). The political theorist is, thus, necessarily engaged in a theoretical analysis of power and legitimacy as well as in a call for a practical-political discourse about the circumstances of democracy among the very individuals and groups who are embraced by the analysis (see Held, 1980, pp. 346–9; and § 12.3).

It is important to enter a qualification about the standing of the democratic thought experiment. As a framework for an immanent critique of democratic society, it fosters a critical exploration of the relationship between political principles, conditions of partici-

[4] This passage is cited by Benhabib (1992, pp. 9–10), who draws out its implications in both a critical and a subtle manner (pp. 121–47). Benhabib's own procedural reformulation of the principle of universalizability, along the model of a moral conversation in which the capacity to reverse perspectives and explore the position of others is central, is compatible with elements of the position set out above. However, there are differences as well. In laying more emphasis on the process for the attainment of practical judgements in an 'open-ended moral conversation', rather than on what all would or could agree under ideal deliberative conditions, Benhabib presents an account of the limits of counterfactual reasoning in political and ethical discourses (1992, esp. pp. 23–67). Her reservations on this matter are important, especially those concerning an overgeneralized use of the model of counterfactual reasoning in ethical discourse. However, they do not undermine the efficacy and validity of the democratic thought experiment; for the latter is, as stressed above, a requirement of an examination of the foundations of political authority and of the possibility of democratic legitimacy. A democratic thought experiment is necessary in order to investigate the worthiness of the major institutions of society to be recognized from the point of view of all parties, although its results must necessarily be interpreted tentatively and as part of an overall argumentative strategy (see §§ 9.3 and 12.3).

pation and types of compliance. As such, it is misleading and unnecessary to think of it as grounded ultimately in all discourse (as Habermas has characterized a parallel notion (see McCarthy, 1991, pp. 195–9)) or in a tradition-free discourse (as Rawls, for instance, understood the original position in *A Theory of Justice* (1971)). For there is no fixed observation point, philosophical position or wholly neutral stance which would allow one to claim that, if only we were to conduct a democratic thought experiment, an agreement could be arrived at which would be the same irrespective of time and place. A thought experiment is a moment in the hermeneutic dialogue of which everyone is a part; it can only be conducted within the concepts and categories of the interpretative systems obtaining at particular historical times (see Gadamer, 1975). These can, of course, be enriched by an awareness of a wide range of cultural and historical circumstances and traditions. But political understanding cannot escape the history of traditions. Knowledge is generated within the framework of traditions; and the discernment of truth always has a temporal structure. As a consequence, there can be no such thing as the correct or the final understanding of autonomy; its meaning is always open to further interpretations from new perspectives. When an interpretation is offered of the actual and possible nature of autonomy, it necessarily involves a hypothetical projection bound by the constraints of political tradition.

This does not mean that the evaluative or practical basis of political theory is simply invalidated. For the differences among evaluative stances are never merely those between discrepant 'ultimate values' – or 'warring Gods' as Weber put it – which one must simply accept or reject (Weber, 1972a, pp. 152–3). The meaning of evaluative standpoints is always in part given by the framework of concepts, beliefs and standards within which they are embedded – the web of concepts and theories in and through which the factual and normative inform one another. These interpretative webs are open to appraisal in both philosophical and empirical terms (see Hesse, 1974; Giddens, 1977, pp. 89–95; Held, 1991b, pp. 11–21). The evaluative stance of the thought experiment is, as the following sections seek to show, both an inescapable and a practical element of political understanding.

It could be objected at this point that, given the plurality of interpretative standpoints in the contemporary world, it is unwise to construct an analytical mechanism, like the democratic thought experiment, which depends upon a notion of rational agreement:

an evaluative stance which all could, in principle, will as participants in an ideal political discourse. For it is doubtful, the objection could continue, that a bridge can be built between 'the many particular wills' and 'the general will' (see McCarthy, 1991, pp. 181–99; cf. Lukes, 1982). In a world marked by pluralism and a diversity of value orientations, on what grounds, if any, can we suppose that all parties could be argumentatively convinced about fundamental political questions?

In response, it can be noted that the democratic thought experiment is not constructed on the supposition that unanimity is always attainable on practical-political questions – far from it. It is not an experiment engaged in seeking a general and universal understanding on a wide spectrum of issues concerning the broad conditions of life or diverse ethical matters (for example, animal rights, the role of voluntary euthanasia). Rather, it is a more restrictive exercise aimed at reflection on the conditions of liberal democracy and the conditions of possible participation. And it is constructed on the assumption that ground rules for dialogue, procedures and dispute settlement are not only desirable but essential precisely because people's views on a wide range of moral-political questions will conflict.

Thus, the democratic thought experiment does not seek to stipulate what people should 'really' think is in their best interest in many everyday, practical matters but, rather, seeks to elucidate the basis of an agreement about the framework that might allow conflicting interpretations of value, interest and judgement to be explored without resort to coercion, force or violence. It is, therefore, about the conditions of democratic dialogue, not about what should be said in such dialogue. At stake is the conceptualization and generation of the necessary background conditions for the pursuit of democratic politics; that is, for the pursuit of argument, compromise and the containment of conflict in public affairs.

8.2 Power, life-chances and nautonomy

The test of impartiality can reveal the incompatibility of democracy with circumstances characterized by the severest forms of inequality, including slavery, apartheid and virulent forms of racism (cf. Barry, 1989, p. 347). For none of these phenomena would be acceptable to all parties in the absence of coercion and force, and under ideal deliberative conditions. They are backed by coercive power and sustained by such power. A democracy which sought to embrace any of these phenomena would be a form of rule in which, as in classical Athens, the participation of the few was linked directly to the limited or non-participation of the many. Athenian democracy, despite its significant innovations, would not have passed the test of impartiality: inequalities existed which would not have been acceptable to all parties. Even if, for example, Athenian citizens had explored the points of view of Athenian slaves (for whose condition they would have had strictly limited sympathy, of course), they would have rejected any thought that the inequalities of slavery were remotely appropriate to them as citizens, and would surely not have accepted slavery as fair and just without prior knowledge of whether or not they would be secure as citizens. In the discourse of an ideal deliberative situation, they could not have known whether their present or future roles might be reversed, and whether their status positions might alter radically. Under such conditions, slavery would have to be rejected.

Irrespective of what Athenian citizens themselves would have considered fair and appropriate under altered circumstances, it is clear that the inequalities of slavery were sustained largely by the application of coercive power. The history of slave rebellion and revolt, alongside the brutal history of slave repression, is adequate testimony to this state of affairs (see Ste Croix, 1981). In contemporary democracies, certainly, it is highly improbable that most people would accept arguments for slavery or its nearest modern equivalent: apartheid. Most would consider that these conditions contradict the very terms of democracy: that is to say, that they are fundamentally incompatible with a belief in self-determination and its requisite minimum conditions: civil and political rights. However, the issue is not primarily one of belief; for the grounds for rejecting slavery and apartheid are properly ascertained by their failure to meet the test of impartiality. If the terms of the thought experiment are applied, inequalities can only be accepted as legitimate when, in the absence of coercion or force, there are good grounds for believing that they would be equally acceptable to all groups. There seem no good grounds for believing that the inequalities of slavery or apartheid would, under contemporary conditions, be acceptable to those who would do worst under them. Accordingly, slavery and apartheid may be regarded as illegitimate background conditions for any form of political life that claims to be a democracy. But would less virulent forms of power and political inequality also be ruled out by the requirement of impartiality?

Can a democratic political order be regarded as legitimate if it is marked by structured discrepancies with respect to power, opportunities and choices? The issues involved can be unfolded initially through a series of indicative questions.

If one engaged in a democratic thought experiment about the proper form of public power, is it likely that one would accept as legitimate a political order in which the capacity for self-determination was shaped by asymmetries of power, unequal life-chances and radically unequal political opportunities patterned by one's country of origin, race, sex and class? In such a thought experiment, would one regard as justified a polity in which autonomy was formally enjoyed by many, but where access to political opportunities were enjoyed only by a relatively privileged few? If one did not know one's future social and political position, would one accept a decision-making process in which many life-determining issues were not open to public scrutiny and deliberation; and where, despite the existence of nominally democratic decision-making centres, decisions were often taken which affected large numbers of people who had no direct democratic stake in those centres? Further, if people did not know where they would find themselves when the 'social dice' finally fell, would they not seek or choose certain minimum levels of political opportunity and need-satisfaction? Would they not define their good or interest in direct relation to the rules and resources that would be necessary for them to cooperate or compete fairly with others – subject to the limits of their life-plans and abilities[5] – as equal members of their political community? (Cf. Doyal and Gough, 1991, p. 132.)[6] Accordingly, would they not define their good or interest in terms

[5] The recognition of differential human abilities and talents raises difficult questions, which will be taken up in the following chapter.

[6] Dahl states that a person's good or interest 'is whatever that person would choose with the fullest attainable understanding of the experience resulting from that choice and its most relevant alternatives'; and that an essential element in the meaning of the collective interest or common good among the members of a group is, again, 'what the members would choose if they possessed the fullest attainable understanding of the experience that would result from their choice and its most relevant alternatives' (1989, pp. 307–8). While both these formulations are helpful, Dahl does not provide an analytical mechanism to help separate out individual or collective beliefs about the good from the 'fullest attainable understanding' of the good, or from, what I prefer to denote as, the hypothetical ascription of the good.

of a common structure of political action, which would shape and bind all forms of public power, and which would create the basis for an association of equally free persons? Or, to put the point somewhat differently, is a system of power which generates systematic asymmetries of life-chances and political opportunities compatible with the principle of autonomy?

What is power? At one level, the concept of power is very simple: it refers to the *capacity* of social agents, agencies and institutions to maintain or transform their environment, social or physical; and it concerns the resources which underpin this capacity and the forces that shape and influence its exercise. Accordingly, power is a phenomenon found in and between all groups, institutions and societies, cutting across public and private life. It is expressed in all the relations, institutions and structures that are implicated in the production and reproduction of the life of societies and communities. Power creates and conditions all aspects of our lives and it is at the core of the development of collective problems, and the modes of their resolution. While 'power', thus understood, raises a number of complicated issues, it usefully highlights the nature of power as a universal dimension of human life, independent of any specific 'site' or set of institutions (see Held, 1989).

But the power of an agent or agency or institution, wherever it is located, never exists in isolation. Power is always exercised, and political outcomes are always determined, in the context of the relative capabilities of parties. Power has to be understood as a relational phenomenon (Giddens, 1979, ch. 2; Rosenau, 1980, ch. 3). Hence, power expresses at one and the same time the intentions and purposes of agencies and institutions and the relative balance of resources they can deploy with respect to each other.

The power manifest in political and social relations cannot be fully grasped if attention is restricted to what people do or to what apparently occurs (decision-making). For power can also be manifest when agents and agencies appear to do nothing (non-decision-making) (Bachrach and Baratz, 1962). Moreover, power cannot simply be conceived in terms of what agents or agencies do or do not do. For power is also a structural phenomenon, shaped by and, in turn, shaping the socially structured and culturally patterned behaviour of groups and the practices of organizations (Lukes, 1974, p. 22). Any organization or institution can condition and limit the behaviour of its members. The rules and resources, that is, the recursive relations, which such organizations and institutions embody rarely constitute a neutral framework for action, for they establish patterns of power and authority and confer the right to take decisions on some and not on others; in effect, they institutionalize a power relationship between 'rulers' and 'ruled', 'subjects' and 'governors'. Thus, those who are powerful need not routinely display their power if their dominant position is already secured in the prevailing structures of rules and resources (see McGrew, 1988, pp. 18–19).

Where relations of power systematically generate asymmetries of life-chances they may create a situation which can be called 'nautonomic'. Nautonomy refers to *the asymmetrical production and distribution of life-chances which limit and erode the possibilities of political participation*. By life-chances I mean the chances a person has of sharing in the socially generated economic, cultural or political goods, rewards and opportunities typically found in his or her community (see Giddens, 1980, pp. 130–1). Nautonomy refers to any socially conditioned pattern of asymmetrical life-chances which places artificial limits on the creation of a common structure of political action.

Nautonomic structures are shaped by the availability of a diverse range of socially patterned resources, from the material (wealth and income) through the coercive (organized might and the deployment of force) to the cultural – the stock of concepts and discourses which mould interpretative frameworks, tastes and abilities. The availability of such resources in a community depends evidently enough on the capability of groups to exclude 'outsiders' and to control resources denied to others. The attempt to control, if not monopolize, any range of resources according to particular social criteria, such as class, race, ethnicity or gender, can be denoted a form of 'social closure' (Weber, 1978, pp. 341ff; see Parkin, 1979). Closure can be effected by a variety of means including 'exclusion'. The latter is the principal mode in which, for instance, social classes developed: the formation of dominant classes in different types of society was achieved via decisive control of resources, which often included not only land or capital but also armed force and 'esoteric knowledge' (see chapters 2 and 3). Any system of power in which particular life-chances and opportunities are subject to closure can create nautonomic outcomes and, thereby, undermine or corrode the principle of autonomy.

When power, relational power and structural power are interlinked in such a manner as to generate nautonomic outcomes, participation is involuntarily restricted. To the extent that nautonomy exists, a common structure of political action is not possible, and democracy becomes a privileged domain operating in favour of those with significant resources. In such circumstances, people can be formally free and equal, but they will not enjoy rights which shape and facilitate a common structure of political action and safeguard their capacities. People's equal interest in the principle of autonomy will not be protected; and the claims which they might legitimately make, and which might legitimately be made upon them, will not be adequately entrenched. Accordingly, the demonstration of nautonomy provides a criterion for the critical assessment of the operation of power in particular places or sites.

To the extent that a domain of activity operates to structure and delimit systematically life-chances and participative opportunities, 'deficits' are disclosed in the structure of action of a political association. These deficits can, furthermore, be regarded as illegitimate to the extent to which they would have been rejected in a democratic thought experiment. If people did not know their future social location and political identity, it is improbable that they would find the self-interested defence of specific exclusionary processes and mechanisms convincing. These justificatory structures cannot easily be generalized and are, thus, weak in the face of the test of impartiality. The latter's emphasis on the necessity of taking account of the position of the other, of only regarding political outcomes as fair and reasonable if there are good reasons for holding that they would be equally acceptable to all parties, and of only treating socio-political roles as legitimate if they are acceptable to all groups irrespective of where they come in the social hierarchy, does not provide grounds on which nautonomy could easily be accepted. Unless exceptional arguments are available to the contrary (see §§ 9.2–9.4), nautonomy falls to the requirement of impartiality. Therefore, a theory of power which discloses nautonomic structures and processes is potentially a theory which can highlight obstacles to the empowerment of persons as equally free agents in a community and which can, conversely, delineate the necessary elements of a democratic public law.

8.3 Power clusters

In order to examine further the conditions of, and questionable restrictions upon, a democratic political association, it is necessary to extend the account of power to illuminate some of the main obstacles to autonomy. What is at issue is the specification of the key *sites of power* in a community, since any attempt of flesh out the conditions of a common structure of political action must explicate these arenas and tease out the roots of nautonomy.

A 'site of power' is an interaction context or institutional milieu in and through which power operates to shape the capacities of people; that is, to mould and circumscribe their life-chances, effective participation and share in public decision-making. Sites of power can be distinguished from 'sources of power' which create, sustain and transform the production and distribution of power – through the organization and control of certain rules and resources – in and across other sites. Elements of the interaction context of a particular site may operate 'independently'; that is to say, the relations and structures of power on that site may be *internally* generated and applied. Examples of this include aspects of military or bureaucratic organization in which internal hierarchies can generate resources, entrench authority and develop clear powers of intervention in tightly circumscribed realms. However, some sites of power may generate pressures and forces which extend beyond their 'boundaries', and shape and delimit other sites. Certain networks of interaction have greater capacity than others for organizing intensive and extensive, or authoritative and diffused, social relations (see Mann, 1986, p. 27). These sites of power become to a degree the sources of power for other sites. The reach of the medieval church into economic life, or the influence of powerful MNCs on governments in the contemporary era, are cases in point. Against this background, a system of structural power or of social stratification can be said to be established when groups or collectivities exist in a political community which, through their organization and control of particular clusters of rules, peoples and material stemming from one (or more) site of power, can extend and entrench their control across other sites. The variables involved are depicted in figure 8.1 (p. 174).

Traditionally, liberals have conceived the state as the key site of power in the community. On the one hand, the state must have a monopoly of coercive power in order to provide a secure basis upon which trade, commerce, family life and religion can prosper. On the other hand, by granting the state a regulatory and coercive capability, liberal political theorists recognized that they had accepted a force which could and frequently did deprive citizens of political and social freedoms. While liberals affirmed the necessity of the state to govern and regulate society, they also came to

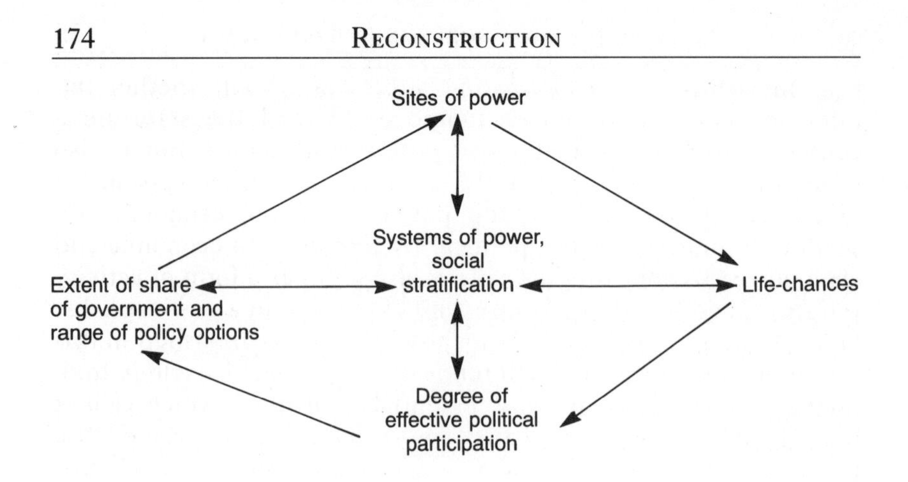

FIGURE 8.1 Power and political participation

conceive of civil and political rights as essential for the regulation of this regulator (see §§ 1.1 and 3.3).

In contrast to this view, Marxists have typically placed emphasis upon the centrality of economic and productive relations in public and private life. The key source of contemporary power – private ownership of the means of production – is, they hold, ostensibly *depoliticized* by liberalism; that is, it is arbitrarily treated as if it were not a proper subject of politics. The economy is, as a result, regarded as non-political, in that the massive division between those who own and control the means of production, and those who must live by wage-labour, is conceived as the outcome of free private contracts, and not a matter for the state. But it is the liberal claim that there is and ought to be a clear distinction between the world of civil society and that of the political which Marxists reject. For them, one of the consequences of the capitalist relations of production is the creation of inequality of such magnitude that it corrodes liberty. The challenge to liberty derives from inequality, or from liberty of a distinctive kind: liberty to accumulate unlimited wealth, to organize economic activity into hierarchically ordered enterprises, and to make the exigencies of capital the imperatives of society as a whole (cf. Dahl, 1985). Accordingly, for Marxists, it is only when the capitalist relations of production are superseded that it becomes possible for people, as free and equal agents, to enjoy autonomy.

The Marxist critique of liberalism raises important questions – above all, about whether markets can be characterized as 'powerless' mechanisms of coordination and, thus, about whether the interconnections between economic power and the state are a central matter in the analysis of power and politics. But it also raises difficulties by postulating (even in its subtler versions) a direct connection between the political and the economic. By seeking to understand the political by reference to economic and class power, by rejecting the notion of politics as a form of activity *sui generis*, and by calling for the 'end of politics' in a post-capitalist order (for politics will be redundant when class is abolished in this interpretation), Marxism itself tends to marginalize or exclude from politics certain types of issue: essentially, all those which cannot be reduced to class-related matters. Important examples are the power of public administrators or bureaucrats over their clients, the role of authoritative resources which build up in most social organizations, and the form and nature of electoral institutions. It is no accident that Marxism does not offer systematic accounts of the dangers of centralized political power or of the problem of political accountability, accounts which represent the very strengths of liberal analysis (see Held, 1987, pp. 132–9).

The accounts of power in both liberal and Marxist political theory are too narrow to encompass adequately the range of conditions necessary for the possibility of a common structure of political action. Generally, these two political traditions have failed to explore the impediments to participation in democratic life other than those imposed, however important these may be, by the axes of state and economic power. The roots of the difficulty lie in narrow conceptions of power itself. In the liberal tradition power has often been equated with the world of government and the citizen's relation to it. Where this equation is made and where power is regarded as a sphere apart from economy or culture, a vast terrain of power is excluded from view, including the spheres of productive and reproductive relations. The Marxist conception raises related difficulties through its exclusion or underestimation of forms of power – and of forms of social structure, collective organization, agency, identity and knowledge – other than those rooted squarely in production. In order to grasp the conditions necessary for the entrenchment of the principle of autonomy, a broader conception of sites of power is required than can be found in either of these traditions.

Any domain of action which disrupts systematically people's equal interest in autonomy, that is, their standing as citizens with equal entitlements to self-determination, requires critical examination. The compatibility of democratic autonomy has to be explored with respect to any organization of life-chances and participative opportunities which systematically stratifies collectivities or groups in relation to a wide array of phenomena, including: their security of personhood; physical and psychological wellbeing; opportunities to become active members of the community; security of cultural identity; ability to join civic associations; capacity to influence the economic agenda; ability to participate in political debate and electoral politics; and ability to act without becoming vulnerable to physical force and violence. Disadvantage in any of these domains could weaken or demobilize the capacities of individuals or groups. A diverse set of sites of power needs, therefore, to be considered – encompassing realms of action which will be referred to as the body, welfare, culture, civic associations, the economy, organized violence and coercive relations, and regulatory and legal institutions. To anticipate the main argument which follows: people's equal interest in the principle of autonomy requires protection across each of these sites; and unless it is so protected a common structure of political action cannot be fully entrenched.

8.4 Seven sites of power

The prevalence of nautonomy in any given site of power can be assessed by a number of indicators including whether and to what extent people have *access* to that site; whether *opportunities* within it are open or closed; and whether *outcomes*, be they assessed in terms of education levels, jobs or a range of cultural activities, are biased in favour of certain groups or interests. What follows below is an account of these issues across each of the sites of power, but an account which is enumerative and illustrative rather than fully systematic. It is intended to disclose the way nautonomy provides a benchmark against which the nature and scope of autonomy can be assessed, and the extent to which nautonomy highlights artificial limits or constraints upon political agency. The analysis shows how the study of power and nautonomy can be pursued, rather than revealing every domain of action to which it might in principle be extended.

The first site of power to be considered, the body, refers to the way in which physical and emotional wellbeing is organized through distinctive networks and institutional milieux, informal and formal, across intersecting social spaces from the local to the international. Relations of power operate in this domain to produce and reproduce a pattern of wellbeing which is structured asymmetrically within nations and across them. Although the latter claim will not be documented here at any length, it is not difficult to illustrate it. Life or survival chances (measured by life expectancy and age-specific mortality rates), physical ill-health (assessed by the prevalence of serious diseases, disabilities and developmental deficiencies) and mental illness (indicated by the frequency of severe psychotic, depressive and other psychological illnesses) all tend to be correlated directly with geography, class, gender and race and, accordingly, with particular clusters of deprivation found – most dramatically – among countries of the South, among non-whites, among the poor and working classes and among women (see UNICEF, 1987; World Bank, 1988; Sivard, 1989; Doyal and Gough, 1991, pt. 3). (Although women live longer than men on average, they generally suffer greater ill-health, which is underpinned by greater physical and emotional stress and by poorer nutrition (Graham, 1984).) These correlations and clusters are not, however, restricted to countries of the South, and can be found widely in the North as well.[7] The patterns of social closure and opportunity among men and women, working, middle and upper classes, blacks and whites, and various ethnic communities profoundly affect their wellbeing across all categories of health both in the United States and in Europe (see, for example, Cohen, J. and Rogers, 1983; Bradley, 1992).

In this context, groups of people find themselves in nautonomic circumstances if they do not have access to the conditions – that is, appropriate food and nutritional levels, clean water and other fluids, adequate health amenities and resources, and sufficient health services – which allow them 'to play the roles, participate in the relationships and follow the customary behaviour which is expected of them by virtue of their membership of society' (Townsend, 1987, pp. 130 and 140; and see Doyal and Gough, 1991, p. 211). In the domain of the body, nautonomy can be defined as a lack of resources (typically nutritional, housing and financial)

[7] Recent investigations by the Carnegie Corporation and the General Accounting Office (a Congressional investigative agency in the United States) have found, for instance, that the long-term development of up to a quarter of American children under the age of three is threatened by severe poverty and social deprivation (*Guardian*, 1994).

and a lack of opportunities (typically educational and health-related) which prevent people from obtaining the conditions necessary for participation across a range of 'goods' in public and private life.

A stark example of nautonomic structures, which pervade the health of over half the globe's population, is revealed in the pattern of maternal mortality rates, the availability of contraception, the distribution of pre-natal facilities and levels of reproductive health care more generally (see Doyal and Gough, 1991, p. 250; UNDP, 1990). The pattern discloses that vast numbers of women do not have access to the medical and social facilities necessary to prevent or assist pregnancy, and to enjoy access to the general material conditions which would help make the choice to have a child a genuinely free one. Accordingly, a central condition for women's wellbeing as potentially 'free and equal' members of the community is commonly absent (Petchesky, 1986). This absence, combined with the continuing pervasiveness of 'male sex-right', simultaneously ensuring male domination within the family and violence against women (from routine sexual harassment to rape) in public and private spaces, has devastating consequences for the potential autonomy of women (see Kelly, 1988; Pateman, 1988; Delphy and Leonard, 1992). While there are some countries in which women's autonomy is severely restricted, participation rates in nearly all domains of public activity – from paid employment to involvement in the legislature – still indicate substantially lower levels for women than men in virtually all contemporary societies (see below).

By welfare, the second site of power, I refer to the organization of the domain of goods and services that aids the transition of the citizen from private person to full membership of the community. The domain of welfare denotes the organization of those capacities that people require in order to ensure that they are 'competent to take part in both economic and political life' (Miller, 1989, p. 318). While it clearly overlaps with the domain of the body, the focus here is primarily upon those social and political arrangements in society which are preoccupied with the *bildung* or cultivation of the citizen – the arrangements in and through which a child slowly becomes a participating member of and contributor to society. In full-fledged welfare states the realm of welfare refers to everything from birth registration to death certification, from schooling to higher education, and from the organization of social security to the provision of a large range of community services. Although this domain remains largely the province of the state in most advanced industrial countries, it is important to stress that many welfare functions, both of an educational and of a non-educational sort, are carried out in the private as well as public sectors (see Pierson, 1991). Many voluntary groups in civil society are actively engaged in the organization and provision of welfare (see Hirst, 1993). In traditional societies, and in many rural or agricultural societies today, the role of such groups is often more extensive; welfare can be organized as much by small local communities as by kinship networks. However, even in advanced societies the informal networks of family and kinship often provide vital mechanisms which interlock and interpenetrate with the welfare provision organized by the state.

The absence of welfare provision, or its asymmetrical distribution in any given context, can contribute to the generation and maintenance of nautonomic structures. In nearly all 'Third World' countries, for instance, the participation rates of females in schools, primary and secondary, is markedly lower than for males (although the female participation rates are increasing significantly in rapidly developing countries) (see UNDP, 1990). But in nearly all countries, irrespective of whether they are in the North or South, East or West, educational opportunities and outcomes are heavily stratified by class, race, ethnicity and gender, with the consequential 'underdevelopment' of the capacities, abilities and talents of the many (see, for example, Halsey, Heath and Ridge, 1980; Heath, 1981; Erikson and Goldthorpe, 1986). Stratified education systems, moreover, directly affect the degree to which citizens become committed and active. Political efficacy, people's estimation of their ability to influence government, and their declared interest in government itself are known to be related to the extent of formal education (see Pateman, 1970, 1983; Held, 1989, ch. 4). Divisions between the politically active and passive can, therefore, partly be accounted for by the lack of adequately developed opportunities for groups of citizens to develop their talents and confidence.

Of course, the development of talents and confidence depends on more than simply formal education; it depends also on the dense network of social provision which can encourage or erode autonomy or independence. For example, the provision of childcare facilities for single parents with young children enables such parents to pursue labour-market and other opportunities. By contrast, if there is little or inadequate provision of this kind, single parents can be locked into a 'poverty trap' which simultaneously places the cost of childcare beyond their reach, prevents their entrance into the labour market and erodes their capacity for active involvement in civil and political affairs (see Dominelli, 1991; cf. Giddens, 1994).

The third site of power, the site of culture or cultural life, refers to those realms of social activity where matters of public interest and identity can be discussed, where differences of opinion can be explored and where local custom and dogma can be examined (see Habermas, 1989). These realms can be ordered formally through churches, the media, or the state's efforts at public relations, as well as informally through local meetings and interchanges. More broadly, the domain of culture denotes the organization of concepts and categories of meaning which are essential to the mobilization of a community. It comprises symbolic orders, norms, standards and types of discourse which together generate accounts of everyday practices and events. Such accounts or interpretative schemes determine what can be apprehended, and what can be noticed and registered as important. Furthermore, they shape attempts to understand and assess political actions and processes; for they carry with them general views about human capacities, needs and motives and about the mutability or otherwise of human institutions which are charged with political implications (see Taylor, 1967). Patterns of meaning also include aesthetic or ritual practices, which can be organized in a variety of ways through secular or 'sacred' forms of authority. Through these authorities, frames of meaning are produced and reproduced which can inform the development of political and social identity.

Asymmetrical access to the production and distribution of interpretative schemes and practices, as well as to rhetorical abilities and skills, are a mark of nautonomy in the sphere of culture. Where collective power operates to control or manipulate a claim to meaning, or to set tight limits on how people might act morally in relation to each other and to nature, nautonomic forces may be present. Such forces can result in circumstances whereby some groups are denied access to dominant cultural codes or are expected to be mere 'receivers' of them, and in circumstances whereby organs of communication and discourse are distributed asymmetrically. In the latter case, such organs may be in the hands of distinctive social groupings, religious hierarchies or the economically privileged, who may control or prevent access to them. Where systems of signification or meaning are mobilized to sustain asymmetrical power relations in the interests of dominant or hegemonic groups, distinctive forms of ideology can take root (see Thompson, 1984, pp. 126–32). Such circumstances are in marked contrast to a situation where, for example, each section of the population has access to, or has its own, organs of communication and is able, in principle, to participate in public deliberation and to criticize existing conventions and dogmas openly.

The fourth sphere of power, the sphere of civic associations, has to be understood closely in relation to the concept of 'civil society' (see Bobbio, 1985; Pelczynski, 1985; Keane, 1988a). There is a profound sense in which civil society and civic associations are never separate from the state; the latter, by providing the overall legal framework of a society, to a significant degree constitutes the former. Nonetheless, it is not unreasonable to claim that civil society retains a distinctive character to the extent that it is made up of areas of social life – the domestic world, social activities, economic interchange and political interaction – which are organized by private or voluntary arrangements between individuals and groups outside of the direct control of the state. It is in this sense that the notion is used here. However, because the economy constitutes a very distinctive site and pattern of power (see below), the sphere of civic associations is usefully separated out from civil society more broadly conceived. The realm of civic associations, thus, refers to the array of institutions and organizations in and through which individuals or groups can pursue their own projects independently of the direct organization of the state or of economic collectivities such as corporations or trade unions. Within this sphere can be counted those bundles of organizations from voluntary groups, charities and churches to political organizations and social movements.

In the realm of civic associations nautonomy is manifest either when background conditions prevent access to such associations or when they are ordered internally in a manner which systematically distorts opportunities and outcomes in favour of particular sectional interests or groups. The former occurs when some groups do not have access to certain capacities and resources (of health, schooling, income, wealth and so on) and, thereby, cannot enter or participate in a range of organizations and institutions. The latter results when organizations and institutions take on a 'life of their own' which may lead them to depart from the wishes and interests of their members. Such may be the case when they generate oligarchic tendencies – organizational structures which ossify and leaders who become unresponsive elites to those in lower echelons, whether they be in the public or private sectors (see Held, 1987, ch. 5).

As the fifth site of power, the economy comprises the collective organization of the production, distribution, exchange and consumption of goods and services. The resources which are central to these processes include the material features of the environment (raw materials, power sources); the means of production (including labour, technology and other instruments of production); and the produced goods and artefacts themselves. These resources are organized through patterns of social relations and divisions of labour which take a variety of forms in different socio-spatial contexts. They are enmeshed in circuits of activity which can, as they do in contemporary capitalism, blend extensive and intensive power networks, stretching over significant territorial spaces and involving millions of people, on the one hand, and organizing the minutiae of economic life, on the other (see Mann, 1986, pp. 24–5).

The economy is the site of one of the main sources of stratification and nautonomy: social class. While classes are groupings formed around economic activity, their position is often reinforced and sustained by power positions in and across other sites (see Giddens and Held, 1982, pt II). In many traditional non-industrial societies, it was taken for granted that the peasant or worker had a significant degree of control over the process of labour and the routines of everyday life. But with the birth of industrial capitalism this substantial degree of control was lost. Once citizens entered the factory gates, their lives were largely determined by the directives of capital: the rights of the citizen to elect or stand as a representative were not extended to work and, accordingly, the sphere of politics was not extended to industry. One of the results of the capitalist form of ownership and control has been the creation of a plethora of forms of inequality, many of which threaten the entrenchment of the principle of autonomy; for they affect the production and distribution of life-chances and participative opportunities (see Cohen, J. and Rogers, 1983; Scott, 1991; Bradley, 1992; Crompton, 1993). As Dahl succinctly put it, 'ownership and control of economic enterprises . . . contribute to the creation of great differences among citizens in wealth, income, status, skills, information, control over information and propaganda, access to political leaders. . . . After all due qualifications have been made, differences like these help in turn to generate significant inequalities among citizens in their capacities and opportunities for participating as political equals' (1985, p. 55). To the extent that modern capitalist relations produce systematic inequalities in economic and social resource, the structure of autonomy is profoundly affected.[8]

The nature of the challenge to political equality and to the democratic process, however, goes beyond the immediate impact of economic inequalities. For the very capacity of governments to act in ways that individuals and groups may desire is constrained. The constraints on democratic governments and state institutions – constraints imposed by the requirements of private accumulation – systematically limit policy options. To remain in power in a liberal democratic regime, governments must take action to secure the profitability and prosperity of the private sector, since they are dependent upon the process of capital accumulation which they have for their own sake to maintain (see Lindblom, 1977). Thus, welfare, taxation and economic policies more generally must function in the context of powerful pressures to keep productivity costs and wage/profit ratios competitive and to keep the economy in step with broad international trends (see § 6.2). A government's policies must follow a political agenda that is at least favourable to, that is, biased towards, the interests of private enterprise and corporate power if its own financial basis and legitimacy are to be protected in the long run. Of course, what alternatives, if any, exist to this system of economic constraints is another question (a question approached directly in chapter 11).

The organization of violence and coercive relations constitutes an additional, sixth, site of power which interpenetrates with other domains and directly affects life and death chances in and across communities. Concentrated physical force can function on behalf of a community, acting for its preservation or defence, or against it, eroding security and undermining pre-established regulatory mechanisms. Prior to the emergence of the modern state, political authorities often faced rival centres of power backed by organized force. Most traditional empires, historic states and feudal polities were wracked by overlapping claims upon people, territory and resources: they did not possess a monopoly of the means of vio-

[8] To claim that the institutionalized separation of the economic from the political has generated a privileged position for those with capital, whether industrial or financial, is by no means to claim as well that this division of spheres has failed to generate significant opportunity for the realization of political liberty and rights, above all for certain sectors of society (see § 3.3; Held, 1989, pp. 203–6; Turner, 1986, pp. 37–44).

lence and many did not even claim it (Mann, 1986, pp. 11 and 25–6). In fact, access to military power and organization often became the basis of new patterns of state formation and development (see chapters 2 and 3). The 'pacification' of peoples and the dismantlement of rival centres of power made possible the progressive concentration of the means of violence in the nation-state throughout the eighteenth and nineteenth centuries. But this process remained incomplete among many of the states of Europe and much contested beyond this region. In the first instance, a tension is manifest frequently between military power and the state; since these are organizationally distinct spheres for many purposes, a capacity exists for those who wield organized force to launch attacks on state institutions and *coups d'état*. Further, some states have clearly disintegrated in the face of armed challenges from separatist groups and minorities, while others, still claiming a monopoly of legitimate force, have had this monopoly challenged over a sustained period (for instance, Britain in Northern Ireland). Furthermore, the state's organization of the means of violence often faces disruption from a diverse set of politically inspired groupings who are prepared to commit violent acts against citizens (frequently randomly targeted) in order to force a political point onto the public agenda (see Cassese, 1991).

Severe limits are placed on democracy by the organization of physical force, the pursuit of military policies and the states system of defence. Even without the direct outbreak of large-scale violence or war, the security dilemma of modern states – whereby they must secure peace by preparing for war – creates a pervasive, generalized insecurity, as noted in chapters 3 and 5. Accordingly, national security policy in one country has direct consequences for another; and the dynamics of the security system of states as a whole has consequences for each and every national government. In addition, the system of organized violence and militaristic values creates a decision-making process that is too often secretive and beyond public review, skewed in favour of strong, sectional, military interests, and corrosive of public accountability and democratic participation more generally (see Johansen, 1993a). In the realm of organized force, nautonomic processes and structures go beyond the direct human casualties of war and shape both the form and nature of the polity – eroding the scope of public deliberation, limiting the range of opportunities for public participation and restricting policy considerations within the state.

The organization of violence as a site of power requires differentiation from the seventh and final sphere of power: the sphere of regulatory and legal institutions – the state as an independent corporation, made up of an ensemble of organizations coordinated by a determinate political authority. The state, as emphasized earlier, is the realm of those powers and forces which derive from the institutionalized regulation and demarcation of a people and territory. Nautonomic processes and structures can become entrenched here for many reasons. Most obviously, such processes and structures can be rooted in the exclusion of subjects and citizens from state politics as a result of the despotic use of political power or authoritarian rule. Or, they can be rooted in circumstances in which access to the polity is highly restricted to certain groups or subjects – owners of property, white men, educated men, men, those with particular skills and occupations. Or, they can be embedded in restrictions on the role of citizens, in limited channels of participation, or in a system of highly uneven incentives and disincentives, benefits and costs, for political involvement in national or international affairs. Or, nautonomy can result from a political process in which the meaning of 'rule' is construed very narrowly, leaving key sites of power – for instance, the economy and culture – outside the sphere of political consideration and intervention. Finally, nautonomy can be the outcome of the exercise of political power in a manner which is, intentionally or unintentionally, skewed to other sites of power (for example, the military or corporate interests). Any one of these factors can serve to limit the entrenchment of the principle of autonomy within and beyond the state.

In conclusion

Nautonomy can be embedded in one of the key sites of power but is likely to be embedded in and across many of them. While sources of nautonomy vary over time, and can be found in shifting clusters of power relations, they are most often locked into a number of such sites, creating self-reinforcing mechanisms. Social stratification is one of the chief means in and through which sites of power can be articulated and rearticulated to produce nautonomic outcomes. The dynamics and interrelations of sites of power have direct implications for the degree to which autonomy can be enjoyed. Autonomy is, in short, structured through power.

Would anyone who would be systematically disadvantaged as a result of nautonomic forces and outcomes accept them as legitimate in an ideal deliberative discourse? Would any group of people who would fare badly under them accept them if they did not in some sense have to do so? In a democratic thought experiment, could one accept without contradiction a commitment to persons as equally free within the process of self-determination, and a commitment to mechanisms for distributing life-goods based upon the privileges of birth (that is, the social, cultural and economic resources of one's family) and/or upon the systematic advantages established in relation to, for instance, race, ethnicity and gender? A commitment to the principle of autonomy, on the one hand, and to the luck of the 'social dice' in the determination of what resources are available to whom within and across each site of power, on the other, seems a contradiction in terms. That is to say, a commitment to equal political freedom in a democratic community and to distributive mechanisms which hinder or undermine such freedom cancel each other out. In the absence of alternative arguments (see §§ 9.2–9.4), the legitimacy of the organizational principles of nautonomic systems of power would be called into question and their transformation sought.

It could be contended that one could conduct a democratic thought experiment and come to a very different conclusion – for instance, one which recognized that while people should be equally free in the democratic process, they should be at liberty to pursue self-chosen ends and the opportunities necessary to realize these outside the political realm. Thus, the pursuit of economic activity employing private capital in a market-based economy, or the development of occupational hierarchies and structures, is quite compatible with a commitment to democratic politics. Further, any conclusion to the contrary, it might be suggested, simply confuses different spheres of activity which have their own organizational principles and mechanisms of operation and which, ultimately, provide some checks and balances against the excessive accumulation of power in any one domain (see pp. 9–11 for a version of this argument; cf. Zolo, 1992).

Put in this way, however, these points do not amount to a serious objection to the arguments offered so far. For it does not follow that the advocacy of a thoroughgoing entrenchment of the principle of autonomy entails a commitment to challenging the pursuit of economic activity utilizing private capital, or to challenging hierarchy in all domains of public and private life. Nor does it necessarily entail a commitment to questioning the division of labour or to criticizing the role of expertise. All these phenomena (and many more besides) are only of interest to a democratic thought experiment to the extent to which they generate concentrations of power that produce asymmetries of life-chances that, directly or indirectly, are corrosive of the possibility of democratic autonomy. The focus on nautonomy is a focus on the foundations of those unequal life-chances which undermine political liberty itself. Thus, the device of the democratic thought experiment presents a form of argument, not for the exploration of inequalities of power and resource *per se*, but for an assessment of those inequalities, and only those inequalities, that hinder or erode the establishment of equal participative political opportunities.

A further objection could be levelled at the characterization of the relationship between the principle of autonomy and nautonomy as one of 'contradiction', on the ground that such a characterization would be unconvincing to those life gamblers who are prepared, if not happy, to take their chances on the 'wheel of socio-economic fortune'. That there are some who would take such a view is undeniable, although holding this view does not necessarily mean failing to grasp the tensions between the opportunities and constraints at issue. Life gamblers accept that there are odds, and are aware that there are winners and losers; it is just that they see nothing inherently wrong in this state of affairs. They are content to gamble on a successful result and to wait for the outcome. But while this may be a satisfactory position for an individual to hold concerning the use of personal resources, it is not an adequate response to the existence of systematic asymmetries of life opportunities which undermine ranges of choice for groups and parties.

The pursuit of risk and need satisfaction by individual chance takers cannot address or undo the systematic disadvantages experienced by those who do worst under existing nautonomic circumstances. Life gamblers cannot secure the rules and resources that would be necessary for people to associate and cooperate fairly with each other and, accordingly, their rationalizations and strategies are hardly likely to be convincing to life's non-gamblers, especially those who, under ideal deliberative conditions, would recognize that they are least served by the inequalities which marginalize or exclude them from public life. Just as democratic processes depend on a framework in which non-violent disagreement and conflict resolution can occur, they depend also on a framework in which all citizens can, in principle, enjoy an equal entitlement to self-determination. Such a framework requires careful delineation and entrenchment, and is not sustainable in a context in which 'inputs' and 'outputs' depend on the luck of the draw.

Of course, there may be those who would prefer an indeterminate political process, or who would be content neither to participate in a democratic dialogue nor to engage in a democratic thought experiment. Clearly, if democracy is rejected, the politics of other forms of governance will come into play. No one can be persuaded to accept democratic processes and outcomes if he or she rejects the idea of self-determination altogether. But the participants of a democratic thought experiment are not in this position; for the parties to the thought experiment have a pre-commitment to democracy, that is, to examining the conditions people would accept as reasonable for their status to be met as equally free. It is this pre-commitment – an historically generated pre-commitment – which motivates the search for the appropriate conditions of enactment of the principle of autonomy.

9

DEMOCRACY AND THE DEMOCRATIC GOOD

The seven sites of power are the key spheres of human interchange in and through which the organization of nautonomy takes effect. Although the spheres demarcate distinctive domains of interaction, they interconnect with one another in actual communities and societies. The latter can be conceived, in fact, as intersecting and overlapping domains of power. The organizations and collectivities which constitute each domain weave across each other, forming distinctive constellations in the historical process. Moreover, sites and sources of power are not necessarily formed by a fixed set of stable elements, and can give rise to shifting organizational configurations (cf. Mann, 1986, pp. 17–28). In addition, some networks of power have greater capacity for organizing social cooperation and competition than others, within and across borders.

It is important to emphasize that even though peoples and groups may be empowered to act in and across some sites of power, they may not be able to enjoy adequate protection of their interest in the principle of autonomy – that is, their equal entitlement to self-determination – if they experience asymmetrical life-chances and severe disadvantages stemming from other sites. The entrenchment of the principle of autonomy can be disrupted by forces which are rooted in any one of the domains of power. A common structure of political action is incompatible with nautonomic processes and structures which – as a result of systematic inequalities in, for instance, the security of personhood and/or physical and emotional wellbeing and/or access to economic and political associations – undermine participative possibilities across a range of activities.

It follows that a democracy would be fully worth its name only if citizens had the actual power to be active as citizens; that is to say, if citizens were able to enjoy a bundle of rights which allowed them to command democratic participation and to treat it as an entitlement (cf. Sen, 1981, ch. 1). Such a bundle of rights should not be thought of as merely an extension of the sphere of accumulated private demands for rights and privileges over and against the state, as many liberal thinkers have conceived rights; nor should it be thought of as simply redistributive welfare measures to alleviate inequalities of opportunity, as many of the theorists of welfare have interpreted rights. Rather, it should be seen as entailed by, and integral to, the very notion of democratic rule itself. If one chooses democracy, one must choose to operationalize a structural system of empowering rights and obligations, for such a system constitutes the interrelated spaces in which the principle of autonomy can be pursued – and enacted.

9.1 The democratic public law

It is usually accepted that democracy entails certain substantive goods in the form of primary civil and political rights. By these is typically meant all those rights – from freedom of speech, press and assembly to the right to vote in a free and fair election and to form opposition political parties – that are necessary in order for citizens to be able to govern themselves. They are the packages of rights which follow from the right to democratic government. Without entitlements to speak freely, to criticize other standpoints, to mobilize opposition and to participate in a political process in which votes are allocated equally among citizens, there can be no democratic political process. Accordingly, it can be said that 'to the extent that the democratic process exists in a political system, all the primary [civil and] political rights must also exist. To the extent that primary [civil and] political rights are absent from the system, the democratic process does not exist' (Dahl, 1989, p. 170). However, civil and political rights alone cannot create a common structure of political action – a framework of equal autonomy for all participants in public life. Bundles of rights and obligations which are pertinent to each of the spheres of power must be regarded as integral to the democratic process. If any one of these bundles is absent from the democratic process it will be one-sided, incomplete and distorted. If any one of them is missing or unenforced, people's equal interest in the principle of autonomy will not be fully protected. It does *not* follow, it should be stressed, that democracy is an all-or-nothing affair. The entrenchment of civil and political rights alone is, of course, of great moment (see § 3.3). Nonetheless, democracy must be understood as a continuum across which particular rights *within* clusters will be more or less enforced, and *different* rights clusters will be more or less entrenched (cf. Beetham, 1993a).

Seven clusters of rights are, accordingly, necessary to enable people to participate on free and equal terms in the regulation of their own associations: health, social, cultural, civic, economic, pacific and political rights.[1] Primary political rights might be robust in a political community, but unless other rights clusters are recognized there will be significant areas in which large numbers of citizens will not be 'free and equal' and areas in which, although citizens may well enjoy equal rights in principle, they will not be able to take advantage of these equally in practice. If citizens, for example, enjoy social, cultural and political rights and yet suffer marked disparities in physical security and/or control over their bodies due, for instance, to little or no control over fertility and reproduction, a strong case can be made that for large numbers of citizens – in this case, women – the efficacy of their rights will fall far short of that of men. In brief, people's equal interest in the principle of autonomy can only be protected if they enjoy a common structure of political action across each of the sites of power. See table 9.1.

[1] The concept of the 'political', in this context, denotes the realm traditionally associated with the form, organization and operations of the state or apparatus of government, and the latter's relation with its citizens. This 'narrow' usage should be distinguished from the 'broader' use of the concept which treats the political as coextensive with the whole range of sites and sources of power. Politics, in this broader account, is about power in general; that is to say, it is about the *capacity* of social agents, agencies and institutions to maintain or transform their social or physical environment. It is about the resources which underpin this capacity and about the forces that shape and determine its exercise. I use the notion of the political in both senses in this volume. The context in which the different conceptions of politics are used should, I hope, leave no ambiguity as to their meaning.

TABLE 9.1 Sites of power, types of rights

1 Sites of power	*2 Categories of rights*	*3 Examples of rights*	*4 Particular domain of action which right helps empower*
1 Body	Health	(i) Physical and emotional wellbeing	Pursuit of bodily needs and pleasures
		(ii) Clean, non-toxic, sustainable environment	Physical continuity
		(iii) Control over fertility	Biological reproduction; freedom to be or not be a parent
2 Welfare	Social	(i) Universal childcare (ii) Universal education (iii) Community services	Development of abilities and talents
3 Culture	Cultural	(i) Freedom of thought and faith (ii) Freedom of expression and criticism (iii) Toleration	Pursuit of symbolic orders and modes of discourse
4 Civic associations	Civic	(i) Ability to form or join autonomous associations (ii) Active membership of civic associations (iii) Freedom of information	Individual and group projects

TABLE 9.1—*continued*

5 Economy	Economic	(i) Guaranteed minimum income (ii) Diverse forms of consumption and productive property (iii) Access avenues to productive and financial resources	Ability to pursue economic activity without immediate financial vulnerability
6 Coercive relations and organized violence	Pacific	(i) Peaceful coexistence (ii) Lawful foreign policy (iii) Accountability of political leaders for crimes, civil or criminal	Physical security and non-coercive relations
7 Legal and regulatory institutions	Political	(i) Due process and equal treatment before the law (ii) Adequate and equal opportunities for deliberation	Participation in public agenda-setting, debate and electoral politics

TABLE 9.1—*continued*

			(iii) Direct involvement, and/or elector of representatives, in political bodies with overlapping membership in cross-cutting political communities

The framework set out in table 9.1 is as follows. Column 1 lists the sites of power analysed in the previous chapter; column 2 lists the corresponding categories of rights which must be articulated if nautonomy is to be rooted out in particular sites. These categories are fundamental to the specification of democratic public law. Column 3 provides an illustration of those particular rights that would fall under each category. A complete list of these rights would be a list of all claims that successfully disclosed sources of nautonomy and, therefore, the necessary capacities to avoid them. The list included in table 9.1 is a list of necessary components of democratic public law. (A complete account must await another study.) Column 4, finally, designates the domains of action which the specified rights, in principle, empower.

Health rights concern the basic conditions of human agency, the absence of which destroys the great bulk of choices human beings might enjoy (cf. Gerwith, 1978). The range and quality of life-chances are directly related to the presence or absence of these rights. Three examples of such rights illustrate the paramount significance of them if the body is to be an active site of pleasure and activity. A right to physical and emotional wellbeing is perhaps the most elemental of all the health rights, if not of human rights more generally; it lays down an entitlement to those resources (or, as referred to later, those 'intermediate needs' (pp. 210–12)) without which human beings cannot function fully. It is the condition of all agency and of the pursuit of autonomy.[2] Closely related to it is a right to a clean, non-toxic, sustainable environment, which signals how the pursuit of life, liberty and opportunities must take place without damage or destruction, or without a serious, demonstrable risk of damage or destruction, to the earth's eco-systems and environmental balances, many aspects of which alone could, of course, erode the conditions of autonomy. The protection of the 'common heritage of humankind' and 'the global commons' (discussed in § 5.1) depends on upholding this right. Finally, control over fertility, creating the possibility of freedom of choice with respect to biological reproduction, parenthood and child-rearing, is a further important determinant of the nature and range of participative possibilities faced by citizens and, particularly, female citizens. Its common absence, as highlighted in the previous chapter, can be linked directly to inequalities between men and women with respect to political participation.

A right to welfare directly affects the nature and range of opportunities and skills citizens can enjoy and develop as members of a political community. To develop talents and abilities depends on a lifetime of informal and formal education – an indispensable element of the conditions required to become an active member of a polity and society. The particular rights involved include universal childcare and education, both of which are necessary for a learning process which is available to all citizens irrespective of class, race, gender and age. These rights are also critical conditions for the establishment of equal opportunities for women to enter non-domestic work and the broader framework of civic associations and political life. The third example of a right to welfare refers to community (or social) services – those organizations and institutions which provide crisis management in the event of a severe disruption of household, family and social life. These services are the necessary basis of emergency provision to ensure that a crisis in the development of people's life opportunities and abilities does not, in principle, become permanently fixed as a barrier to development and the pursuit of participative opportunities.

[2] While physical and emotional wellbeing is not, of course, a wholly social matter, the quality of human health depends to a very large extent on socially organized phenomena, from food availability and health-care institutions to the degree to which the environment is protected. It is these matters which are at stake here (see § 8.4; and Hall, R. H., 1990).

Cultural rights concern those domains of activities and capacities without which people could not learn to express themselves, to explore diverse symbolic forms, and to develop diverse individual and collective identities. Clearly, the cultural sphere overlaps with that of welfare, as defined here. However, it contains at its core a distinctive set of conditions and principles without which citizens would be unable to pursue and test freely the nature of symbolic orders and different modes of discourse. These conditions and principles concern such matters as freedom of thought and faith, and freedom of expression and criticism. Within the framework of democratic autonomy, such rights should not be mistaken for an unlimited licence to express oneself; for such a licence fails to recognize barriers which ought to be created in order to protect the equal autonomy of others. Cultural rights must, in short, be linked to a concept of democratic toleration if they are to be adequately specified. Such a concept entails that toleration be based on respect for the equal entitlement capacity of all citizens, that is, on respect for their capacity for autonomy and independence. To foster democratic criticism, culture and tolerance is, in this view, to foster a common culture of respect for autonomy. Accordingly, cultural rights meet a legitimate limit if this culture is threatened or abrogated. Intolerance, therefore, can be understood as the treatment and/or representation of categories of persons as inadequate or incapable of autonomy. Anti-semitism and racist literature are examples of material which so acts on categories of persons. It is important to separate out caricature, humour or ironic comment about an individual from an illegitimate portrayal of the position or abilities of distinctive groups. Cultural expression or criticism is unacceptable if it erodes the position of people with respect to democratic autonomy and the culture necessary to support it. 'Freedom of thought and faith' and 'freedom of expression and criticism' must take their meaning from this context.

Civic rights refer to those necessary conditions for people to be able to pursue their self-chosen life styles and activities in the context of the diverse forms of associations which make up the realm of civil life. The quality of access to these associations and the nature of their accountability to their members are among the particular conditions which determine the form and scope of participation in this realm. Such conditions must translate into distinctive rights to permit, in principle, universal access to and accountability of civic associations. The particular model of such accountability would have much to learn from associationalist doctrines which suggest that autonomy and human welfare are best served when as many of the activities of society as possible are organized by voluntary and democratically run associations (see Hirst, 1993, 1994). Associationalist relations can be built by citizens' initiatives and groups formed freely by committed individuals. However, associationalist principles do not provide a blueprint for the single most appropriate model of participation and involvement in diverse organizations. The state of democratic theory and the knowledge we have of democratic experiments do not allow wholly confident predictions about the most suitable strategies for organizational change (see Held and Pollitt, 1986). The rights clusters which fall under the civic category are, like those under each of the other categories, essential statements of guiding principles, but they do not in themselves specify their appropriate conditions of enactment; nor could they.

The origins of economic rights can be traced to the struggles of working-class and trade-union activists to gain some degree of autonomy and control in the workplace. The right to form trade unions, a right of continuing significance for most employees, was not gracefully conceded, and was achieved and sustained only through bitter conflicts. The same applies to the extension of the activities of unions to secure regularized bargaining and the entitlement to strike. Accordingly, economic rights have meant all those rights which have been won by the labour movement over time and which create the possibility of greater control for employees over the workplace (see Held, 1989, ch. 7). But while this conception of economic rights is not unhelpful, it does not adequately embrace all the elements which must be regarded as integral to economic rights. The aspiration to protect people's equal interest in the principle of autonomy does not translate into any simple, work-based conception of economic rights, for the latter alone forecloses the concerns and interests of others who are significantly affected by what happens in economic organizations, including those in other workplaces, in households and in consumer groups. The illustrative list of economic rights in table 9.1 – guaranteed minimum income, diverse forms of consumption and productive property, and access avenues to productive and financial resources – is concerned at root with the ability of people to pursue economic and other forms of activity without the threat of immediate economic vulnerability, whether they be producers or consumers. (The issues raised by economic rights are far-reaching and are discussed directly in chapter 11.)

The penultimate category of rights is pacific – a right to a non-violent and peaceful polity and life style. Coercion and violence are incompatible with democratic forms of decision-making, deliberative procedures and debate. In fact, peaceful coexistence is one of the most fundamental requirements of democracy; for without it the deliberative, representative and aggregative elements of democracy cannot function satisfactorily. It is no accident that democracy is frequently suspended during war or set aside in *coups d'état*. Likewise, in forms of local democracy from the household to the workplace, coercion and force frequently take the place of deliberative and consensual mechanisms when one party or another seeks to halt discussion and impose a 'settlement' in favour of their interests. If peaceful coexistence is a condition of democracy, it is a condition, like many of the others listed in table 9.1, that can only be adequately enacted if it is entrenched in diverse legal settings, from the national to the international. For example, an important articulation of a pacific right would be a right of all citizens to a legal foreign policy; that is, to a foreign policy that is tied to open and accountable procedures (Falk, 1991a). In addition, a further right that helped to ensure the accountability of political leaders for crimes of state, civil or criminal, would enhance the prospects of peace. Moreover, if these rights were linked to an enforceable constraint on violence in international law through such provisions as compulsory jurisdiction before the International Court, the prospects of peace would be all the stronger (see chapter 4; and chapters 10–12 for a fuller discussion of these problems).

Political rights, finally, include all those rights which traditionally fall under this heading (as well as some of those which are conventionally referred to as civil rights, such as due process and equal and consistent treatment before the law),[3] and which are essential

[3] The conventional conception of civil rights refers to the category of rights which define the liberty of the subject and which provide a fundamental counterweight to the political – an independent basis of liberty which circumscribes, delimits and underpins the proper sphere of politics. The categories developed above do not undermine this basis of liberty; rather, they seek to strengthen it, despite grouping some civil and political rights together. First, in explicating the many different bases of rights clusters, they show how autonomy needs to be nurtured and protected against many different forms of power

for participation in the exercise of political power either directly as a member of a political association invested with political authority or indirectly as an elector of the members of such an association. The full implementation of these rights in the affairs of state and civil society depends on the creation of the conditions for democratic autonomy in general. However, it also depends on the opportunities for public deliberation and dialogue, and on the proper balance between direct involvement in political decision-making and the legitimate allocation of this task to representatives, which will vary according to the nature and scope of public issues. In other words, the model of democratic autonomy requires the careful examination and pursuit of the conditions of enactment of political rights across diverse sites of collective association in order to ensure appropriate forms of participation in public agenda-setting, debate and electoral politics. How one should conceive these matters is analysed further below and in the chapters which follow.

Taken together, the seven categories of rights constitute the interrelated spaces in and through which the principle of autonomy can be entrenched. Each bundle of rights represents a fundamental enabling condition for political participation and, therefore, for legitimate rule. Unless people enjoy liberty in these seven spheres, they cannot participate fully in the 'government' of state and civil affairs. To repeat an earlier argument, the seven categories of rights do not articulate an endless list of goods; rather, they articulate necessary conditions for free and equal participation. A key con-

– not just the political. Secondly, in relocating certain 'civil rights' to other domains of power – for example freedom of expression and freedom to form autonomous associations – they show how these belong to a variety of different realms with their own dynamics and logics, although they all overlap, of course, in fundamental ways as well. Thirdly, in elaborating the notion of a democratic public law, which links the rights clusters across different sites of power, the aim is to unfold in a systematic way the conditions of autonomy which must be met if citizens are to enjoy autonomy in equal measure, and if the political sphere is to be an independent, democratic sphere. It would be possible to sub-divide the rights under the heading of 'the political' into 'legal' rights (such as equal treatment before the law) and, more narrowly conceived, 'political' rights (such as voting entitlements). But I have not done this, in order to avoid a proliferation of categories, and because the 'legal' rights which would be included here seem an essential ingredient of effective political involvement.

dition for the possibility of democracy is, therefore, a constitutional structure which articulates and entrenches rights across the seven spheres. Such a structure would enhance the ability of citizens to take advantage of opportunities formally before them. It would help constitute an empowering legal order, circumscribing a common structure of political action. A legal structure, moreover, which recognized citizens in their capacity as citizens in and across the seven domains of power could justifiably be regarded as democratic public law.[4]

Democratic public law sets down criteria for the possibility of democracy – a range of entitlement capacities for members of a democratic society. It is, therefore, the 'grand' or meta-framework which can legitimately circumscribe and delimit politics, economics and social interaction. It specifies the conditions necessary for members of a political community to be free and equal in a process of self-determination. It provides, thereby, criteria by which one can judge whether or not a given political system or set of arrangements is democratic. By inscribing a set of democratic rights into a constitution, a political community commits itself both to safeguarding individuals in certain ways and to protecting the community as a democratic association; for these rights are the rules and procedures which cannot, without inconsistency and contradiction, be eliminated: they are the self-binding conditions of democracy.

The rights that are entrenched in democratic public law, and the corresponding obligations to uphold the autonomy of others across each site of power, must be defined broadly, without regard to specific interests, in order that they can be used to guide and resolve disputes among such interests in particular conflict situations (see Miller, 1989, p. 308). In addition, they must be framed in sufficiently abstract and general terms so that the exact way in which they are met can reflect the diverse material and cultural circumstances of distinct political communities. The universality of democratic rights should be distinguished from specific 'institutional' or 'organizational' prerogatives, often themselves incorporated as rights in law in individual communities (see Bellamy, 1993, pp. 43–76). Thus, while democratic public law must entrench rights of a general type, such as physical security, control over

[4] I leave open here the whole question of the enforcement of democratic public law, although I return to this matter in §§ 9.2, 10.3 and 12.1.

fertility, liberty of expression and criticism, access avenues to or accountability of productive resources, these require institutional and organizational specification if they are to be successfully embedded in political communities. Democratic public law lays down an *agenda* for democratic politics, but necessarily leaves open the exact interpretation of each of the items on the agenda.

For example, democratic public law would stipulate that, through pacific rights, the physical security of men and women should be guaranteed, but would leave components of this to be determined locally: different peoples and communities would need to decide whether physical security would be achieved via increased policing, community 'watch schemes', a curfew on those with violent records, increased street lighting and so forth. Likewise, democratic public law requires that women and men enjoy control over fertility, but the enactment of this right depends on decisions about such matters as free abortion on demand, the availability of contraception, sex education and so on which must involve local considerations and community deliberation. The general issue of principle specified by each democratic right can be distinguished from the particular conditions of its enactment, although the latter must constitute arrangements which are not open to arbitrary abuse and alteration.

The separation of democratic public law from the particular conditions of its enactment generates a guiding framework for political activity which can remain sensitive to the traditions, values and levels of development of particular societies (cf. Parekh, 1993, esp. pp. 167–75). It allows space for the mutual delimitation of democratic principles and practices, while recognizing that democratic principles provide a non-negotiable set of orientation points for political practices. For without this recognition, democratic rights would be no more than rhetorical, and democratic politics would be without a *constitutive core* which precisely permits its characterization as democratic.

9.2 The obligation(s) to nurture self-determination

If people are to be equally free, they must enjoy rights which safeguard their capacities, that is, which shape and facilitate a common structure of political action. These rights must demarcate the minimum rules and resources necessary for participation, in principle, in the determination of the conditions of their own association. These requirements correspond to a share of those facilities necessary for the protection of people's equal interest in the principle of autonomy. They set out, as previously noted, a claim upon resources as well as a basis to be claimed upon. Further, if people's equal interest in the principle of autonomy is to be safeguarded, it will mean giving very particular attention to those groups of people who are disabled by social institutions and structures from fully participating in the determination of their own lives. Accordingly, extensive redistribution of resources may be required in order to ensure that people who have been disadvantaged through nautonomic circumstance receive the support needed to further their status as equally free within the process of self-determination.

Moreover, giving equal weight to each person's interest in autonomy will mean giving very particular attention to those groups who, by virtue of some physical or mental characteristic, are also disadvantaged within existing structures from participating in the determination of the conditions of their association. Not all of those who are disadvantaged in this way could enjoy full and equal participative opportunities with others across each site of power, but only a very few of those who are so handicapped – notably, those who suffer the severest forms of psychotic or physical impairment – cannot come to enjoy the status of equal freedom. Although people's learning abilities and willingness to learn clearly vary, most of those who currently slip below a floor of participation in their communities do so because of formal barriers to entry and disadvantage, stemming from their social environment, which can be compensated by some additional resource – whether material, cultural or physical (cf. Jenks, 1988; Cohen, G. A., 1989; Lukes, 1991). Such resource is the necessary means to a successful development of a range of capabilities and opportunities; and, properly allocated, would allow equal weight in principle to be given to each person's interest in autonomy (see Miller, 1989, pp. 72–3; Dworkin, 1978).

If the principle of autonomy is to be entrenched in a manner which sustains institutional neutrality between individuals' and groups' conceptions of the good, then a commitment follows both to the creation of a common structure of political action and, at the same time, to the differential treatment of members of a political community in order to ensure that they can enjoy such a structure of action. The principle of autonomy lays down an *obligation* to ensure that those who cannot fully enjoy autonomy under existing circumstances are enabled so to do in the long term. A common structure of political action can only be created by policies premised on the recognition of *unacceptable structures of difference* which they seek to overcome. To secure the conditions which enable citizens to play an active role as citizens requires different strategies and policies for different sets of people in need. Democracy will only operate in a manner consonant with the model of democratic autonomy if its conditions are progressively developed and reinforced. Elsewhere, I have referred to this commitment as a 'double-sided' policy process necessarily aimed at alleviating the conditions of those who have the least resource and capacity while restricting the scope and circumstances of the most powerful (1987, pp. 295–9). Accordingly, the liberty of each person within the framework of democratic autonomy must be one of progressive accommodation to the liberty of others.

The obligation to nurture self-determination can be thought of as a multidimensional obligation, or as a diverse set of related obligations to nurture autonomy wherever its possibility is systematically challenged. For each right carries with it not only the obligation to respect and honour the rights of others in each domain of activity, but also the obligation to nurture self-determination wherever its conditions fail to be met. All members of a democratic political community have, thus, both autonomy-based obligations as well as autonomy-based rights – obligations to support and provide others with the means of autonomy wherever possible and necessary. These obligations or responsibilities cannot all be fulfilled with the same types of initiative (personal, social or political) or at the same level (local, national, regional or international), but whatever their mode of realization, all such efforts have one thing in common: the concern to discharge obligations we all take on by virtue of the claims we make for the recognition of democratic rights (cf. Raz, 1986, chs 14–15, esp. pp. 407–8 and 415–17).

This meshing of rights and obligations could be portrayed as a programme for the coercive limitation of individual opportunity, 'forcing some to aid others' (see chapter 11); but not for good reason. In all liberal political systems there are limits on the extent of liberty which citizens can enjoy. Liberals have always argued that 'the liberty of the strong' must be restrained. The difficulty is that the dominant accounts of political analysis have provided highly partial and one-sided accounts of who constitutes 'the strong' (see § 8.3). In contrast, the model of democratic autonomy is distinguished by a commitment to the principle that the liberty of some individuals must not be encouraged at the expense of others, where others may, under certain circumstances, even be a majority of citizens. Rights and obligations, liberties and responsibilities must, therefore, meet in the analysis of power and resource, and in the specification of the conditions under which citizens' equal interest in self-determination can be protected. Thus, for instance, if women are ultimately to enjoy 'free and equal' autonomy conditions, the traditional privileges of men with respect to jobs, income, cultural activities and political opportunities will have to be transformed, while the typical circumstances under which women bear and raise children will have to be altered progressively. This double-side policy process, a process marked by unpacking both autonomy-rights and -obligations, can, in principle, be applied to all areas of systematic inequality (from wealth and economic power to race and ethnicity), where it could be shown that such inequality undermines the entrenchment of democratic autonomy. In this particular sense, the pursuit of the principle of autonomy would involve new limits on the scope of action for some, while it would create new opportunities for many, and different kinds of opportunity for all.[5]

Of course, the ideal process of accommodation to autonomy conditions, like the ideal amount of resource available for the compensation of the disadvantaged, may not always be the same as that which is feasible in the first instance (see § 9.3 below). But to the extent that accommodation is possible, it is an essential component of a democratic polity concerned with the eradication of arbitrary forces in the determination of democratic processes

[5] To argue that members of a democratic political community have both autonomy-based rights and obligations is not to argue, of course, that everyone has to discharge the latter in identical ways. There is no reason to believe, as Shue has argued, that everyone has equally 'burdensome duties toward everyone else' even if everyone else has 'meaningful rights' (1988). As he put it: 'For every person with a right, and for every duty corresponding to that right, there must be some agents who have been assigned that duty and who have the capacity to fulfil it.' In certain cases these agents are rightly individual citizens or certain delimited groups, but in other cases they can and ought to be collective agents such as governments and other political bodies. 'On the side of duties there can be a division of labour' (1988, p. 689; cf. O'Neill, 1991).

and outcomes. To reject the process of accommodation would be to leave intact substantial 'deficits' in life-chances and participative opportunities – circumstances which would not sit easily with the test of impartiality (see §§ 8.1–8.2).

In short, democratic public law sets out the basis of the rights and corresponding obligations which follow from a commitment to the principle of autonomy. It sets the form and limits of public power – the framework in which public debate, deliberation and policy-making can be pursued and judged. Rules, laws, policies and decisions can be considered legitimate when made within this framework; that is, when made bearing 'the democratic good' in mind. The principle of autonomy, entrenched in a common structure of political action, demarcates the nature and form of legitimate rule. The 'artificial person' which constitutes the legitimate subject of political action is properly formed when enshrined in democratic public law. The latter lays down a range of criteria which may be deemed to conflict with a country's or community's actual institutions, organizations and practices. It sets up, thereby, an agenda for change and a direction for policy to which 'offending' institutions, laws and policies could, in principle, adapt if they are to claim justifiably the mantle of democracy.

Among candidates for such adaptation would be all newly proposed legislation which would need to be considered in relation to democratic public law, opening up the possibility of a judicial review or hearing before a constitutional court should clashes occur between the former and the latter. While there would have to be different mechanisms and procedures for the enforcement of democratic public law in different areas, the enforcement procedures themselves would need to be clear cut if democratic rights and obligations were to be upheld (see Plant, 1992; Coote, 1992, 1994). At the minimum, democratic public law has to be embodied within the constitutions of parliaments and assemblies; and the influence of judicial 'review boards', the courts, and designated complaints and appeals procedures has to be extended so that groups and individuals have an effective means of suing political authorities for the enactment or enforcement of key rights both within and beyond political associations. Accordingly, the efficacy of a right, such as an entitlement to a clean environment, could be tested by those who believe existing provision to be inadequate to redeem this right in practice. The toxic emission levels of particular factories, for example, could be examined and alternative courses of policy prescribed if they were found necessary and desirable.[6]

9.3 Ideal, attainable and urgent autonomy

The meaning of autonomy can be unfolded further by returning to the story of citizenship (see chapter 3). Struggles for citizenship have involved groups, classes and movements seeking various degrees of autonomy and control over their lives in the face of various forms of stratification, hierarchy and political oppression. Such struggles have been guided by the anticipation of autonomy and by the anticipation of a political order which does not arbitrarily shape and constrain choices within the context of community. In societies where citizenship has been a developing force, an image has invariably been posited of an 'ideal citizenship' and, thereby, of a goal towards which aspirations can be directed. Within all such societies, the urge to obtain this ideal is an urge towards a fuller measure of autonomy, the enrichment of the stuff of which citizenship is made, and an increase in the number of those upon whom the status of autonomy can be bestowed (cf. Marshall, 1973, p. 84).

The anticipation of an ideal autonomy constitutes a regulative principle – a principle which has guided conflicts over the institutionalization of democracy. It has provided a normative standard which could be turned against existing institutions, as it has been by working-class, feminist and anti-racist activists in the nineteenth and twentieth centuries, to reveal the extent to which the principles and aspirations of equal liberty and equal political participation remain unfulfilled. Fleshed out in a democratic thought

[6] The existing judicial system in most countries is unlikely to provide sufficiently representative personnel to oversee such a judicial process. An alternative would have to be found, comprising perhaps judicial bodies composed of people who were 'statistically representative' of the population – that is, who were statistically representative of key social categories (gender, race, age) – and who could conduct their inquiries along the lines of a deliberative investigation or poll (see Burnheim, 1985, for a discussion of statistical representation; and Fishkin, 1991, for an analysis of a deliberative poll). There is no reason to suppose that such bodies would be less capable of independent judgement than the existing judiciary and many good reasons for believing that their judgements over the specific matter of how to interpret democratic rights would be more representative of collective opinion.

experiment and an analysis of power, the ideal can also be seen to comprise a programme of political action for the creation of a democratic order which, at its most basic, would entrench the principle of autonomy for each and every citizen within and across each and every site of power.

The anticipation of this latter ideal is the anticipation of an involvement in public affairs in which public discourse can prevail free of force or the threat of force, in which all forms of nautonomy are eradicated, and in which participants can enjoy equal standing in the process of collective decision-making. Adapting concepts first developed by Dahl to the terms of the argument presented here, the contours of this involvement can be demarcated formally with reference to five criteria:

1. effective participation – citizens must be equally free to engage in public life, to form their views and preferences, to express reasons for supporting one outcome rather than another, and to debate these in the relevant public domains;
2. enlightened understanding – citizens must enjoy adequate and equal opportunities, providing them with all the knowledge they need, to examine and affirm what choice in a matter before them would best serve their ends and interests;
3. control over the agenda – citizens must have vested in them the authority to decide what matters are and are not on the public agenda, subject to the conditions and constraints imposed by democratic public law;
4. voting equality at decisive stages – each citizen must be assured that his or her judgement will be counted as equal in weight to the judgements of other citizens at the decisive moments of collective decision-making;
5. inclusiveness – the provision of the powers of citizenship to all mature (adult) persons (see Dahl, 1989, chs 6–9; cf. Held, 1991c).

It is very hard to conceive how persons could be politically equal in a democratic process should any one of the criteria be violated; and how any political process that failed to satisfy one (or more) of the criteria could fully entrench the principle of autonomy.

Thus, if citizens did not enjoy the conditions for effective participation and enlightened understanding, systematic obstacles to involvement in public life would persist and the political marginalization of large categories of citizens would in all likelihood continue. If the final control of the agenda were not in the hands of citizens, the reach and control of 'the people' would, at best, be partial and limited. If the right to 'equal votes' were not established, there would be no mechanism that could take equally into account, and provide a decision procedure to resolve differences among, the views and preferences of citizens (even though the latter might decide not to deploy a decision-making system based on voting in all circumstances). If the *demos* did not include all adults (with the exception of those temporarily visiting a political community, and those who 'beyond a shadow of doubt' were legitimately disqualified from participation due to severe mental incapacity and/or serious records of crime), then it would clearly fail to create the conditions for 'equal involvement'. For citizens to be equally free, and to enjoy equal consideration of their interests in a democratic process, the above criteria would have to be met.

A number of points need to be noted about the ideal of autonomy. In the first instance, the ideal is not in itself an ideal of equality in all political, social and economic spheres. Inequality is only significant, as indicated in the previous chapter, to the extent that it bears on participative possibilities and enables or restricts autonomy. In other words, the pursuit of democratic autonomy is not to be conflated with the pursuit of equality *per se*; it is the pursuit of equal participative opportunities. Second, a democratic right or entitlement capacity is not to be confused with the full complement of resources required to pursue one's own life-plans (see Miller, 1976, ch. 4, 1989, pp. 146–8). Within the framework of the principle of autonomy, entitlement capacities have always to be understood as both enabled and constrained by the requirement of political equality; that is, by the requirement that citizens enjoy autonomy in equal measure. A common structure of political action entrenched in democratic public law creates, in principle, the potential for each citizen to participate in public and private life and to assume the burden of rights and obligations which follow from this. When this potential is not established, as Doyal and Gough have written about the disadvantaged, they 'suffer not because they *have* less than others but because they can *participate* less in their respective form of life. It is their impaired agency rather than their inequality as such that should be the focus of . . . concern' (1991, pp. 95–6; see Raz, 1986, pp. 227–40).

Third, the conception of autonomy which embraces the possibility of participation across different sites of power is inevitably a complex one, differentiating between the rules and resources required to sustain people's equal interest in autonomy across each of these sites. The specific conditions which could satisfy the principle of autonomy in the domain of the body (such as a clean, non-toxic environment) are by no means the same as those in the sphere of culture (such as democratic toleration). The 'substance' of autonomy will vary across each sphere of power, although there will, of course, be substantive overlaps necessitated by the operation and dynamics of extensive power systems and the overall need for accountability. The anticipation of an ideal autonomy must, therefore, be the anticipation of a 'complex autonomy' sensitive to diverse conditions in diverse sites (cf. Walzer, 1983; Mulhall and Swift, 1992, ch. 4).

Fourth, the anticipation of an ideal autonomy, and the defence of its desirability, is not to be equated with claims about its attainability and feasibility. For the ideal of autonomy is a hypothetically projected reconstruction of the rules and norms of democracy – a counterfactual posit. Whether or not the empirical conditions can be created for the realization of this ideal is not a question which admits of an a priori answer. The ideal provides both a benchmark against which democratic progress can be measured and a practical hypothesis (cf. Habermas, 1973, pp. 258–9). Arguments about the desirability of the principle of autonomy and the conditions of its enactment do not resolve the many practical issues of politics which it poses. While the model of democratic autonomy circumscribes the legitimate form and scope of public power, it remains to be specified in what precise ways and with what order of priorities it can be enacted.[7] In addition, it can be readily agreed that, although the reduction of forms of nautonomy is an objective towards which democrats have striven and will continue to strive, there is in all probability no chance of its final and total transcendence. This being the case, a number of questions follow, including: what are the legitimate constraints on the transformation of the conditions of autonomy? What priorities can be established to provide a guide through the many pressing domains of power and

[7] To set out the constitutive standards of an ideal autonomy is not to specify the institutions that best meet these. The concept of an ideal autonomy can help guide a judgement about the relative worth of democratic political arrangements. But it will not translate into a single, simple blueprint for democratic institutions (see § 10.3 and chapter 12; see also Held, 1987, ch. 9, 1993c; Held and Pollitt, 1986, ch. 1; cf. Beetham, 1993b; Budge, 1993; Miller, 1993; Phillips, 1993).

nautonomy? The basis of a satisfactory response to these issues lies in distinguishing 'ideal' from 'attainable' and 'urgent' levels of autonomy.

The democratic thought experiment suggests that if people did not know their social destiny, they would seek to determine particular outcomes which were fair and reasonable according to the test of impartiality (see § 8.1). This would mean they would elect conditions of enactment of the principle of autonomy which would cut across the key domains of power. They would, thus, come to an understanding of an ideal autonomy as the necessary and inescapable regulative principle of democracy. However, ideal does not mean immediately attainable, and this would surely be recognized. For there exist, of course, diverse circumstances, from economic scarcity to crisis situations, which constrain and limit actual choices. While it can be argued that only an ideal autonomy is an adequate specification of the ultimate requirements of democracy, a need has to be recognized for criteria of public policy-making which can guide and shape communities in the shorter term. 'Attainable' autonomy is the bridge between the ideal and the real – a comparative vantage point from which to specify the possible levels of autonomy required to lay down a common structure of political action. It sets down a plausible set of objectives for the immediate future. But even 'attainable' levels of autonomy need to be distinguished from what legitimately can be regarded as the most 'urgent' and pressing cases of need. How can these terms be refined?[8]

An 'attainable' level is the level of capacity and resource which is necessary to participate in one's political community without systematic disadvantage and arbitrary constraint within the range of demonstrable alternatives. It provides people with the means to choose the activities they might involve themselves in and to question the practices and beliefs of their respective communities, should this be appropriate (see Doyal and Gough, 1991, p. 160). Put more technically, this 'participative' definition of autonomy can be defined as the necessary level of 'intermediate need-satis-

[8] In making distinctions between 'attainable' and 'urgent' levels of autonomy, I have been influenced by Doyal's and Gough's very useful discussion of 'minopt' and 'constrained minopt' levels of health and autonomy, and the related consideration of the impairment to human agency which follows if these levels are not met (see Doyal and Gough, 1991, esp. chs 7 and 8).

faction' required to produce the 'optimum' use of entitlement capacities, where the optimum is conceived in terms of the actual ability of individuals and groups to best utilize such capacities within their communities.[9] 'Intermediate needs' are those things which have 'universal satisfier characteristics'; that is, properties, whether of goods, services or activities, which enhance autonomy in all cultures (Doyal and Gough, 1991, pp. 162 and 157). Examples of the latter are drinking water, nutritional food, appropriate housing, health care, adequate education and economic security. The significance of the concept of intermediate needs is that it recognizes the many different ways communities might fulfil rights or entitlement capacities across each domain of power, while signalling basic minimum standards if autonomy is to be achieved. For example, food can be prepared according to diverse customs and practices, happily producing an array of tastes and pleasures, but unless it is nutritious, embodying a minimum level of calories a day and a correct balance of proteins and vitamins, it will be insufficient to protect health in the long term – no matter which culture or community people live in. Likewise, birth control and child-bearing can be practised in diverse ways across cultures, but unless they are practised safely and offer clear choices about parenthood, they will not be adequate to provide for control over fertility, irrespective of the context in which people live. Further, economic security provided by a basic minimum income can be organized in diverse ways, yet, again, unless it delivers freedom from immediate economic vulnerability, it will not be adequate to allow advantage to be taken of participative opportunities.

If people's intermediate needs are unmet and they cannot fully participate in their political community, their potential for involvement in public and private life will remain unfulfilled. Their ability to make (or not make) choices and to determine the course of their life projects will have been restricted, irrespective of the choices they would have made about the extent of their actual participation. While the principle of autonomy embodies the aspiration to active citizenship, it does not follow that everyone must,

[9] The relation between rights and needs is, of course, unproblematic in the account of ideal autonomy. In the latter case, it is assumed that all the needs necessary to attain the ideal are met. The circumstances are very different in a discussion of attainable levels of autonomy because the emphasis is on feasible and practical means to meet the conditions of autonomy.

irrespective of individual choice, actually participate: participation is not a necessity. What is at issue is the citizen's *rightful share* of the process of governance – the right and opportunity to act in public life. A provision which falls short of a rightful share can be referred to as a situation of manifest 'harm' in that the participatory potential of individuals and groups will not have been achieved.

The other side of the principle of autonomy is the obligation, already noted, to protect the vulnerable and to avoid related harm where possible. This 'other side' is the principle of public intervention to shape and delimit autonomy. John Stuart Mill gave this idea one of its earliest classic formulations when he argued 'the only purpose for which power can be rightfully exercised over any member of a civilized community, against his will, is to prevent harm to others' (1982, p. 68). In Mill's texts there are significant ambiguities in the account of the proper form and scope of this principle (see Ryan, 1974): in the context of the argument here, however, its meaning can be clarified. Social or political interference with individual autonomy may be justified when, it can be said, an act (or failure to act), whether it be intended or not, 'concerns others' and then only when it 'harms' them; that is, when it diminishes or erodes their rightful share of autonomy within the context of community. The sole end of interference with autonomy should be the alleviation of harm. For the only form of autonomy which deserves the name is, as Mill rightly put it, 'that of pursuing our own good in our own way, so long as we do not attempt to deprive others of theirs or impede their efforts to obtain it' (1982, p. 72). In those activities which are merely 'self-regarding', that is, only of concern to the individual, 'independence is, of right, absolute'; over oneself, over one's own body and mind, 'the individual is sovereign' (Mill, J. S., 1982, p. 69). Privacy should be assumed in all those areas which are not the basis of potential and demonstrable 'harm' to others. The principles of political involvement, participation and intervention are applicable to the array of sites of power and nautonomy, but they are not applicable to what I have referred to elsewhere as the 'sphere of the intimate'; that is, to all those circumstances where people live out their personal lives without systematically harmful consequences to others' autonomy (Held, 1987, p. 293).

I refer to the 'participative' conception of autonomy as an 'attainable' level of autonomy because the measure of optimum participation, and the related conception of harm, can be conceived directly in terms of the 'best practice' or 'highest standard' presently *achieved* in a political community (cf. Doyal and Gough, 1991, p. 169). From schooling to fertility control, from policing to the provision of income-support schemes, attainable levels of autonomy imply a comparative judgement of 'best practice' which can become policy goals within and across sites of power. The comparison need not be restricted to a single political community; for 'attainable' can be conceived of as the 'best practice' achieved in any political community. The notion of 'attainable autonomy' has, thus, a double referent – within and beyond particular nation-states – and creates targets demarcating a range of feasible alternatives (see chapter 10).

But attainable participative levels are not, of course, the same thing as immediately pressing levels of autonomy which define the most urgent need. It is abundantly clear that, within existing communities and countries, certain entitlement capacities, particularly health, education and welfare, are not universally achieved. The 'harm' that follows from a failure to meet such needs can be denoted as 'serious harm', marked as it often is by immediate, life-and-death consequences. This harm constitutes a domain of need and suffering which is both systematic and wholly unnecessary. As it is understood here, serious harm is directly 'avoidable harm'. To maintain such a position is to take the view, as Falk has contended, that capabilities and resources exist 'even within the current frameworks of power and wealth to mitigate and even solve problems'. In the most basic sense, the challenges posed by avoidable suffering are 'political and ethical, and possibly psychological, but do not arise from any absolute scarcity or from an absence of resources and technical capabilities' (Falk, 1995, pp. 56–7). That is to say, with a determined effort circumstances generating serious harm could be largely overcome without fundamentally altering the existing political order and economic structures. To take this view is to insist, moreover, that *politics matters* in the very specific sense that a shift of political judgement, towards the promotion of autonomy and the alleviation of pressing need, could have dramatic consequences.

Among the numerous examples which could be cited in this context are, to take an instance of cross-border concerns first, the quarter of a million small children who die every week of easily preventable illness and malnutrition. Each day, for instance, 8000 children die of measles, whooping cough and tetanus, 7000 children die of diarrhoeal dehydration, and 6000 children die of pneumonia (see UNICEF, 1990, p. 3). For a relatively trivial financial commitment ($2 billion to $3 billion per year according to UNICEF) these deaths could be avoided. Further, about 500,000 women die each year from causes which, while triggered by pregnancy and childbirth, have roots in poverty and related ill-health (UNICEF, 1990, p. 8). The alleviation of such conditions, and of widespread global poverty more generally, could be achieved by restructuring the debt and interest payments of the developing world and through the provision of additional aid: approximately $50 billion a year, or less than half of 1 per cent of the world's gross international product, or about 5 per cent of present military spending. This sum could significantly move the world's population towards the goals of 'adequate food, water, health care and education for every man, woman and child' (UNICEF, 1990, p. 13). It is important to note that while many of the severest forms of poverty and ill-health are concentrated in developing countries, particularly in the countries of sub-Saharan Africa, they are by no means only found there. The polarization of wealth and income in developed countries, a trend markedly exacerbated in the 1980s, has left a significant minority in the severest hardship, often living with little or inadequate shelter, health care and food. These citizens may enjoy formal equality, for example before the law, but for many of them it is rendered virtually meaningless in practice by the absence of satisfactory housing, nutrition and education. For many, opportunities and life-chances are highly limited (see, for instance, Falk, 1995, ch. 2; Commission on Social Justice, 1993, ch. 3).

Changes in the allocation of financial resources could alleviate these problems, but they are by no means the only issue at stake in meeting pressing needs. A shift towards the promotion of autonomy in political life could also direct attention to the extreme suffering that follows, for instance, from routine human rights violations. Table 9.2 shows that, with the exception of only two or three countries, the integrity of the person and political rights generally have been severely compromised in Asia (levels 3–5) in recent times. Comparative evidence from other regions of the world suggests that the state was, in the main, tougher on the individual in Asia than elsewhere (see Potter, 1993). Nonetheless, extensive abuse of civil and political rights has been recorded in over a hundred countries, north, south, east and west (Falk, 1995). While a common structure of political action remains a remote possibility in many places in the short term, it creates an

TABLE 9.2 Observance of integrity of the person in selected Asian countries, 1980, 1988 and 1992

Country	*AI 1980*	*SD 1980*	*AI 1988*	*SD 1988*	*SD 1992*
Afghanistan	5	5	4	5	5
Bangladesh	3	3	3	3	3
Burma/Myanmar	–	3	5	5	5
China	3	3	3	3	3
India	4	3	4	4	4
Indonesia	4	3	3	3	3
Japan	–	1	2	1	1
Kampuchea	3	3	3	4	3
Laos	3	3	3	3	3
Malaysia	2	2	2	2	2
Pakistan	3	3	3	3	4
Philippines	4	3	3	3	4
Singapore	3	3	2	2	1
South Korea	3	3	3	2	3
Thailand	3	3	2	3	3
Vietnam	3	3	3	3	3

AI = based on reports from Amnesty International
SD = based on reports from the US State Department

Level 1: Countries live under a secure rule of law, people are not imprisoned for their views, and torture is rare or exceptional. Political murders are extremely rare.
Level 2: There is a limited amount of imprisonment for non-violent activity. However, few persons are affected, and torture and beating are exceptional. Political murder is rare.
Level 3: There is extensive political imprisonment, or a recent history of such imprisonment. Execution or other political murders and brutality may be common. Unlimited detention, with or without trial, for political views is accepted.
Level 4: The practices of level 3 are expanded to larger numbers. Murders, disappearances and torture are a common part of life. In spite of its generality, on this level terror affects primarily those who interest themselves in politics or ideas.
Level 5: The terrorism of level 4 has been expanded to the whole population. The leaders of these societies place no limits on the means or thoroughness with which they pursue personal or ideological goals.

Source: This table taken from Potter, 1993, p. 368 (original data derived from the Projects for the Interdisciplinary Study of Root Causes of Human Rights Violations Newsletter and Progress Report, 2,2, Autumn 1990, pp. 18–20, and recently updated).

urgent agenda for the direction of diverse forms of resource, whether physical, cultural, educational or material.

9.4 The democratic good

Democracy is constituted by an ideal autonomy the efficacy of which will always be constrained by the availability of both resources and good political judgement – judgement which is shaped by a commitment to the principle of autonomy and the entrenchment of democratic public law. While the ideal notion of autonomy sets a direction for change, and attainable levels set out contemporary possibilities and options for a common structure of political action, pressing levels create an urgent and immediate agenda. But does this mean democracy will always be caught in a vicious circle, requiring a common structure of political action as a condition of possibility but recognizing that such a structure is always a contingent outcome of politics? Far from being vicious, however, this circle is virtuous: an essential and inescapable element in democratic politics and understanding. Democratic politics requires the notion of a democratic *Rechtstaat* that incorporates and lays down the notion of a common structure of political action; only within this framework can it sustain and protect its identity as democratic. In accepting such a requirement, democratic politics would itself acknowledge an ideal autonomy as constitutive of the ultimate meaning of democracy. In so doing, it would anticipate a political future which would place constraints upon the form and limits of political options in the present. And under these conditions, the ideal of autonomy could be said to be, in effect, operative in political life. Routine democratic politics could not be regarded as a wholly contingent matter; conducted and reconducted within the framework of autonomy, it would be pursued with the common good – the democratic good – in mind. As such, a guiding framework would be created to shape and delimit public policy. To the extent that democratic politics kept this framework in view, public debate would be focused on the democratic good of the community – a far cry from conceiving democratic politics as the mere aggregation of individual preferences (see § 8.1; cf. Cohen, J., 1989; Miller, 1993). On the other hand, how exactly this framework can be interpreted and upheld would inescapably be a matter of substantive politics as well.

For instance, scarcity of resources often leads to conflicts over the proper priorities of public policy. In these circumstances, clashes among rights are commonplace. Some critics of rights theory have taken this to be a fatal criticism, asking: 'what metric could we use to say whether housing, health care, or education produces more freedom, or to decide whether one person's liberty would be increased more than another's'? (see Bellamy, 1993, p. 50). To engage with this question, the critics point out, puts in jeopardy the whole concept of rights as entitlements or 'trumps' which cannot be legitimately overruled by minorities or majorities (cf. Dworkin, 1977; Rawls, 1971). Such issues do raise serious questions about how priorities among rights are established, but they are by no means fatal to the conception of rights used here. In the first instance, the distinction between ideal, attainable and urgent levels of autonomy circumscribe an order of priorities. Avoiding serious harm is the primary condition of the development of autonomy; and the pursuit of 'attainable' levels of autonomy the necessary next step in the creation of a common structure of political action that links the ideal and the real. But within this framework there will be difficult questions about which priorities to pursue. It is tempting to argue that democratic public law contains its own priorities – a hierarchy of need from health to welfare and political rights. But such an argument would not be convincing; for the resolution of many basic questions of health, for instance, is often tied up to wider political and economic considerations. To take one example: famines often erupt in the wake of war, but they also occur where there have been no such conflicts and where, as often as not, national and global food availability has been no worse and sometimes better than in previous non-famine years. They even occur where food is being exported from the country concerned (Lappé and Collins, 1979; Sen, 1981).

In complex circumstances such as these, there is no simple metric or decision procedure to establish priorities among rights. On the other hand, a commitment to the principle of autonomy and a common structure of political action sets down not only rights but also, it needs to be emphasized again, obligations – obligations to alleviate the position of the least well off. A commitment to democratic autonomy entails a commitment to meeting the requirements of the disadvantaged with respect to autonomy, as well as to reducing the prerogatives of the powerful to the extent to which these hinder the development of a fully democratic order. While this commitment does not create a decision procedure to resolve all clashes of priority in politics, it does lay down an unambiguous starting point and guiding orientation. Beyond this it is going to be a matter for citizens and their representatives to decide, in dialogue, deliberation and debate, how exactly goods and services are ultimately to be distributed. This element of political indeterminacy is both unavoidable and desirable.

Part IV

Elaboration and Advocacy: Cosmopolitan Democracy

10

POLITICAL COMMUNITY AND THE COSMOPOLITAN ORDER

The principle of autonomy: a résumé and elaboration

The principle of autonomy evokes the possibility of autonomy for all. Such an ideal is a necessary notion – the condition of democracy and a guiding orientation for its entrenchment. Its progressive realization would at once be an achievement and the constant posit of a goal that requires further pursuit. Kant's statement of the kernel of his doctrine of freedom captures well this tension between requirement and practical challenge.

> A constitution allowing the *greatest possible human freedom* in accordance with laws which ensure *that the freedom of each can co-exist with the freedom of all others* . . . is at all events a necessary idea which must be made the basis not only of the first outline of a political constitution but of all laws as well. It requires that we should abstract at the outset from present hindrances, which perhaps do not arise inevitably out of human nature, but are rather occasioned by neglect of genuine ideas in the process of legislation. . . . Even if [a 'perfect state'] . . . should never come about, the idea which sets up this maximum as an archetype . . . still remains correct. For no-one can or ought to decide what the highest degree may be at which mankind may have to stop progressing, and hence how wide a gap may still of necessity remain between the idea and its execution. For this will depend on freedom, which can transcend any limit we care to impose. (1970, p. 191)

The idea of autonomy entails that the individual's exercise of his or her capacity should be free of improper constraint – political, social or economic – and that autonomy be articulated in terms of arrangements underpinning autonomy for all in the political community. Autonomy is, thus, dependent on mutually enabling and constraining conditions; it has to be supported and restricted in its own name. People can, in principle, become autonomous over time if they recognize their equal interest in the principle of autonomy and their mutual dependence.

The entrenchment of democratic public law is the foundation of autonomy, promising protection and security to each and all. It requires the pursuit and enforcement of the seven clusters of rights and obligations in a democratic legal state. A democratic legal state provides the political framework for the development of a common structure of political action. Paradoxically, the enactment of such a framework requires delimitation of the scope of popular rule: the reach of popular sovereignty must be limited. The *demos* must govern, but within the framework of a set of fair social, political and economic conditions which make possible the very nature of democratic life itself. The *demos* must rule, but within the framework of a legal order which is both empowering and limiting. This is the sense in which democratic autonomy lies between state and popular sovereignty (referred to in §§ 7.1 and 7.3).

Further, if the framework of democratic public law is upheld, the modern state's claim to neutrality and impartiality can, in principle, be vindicated. For such a framework, with its immediate requirements and long-term obligations, is the basis of a system of authority which is guided by the democratic good and which can avoid, as an element of its fundamental orientation, systematic bias in favour of sectional interests. Or, to put the point somewhat differently, democratic autonomy represents a set of arrangements for the distribution of benefits and burdens that ought to be acceptable to all parties. In principle, it is a structure and process people 'could live with, wherever they come in the [social] sequence, on condition that all others have played their part by the same rules' (Barry, 1989, p. 199). Thus, it can be thought of, following Kant, as the 'practical idea' of reason, or, as it should now be put within the terms of the arguments offered here, as the practical idea of an ideal deliberative discourse (see § 8.1; and cf. Kant, 1956, pp. 17ff).

Are the clusters of rights entailed by the principle of autonomy citizenship rights, or human rights, or something different again? Behind this question lies the pressing issue of the proper form and nature of political community; that is, the most appropriate and feasible political anchor for rights. As indicated in chapters 7 and 9, I prefer to call rights 'empowering rights' or 'entitlement capacities' because they are integral to the possibility of democracy itself. They are not best conceived either as citizenship rights or as universal rights. Citizenship rights embody a conception of empowerment that is strictly limited to the framework of the nation-state. In modern times, rights have nearly everywhere been enshrined effectively within the institutions of nation-states. To the extent that certain types of rights have become more-or-less commonplace, this has been the result of processes which have spread with the form of the modern nation-state itself (see chapter 3). To the degree that such states are 'democratic' they accord a range of rights, notably civil and political rights, to their citizens. But if it is the case that many types of citizenship rights have become progressively universalized in the wake of the nation-state, it is also the case that the nation-state today is by no means able to guarantee many of these rights (see § 5.1). Furthermore, there have emerged formulations of rights – in treaties, regional documents and international law – which directly transcend the claims of individual nation-states. Therefore, there is a fundamental question about whether the rights embodied in citizenship rights can any longer be sustained simply within the framework that brought them into being.

But can rights be translated effectively into universal or human rights? It has been part of the argument of part II of this volume that the acceleration of globalization has led to pressures to entrench significant 'citizenship rights' within frameworks of international law. However, this process is very far from complete. In addition, the notion that 'rights' advance universal values and are, accordingly, human rights – *intrinsically* applicable to all – is open to doubt. It is clear, for example, that many nations and peoples do not necessarily choose or endorse the rights that are proclaimed often as universal – as has been illustrated in the cultural clash over rights, documented earlier (see § 4.3; cf. Galtung, 1994). The tension between the claims of national identity, religious affiliation, state sovereignty and international law is marked, and it is by no means clear how it will be resolved.

Empowering rights or entitlement capacities are intrinsic to the democratic process. There may be no religious, metaphysical or foundational grounds for becoming a democrat, but if one chooses to be a democrat, one must choose to enact these rights. Democracy and the rights clusters are intimately interrelated. Accordingly, the rights at the centre of the democratic process are best distinguished from any straightforward claim to either citizenship or universality. They can be defended independently of the notion of national citizenship; that is, they can be justified directly in relationship to democracy. And they can be invoked independently of claims to universality. The historical and cultural relativity of democracy can be recognized without sacrificing the claim that if one accepts democracy as the most superior form of governance, its specific and complex conditions must also be acknowledged. To avoid misunderstanding, these arguments need unpacking further in relation to the idea and prospects of the democratic political community.

Throughout the nineteenth and twentieth centuries there has been an assumption at the heart of liberal democratic thought concerning a 'symmetrical' and 'congruent' relationship between political decision-makers and the recipients of political decisions. In fact, symmetry and congruence, as indicated in chapter 1, are assumed at two crucial points: first, between citizen-voters and the decision-makers whom they are, in principle, able to hold to account; and secondly, between the 'output' (decisions, policies, etc.) of decision-makers and their constituents – ultimately, 'the people' in a delimited territory. These relationships can be represented as shown in figure 10.1. It has been assumed, in other words, by democratic theorists (orthodox and radical), that 'the fate

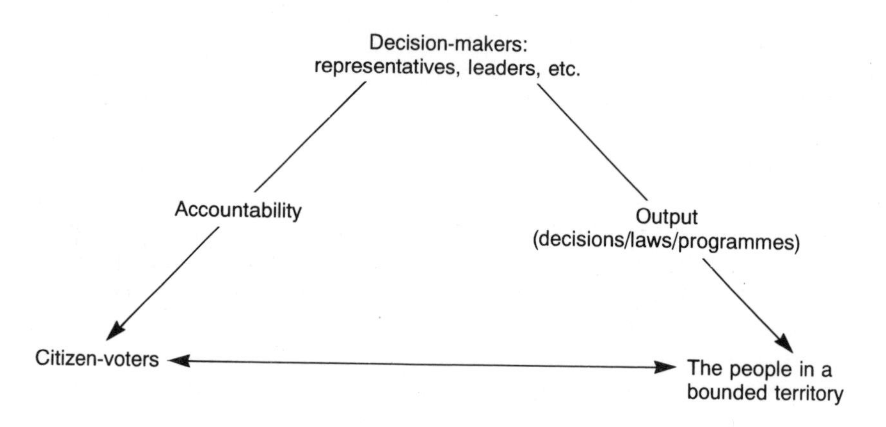

FIGURE 10.1 The democratic political community?

of a national community' is largely in its own hands and that a satisfactory theory of democracy can be developed by examining above all the interplay between 'actors' and 'structures' in the nation-state.

At the centre of this position is a taken-for-granted conception of sovereignty and an uncritically appropriated concept of political community. And the difficulty with it is, to recall arguments made earlier, that political communities have rarely – if ever – existed in isolation as bounded geographical totalities, and they are better thought of as multiple overlapping networks of interaction (see part II). These networks crystallize around different sites and forms of power, producing patterns of activity which do not correspond in any straightforward way to territorial boundaries. The spatial reach of the modern nation-state did not fix impermeable borders for other networks, the scope and reach of which have been as much local as international or global. Moreover, national identities and interaction networks have been criss-crossed by a variety of points of orientation and exchange. Political communities are, thus, locked into a diversity of processes and structures which range in and through them, linking and fragmenting them in complex constellations. It is no surprise then that national communities by no means make and determine decisions and policies exclusively for themselves, and that governments by no means determine what is right or appropriate exclusively for their own citizens.

The assumption that one can understand the nature and possibilities of political community by referring merely to national structures and mechanisms of political power is unjustified. While it is a mistake to conclude from the seeming flux of contemporary interaction networks that political communities today are without distinctive degrees of division or cleavage at their 'borders', they have been shaped by multiple interaction networks and power systems over time (see pp. 135–6). Thus, questions are raised both about the fate of the idea of the political community and about the appropriate locus for the articulation of the democratic political good. If the agent at the heart of modern political discourse, be it a person, a group or a collectivity, is locked into a variety of overlapping communities – 'domestic' and 'international' – then the proper 'home' of politics and democracy becomes a puzzling matter.

10.1 The requirement of the democratic good: cosmopolitan democracy

If freedom is threatened by the behaviour of other nations and states, what is right for a political community, Kant argued, cannot prevail. By contrast, 'right' can prevail, he held, if the rule of law is sustained in all states as well as in international relations (1970, pp. 107–8; and see Reiss, 1970, pp. 33–4). Within the terms of the argument presented here this is an important contention, but it needs to be recast to meet the conditions of autonomy in the context of interconnectedness. Accordingly, it can be maintained, autonomy can prevail in a political community if, and only if, it is unimpeded by threats arising from the action (or non-action) of other political communities, or from the networks of interaction which cut across community boundaries.

Although the threats to freedom derive, in Kant's view, from many forms of violence, they stem above all from war and the preparation for war. 'The greatest evils which affect civilised nations are', he wrote, 'brought about by war, and not so much by actual wars in the past or the present as by never ending and indeed continually increasing preparations for war' (quoted in Reiss, 1970, p. 34). A violent abrogation of law and right in one place has serious consequences for those in many other places and can be experienced everywhere (see Kant, 1970, pp. 107–8). In Kant's account, the establishment of what is right requires the establishment of 'perpetual peace', and the abolition of war as a means of politics. The 'spirits' of commerce and of republicanism provide a clear impetus to this possibility; for commerce generates networks of mutual self-interest which become hostile to the disruption caused by war and war efforts; and republicanism creates politics which depend on consent, and which lead citizens not only to be highly cautious about war (since all its 'calamities' fall directly upon them), but also to respect others whose republics are also consensual and law-abiding (Kant, 1970, pp. 100 and 114).

While the threats to autonomy from war and direct coercion are hard to overestimate, they constitute only one element in the challenge to autonomy. For such challenges can come from any of the diverse sources of nautonomy; and any one of these can undermine the effective entrenchment of democratic law. Moreover, democratic law can prevail only if it is established both within the power domains of particular political communities and within those which cut across them. Sites of power can be national, transnational and international (see chapters 5 and 6). Accordingly, democratic public law within a political community requires democratic law in the international sphere. Democratic public law needs to be buttressed and supported by an international structure of such law or by what I should rather simply call 'cosmopolitan democratic law'. By cosmopolitan democratic law I mean, in the first instance, a democratic public law entrenched within and across borders.[1]

Cosmopolitan democratic law is most appropriately conceived as a domain of law different in kind from the law of states and the law made between one state and another, that is, international law. For Kant, the foremost interpreter of the idea of a cosmopolitan law, cosmopolitan law is neither a fantastic nor a utopian way of conceiving law, but a 'necessary complement' to the unwritten code of existing national and international law, and a means to transform the latter into a public law of humanity (1970, p. 108).[2] Kant limited the form and scope of cosmopolitan law to the conditions of universal hospitality, by which he meant the right of a stranger or foreigner 'not to be treated with hostility' when arriving in someone else's country (1970, p. 105). He emphasized that this right extended to the circumstances which allow people to enjoy an exchange of ideas and goods with the inhabitants of another

[1] In Europe the origins of the term 'cosmopolitan' can be traced to the ancient Greeks and, particularly, to the Stoic ideal of human beings as rational creatures with universal rights as citizens of the 'cosmopolis' (see Heater, 1990). It was a term used commonly for the first time in preindustrial Europe among European intellectual elites, referring to a political or cultural universalism which challenged the particularity of nations and states, on the one side, and the pretensions of religious universalism, on the other. The *Oxford English Dictionary* defines a cosmopolitan as 'belonging to all parts of the world' and as 'having the characteristics which arise from, or are suited to . . . [and] range over many different countries; free from national limitations and attachments' (1971, vol. 1, p. 1032). While this is helpful as an initial orientation, I shall restrict the meaning of cosmopolitan here to a form of law, and to a form of political community which might create and sustain this law.

[2] While the exact meaning of Kant's conception of cosmopolitan law has long been controversial, this controversy need not be of direct concern here. For a representative range of views see Hinsley, 1963, ch. 4; Doyle, 1983; Wight, 1987; Archibugi, 1992.

country, but that it did not extend as far as the right to be entertained, or the right to permanent settlement, let alone the right of citizenship (1970, pp. 105–8). A foreigner ought not to suffer any enmity 'so long as he behaves in a peaceful manner', although he can be turned away 'if this can be done without causing his death' (1970, pp. 105–6). The right of hospitality is, in short, a right to present oneself and to be heard – the conditions necessary 'to *attempt* to enter into relations with the native inhabitants' (1970, p. 106).

Cosmopolitan law, thus understood, transcends the particular claims of nations and states and extends to all in the 'universal community'. It connotes a right and duty which must be accepted if people are to learn to tolerate one another's company and to coexist peacefully. In Kant's hands, these arguments also lead to a striking rejection of colonialism: 'the *inhospitable* conduct of the civilised states of our continent, especially the commercial states' and 'the injustice they display in *visiting* foreign countries and peoples (which in their case is the same as *conquering* them)' (1970, p. 106). For Kant universal hospitality is, therefore, the condition of cooperative relations and of just conduct. But while Kant's opposition to colonialism and arguments for universal hospitality are noteworthy, they do not elaborate adequately the conditions of such hospitality. For without conceiving of cosmopolitan law as cosmopolitan democratic law, the conditions for the protection of freedom and autonomy for each and all cannot be satisfactorily envisaged. The pursuit of individual or collective projects, within the context of a commitment to universal 'good neighbourliness', requires the anatomy of power and nautonomy to be grasped in order that the legitimate boundaries of one's own and of the other's autonomy can be appreciated. Universal hospitality must involve, at the minimum, both the enjoyment of autonomy and respect for the necessary constraints on autonomy. That is to say, it must comprise mutual acknowledgement of, and respect for, the equal and legitimate rights of others to pursue their own projects and life-plans. Moreover, in a highly interconnected world, 'others' include not just those found in the immediate community, but all those whose fates are interlocked in networks of economic, political and environmental interaction. Universal hospitality is not achieved if, for economic, cultural or other reasons, the quality of the life of others is shaped and determined in near or far-off lands without their participation, agreement or consent. The condition of universal hospitality, or, as I would rather put it, of a cosmopolitan orientation, is a cosmopolitan democratic public law.

A commitment to the principle of autonomy entails a duty to work towards the establishment of an international community of democratic states and societies committed to upholding democratic public law both within and across their own boundaries: a cosmopolitan democratic community. In Kant's account, the establishment of a cosmopolitan community depends on the creation of a 'pacific federation' or 'union'; that is, a treaty, among a steadily expanding number of states, to prevent war permanently. As he wrote,

> a *pacific federation (foedus pacificum)*... would differ from a peace treaty (*pactum pacis*) in that the latter terminates *one* war, whereas the former would seek to end *all* wars for good. This federation does not aim to acquire any power like that of a state, but merely to preserve and secure the *freedom* of each state in itself, along with that of the other confederated states... [The union of states will secure] the freedom of each state in accordance with the idea of international right, and the whole will gradually spread further and further. (1970, p. 104)

Kant distinguished between 'pacific unions' based upon federal and confederal structures. A federal association is based, 'like that of the American States,... on a political constitution and is therefore indissoluble', whereas a confederal structure signifies merely 'a voluntary gathering of various states which can be *dissolved* at any time' (1970, p. 171). These terms can be refined further by conceiving of federalism as a political union in which there are common finance, foreign and military policies and no exit clauses for 'sub-federal' entities; confederalism, by contrast, connotes a union in which nations and states retain separate financial, foreign and military policies along with exit clauses which can bring to an end negotiated, coordinated relations.[3]

Kant argued firmly on behalf of confederalism in international affairs on the grounds that a single state of all peoples – a state of nations or an international state – is an impractical and potentially dangerous objective. It is impractical because states are unlikely to agree to a complete surrender of their sovereignty, and the territory of the world is too extensive to be regulated by one supreme authority. It is dangerous because of the potentially

[3] I am grateful to Johan Galtung for clarifying these terms.

tyrannical implications of the formation of a single, centralized state. In some of Kant's writings, he does not dismiss the idea of a world state altogether, and concedes that it is a solution which might have some advantages, but it is a solution he always recognized as unrealistic and politically naive; hence, he affirmed a treaty-based confederation of all states opposed to war as the feasible and right solution (1970, pp. 102–5).[4]

Within the framework of democratic autonomy, the idea of a cosmopolitan community can be located between the principles of federalism and confederalism. A single, unified, international state structure ought not to be regarded as an aim; it is impractical and undesirable for many of the reasons Kant gave. States continue to guard jealously their sovereignty, often seeking ways to protect and enhance it in the face of regional and global flows (see § 4.3). Further, the regulation and development of many aspects of local and national communities properly belong to these communities, and they rightly resist attempts at the further centralization of power and authority (see § 10.3). Such communities do not want to give up the right to self-government across diverse matters. Locke's famous objection to the idea that individuals could only find a 'peaceful and commodious' life with one another if they were governed by the dictates of a single, unified, indivisible sovereign still retains its relevance in the face of attempts to unify and centralize political power (see p. 43).

In addition, the notion of a single federal structure for the governance of all nations is vulnerable to many of the same objections as those levelled against 'bureaucratic command government', acting presumptuously *as if* it knew what people should do and how they should behave in diverse settings, and vulnerable to chronic inefficiency, information overload and despotic practices (see Hayek, 1960; Rutland, 1985). Moreover, the concept of a world state or state of nations all too often presupposes that the world's peoples can come to share a homogeneous culture, a common universe of discourse and a single form of (global) citizenship – a presupposition that seems dangerously naive in the face of people's frequent, intense attachment to their locality as the appropriate forum for self-assertion and democratic association.

[4] Doyle notes usefully that Kant 'develops no organizational embodiment of this treaty, and presumably he does not find institutionalization necessary. He appears to have in mind a mutual non-aggression pact, perhaps a collective security agreement' (1983, p. 227).

The desire to preserve something meaningful and tangible in existing local culture, in the context of profound globalizing tendencies, is what arguably lies behind many of today's most intense political phenomena, from ethnic revivalism to political separatism and movements for local democracy (see § 6.1).

Nonetheless, the idea of a democratic cosmopolitan order is not simply compatible with the idea of confederalism, a wholly voluntary, treaty-based union, constantly renewed through limited agreements. It is the case that the creation of a cosmopolitan democracy requires the active consent of peoples and nations: initial membership can only be voluntary. It would be a contradiction of the very idea of democracy itself if a cosmopolitan democratic order were created non-voluntarily, that is, coercively. If the initial inauguration of a democratic international order is to be legitimate, it must be based on consent. However, thereafter, in circumstances in which people themselves are not directly engaged in the process of governance, consent ought to follow from the majority decision of the people's representatives, so long as they – the trustees of the governed – uphold cosmopolitan democratic law and its covenants. Against this background, commitment to the regulatory procedures of this order would be non-voluntary, and would remain so as long as it was bound and circumscribed by this law (see chapter 12 for a discussion of this condition and of the possible use of referenda in disputed cases). If cosmopolitan democratic law were entrenched and enforced, there would be a clear duty to obey the law. But if those who governed flouted the terms of cosmopolitan law, the basis of political legitimacy would be eroded.

10.2 Democracy as a transnational, common structure of political action

The rights and obligations which inhere in democracy are not naturally given or universally chosen; they require a decision or commitment to the notion that in political communities it ought to be adult citizens who determine freely the conditions of their own association and the course of their polity. Once this decision is made, the conditions for the institutionalization of democracy can begin to be pursued and debated. In the context of regional and global interconnectedness, however, people's equal interest in autonomy can only be adequately protected by a commitment from all those communities whose actions, policies and laws are interrelated and intertwined. For democratic law to be effective it must be internationalized. Thus, the implementation of a cosmopolitan democratic law and the establishment of a cosmopolitan community – a community of all democratic communities – must become an obligation for democrats, an obligation to build a transnational, common structure of political action which alone, ultimately, can support the politics of self-determination.

The whole planet's population could, in principle, be embraced by this framework, but whether it is depends, of course, on the political and cultural resources of a community which determines its ability to engage in a democratic and transnational commitment. In the first instance, cosmopolitan democratic law could be promulgated and defended by those democratic states and civil societies that are able to muster the necessary political judgement and to learn how political practices and institutions must change and adapt in the new regional and global circumstances. Such an association of states and societies would be an association of democratic nations which might draw in others over time, perhaps by the sheer necessity of becoming a member if the system of government in particular countries were to enjoy legitimacy in the eyes of its own population. The theoretical lesson that democratic legitimacy can ultimately only be redeemed transnationally might quickly be learnt in practice, both from the precedents set by the new democratic association and from the difficulty of sustaining a national democracy which acted alone.

Accordingly, the cosmopolitan model of democracy creates the possibility of an expanding institutional framework for the democratic regulation of states and societies. The achievement of taking steps towards the realization of democratic autonomy within a nation-state or region – important as it unquestionably is – would be but a milestone on the road to the establishment of a cosmopolitan democracy with global reach. While, initially, only those communities which enable policy and law to be shaped by their citizenry are likely to pursue such a future, the possibility is held out that the conflict between a person's obligation *qua* citizen to obey the regulations of a particular community, and his or her obligation to obey internationally recognized rules, might eventually be overcome, as more and more states and agencies affiliated to the new democratic order (cf. Heater, 1990, pp. 54–5). The principles of individual democratic states and societies could come to coincide with those of cosmopolitan democratic law. As a consequence, the rights and responsibilities of people *qua* national citizens and *qua* subjects of cosmopolitan law could coincide, and democratic citizenship could take on, in principle, a truly universal status. In these circumstances, it could be said, adapting Kant, that the individuals who composed the states and societies whose constitutions were formed in accordance with cosmopolitan law might be regarded as citizens, not just of their national communities or regions, but of a universal system of 'cosmo-political' governance (cf. Kant, 1970, pp. 47–53 and 128–30). Such a system connotes nothing more or less than the entrenchment and enforcement of democratic public law across all peoples – a binding framework for the political business of states, societies and regions, not a detailed regulative framework for the direction of all their affairs. People would come, thus, to enjoy multiple citizenships – political membership in the diverse political communities which significantly affected them. They would be citizens of their immediate political communities, and of the wider regional and global networks which impacted upon their lives. This cosmopolitan polity would be one that in form and substance reflected and embraced the diverse forms of power and authority that operate within and across borders and which, if unchecked, threaten a highly fragmented, neo-medieval order (see § 6.3).

Against the background of a cosmopolitan polity, the nation-state would, in due course, 'wither away', but this is *not* to say that states and national polities would become redundant. There are many good reasons, noted in part II, for doubting the theoretical and empirical basis of claims that nation-states will disappear. Rather, 'withering away' means that states would no longer be, and would no longer be regarded as, the sole centres of legitimate power within their own borders (as is already the case in diverse settings). States would be 'relocated' within, and articulated with, an overarching global democratic law. Within this framework, the laws of the nation-state would be but one focus for legal development, political reflection and mobilization. For this framework would respecify and reconstitute the meaning and limits of sovereign authority. Particular power centres and authority systems would enjoy legitimacy only to the extent that they upheld and enacted democratic law.

The idea of the modern state itself, it has been argued hitherto, can only be redeemed through the idea of a democratic legal state. However, the latter, it can now be seen, must be extended and recast if the challenges of a highly interconnected world are to be met fully. An impartial and circumscribed system of power must be thought of as a cosmopolitan authority system, or as a cosmopolitan democratic legal framework. The case for such a framework rests in part on the necessity, theoretically and practically, of 'splitting the state', although it is important to separate out arguments about transforming the organizational form of the state from arguments about the pertinence of the concept of the modern state itself. The recognition that some of the duties and functions of the state are and must be performed at and across different political levels – local, national, regional and international – does not entail that the idea of the modern state itself is wholly defunct; it entails, rather, that this idea must be adapted to stretch across borders.

If these distinctions hold, the 'artificial person' at the centre of the idea of the modern state must be reconceived in terms of basic cosmopolitan democratic law. In this conception, sovereign authority or sovereignty would derive its legitimacy from this law: a justified power system would be a system bound and circumscribed by this law. While such a system requires an overarching set of institutions to nurture the entrenchment and application of basic law, it could be composed of a diverse range of decision-making centres which are autonomous; that is, which act within their own sphere of competence subject only to meeting the requirements of democratic law. Such 'centres' could clearly be nation-states, but they need not only be states. Networks of states, that is, regions, could in principle assume this form, on the one hand, while sub-national entities or transnational communities, organizations and agencies might do so, on the other. Thus, sovereignty can be stripped away from the idea of fixed borders and territories and thought of as, in principle, malleable time-space clusters. *Sovereignty is an attribute of the basic democratic law, but it could be entrenched and drawn upon in diverse self-regulating associations, from states to cities and corporations* (see chapter 11). Cosmopolitan law demands the subordination of regional, national and local 'sovereignties' to an overarching legal framework, but within this framework associations may be self-governing at diverse levels. A new possibility is portended: the recovery of an intensive and participatory democracy at local levels as a complement to the public assemblies of the wider global order; that is, a political order of democratic associations, cities and nations as well as of regions and global networks. The cosmopolitan model of democracy is the legal basis of a global and divided authority system – a system of diverse and overlapping power centres, shaped and delimited by democratic law. In this context, secession could take on a new meaning – the break-up of old political entities *within* a common framework of politics, that is, the reshaping of traditional political communities, on the one hand, while, on the other, establishing the possibility of new communities within the framework of a transnational structure of democratic action.

10.3 New forms and levels of governance

However cosmopolitan democracy is conceived, it is based upon the recognition that democracy within a particular community and democratic relations among communities are interlocked, absolutely inseparable, and that new organizational and binding mechanisms must be created if democracy is to develop in the decades ahead. But there is clearly a danger (which the discussion in 1992–3 of 'subsidiarity' in Europe highlighted) that political authority and decision-making capacity will be 'sucked' upwards in any new cross-border democratic settlement (see § 5.2). To avoid this, the principles governing appropriate levels of decision-making need to be clarified and kept firmly in view.

The issues and policy questions which rightly belong to local, workplace or city levels are those which involve people in the direct determination of the conditions of their own association – the network of public questions and problems, from policing to playgrounds, which primarily affect them. The issues which rightly belong to national levels of governance are those in which people in delimited territories are significantly affected by collective problems and policy questions which stretch to, but no further than, their frontiers. By contrast, the issues which rightly belong to regional levels of governance are those which require transnational mediation because of the interconnectedness of national decisions and outcomes, and because nations in these circumstances often find themselves unable to achieve their objectives without transborder collaboration. Accordingly, decision-making and implementation belong to the regional level if, and only if, the common interest in self-determination can only be achieved effectively through regional governance. By extension, the issues which rightly belong to the global level are those involving levels of interconnectedness and interdependence which are unresolvable by local, national or regional authorities acting alone. Decision-making centres beyond national borders are properly located when 'lower' levels of decision-making cannot satisfactorily manage and discharge transnational and international policy questions.

Environmental problems provide an obvious illustration of the necessity of pursuing democratic governance at these different levels. For example, factories emitting various forms of toxic waste can be locally monitored and challenged, nationally regulated and supervised, regionally checked for cross-national standards and risks, and globally evaluated in the light of their impact on the health, welfare and economic opportunities of others. Toxic waste disposal and global warming are examples of two pressing issues which require local as well as global responses if their consequences are to be contained and regulated.

Three tests can be proposed to help filter and guide policy issues to the different levels of governance: the tests of extensiveness, intensity and comparative efficiency. The test of extensiveness examines the range of peoples within and across delimited territories who are significantly affected by a collective problem and policy question. The test of intensity assesses the degree to which the latter impinges on a group of people(s) and, therefore, the degree to which national, regional or global legislation or other types of intervention are justified. The third test, the assessment of comparative efficiency, is concerned to provide a means of examining whether any proposed national, regional or global initiative is necessary in so far as the objectives it seeks to meet cannot be realized in an adequate way by those operating at 'lower' levels of decision-making. The criteria that can be used to pursue the last test include the availability of alternative legislative or administrative means, the cost of a proposed action, and the possible consequences of such action for the constituent parts of an area.[5] Democracy, thus, can only be adequately entrenched if a division of powers and competences is recognized at different levels of political interaction and interconnectedness – levels which correspond to the degrees to which public issues stretch across and affect populations. Such an order must embrace diverse and distinct

[5] The tests of 'extensiveness' and 'intensity' follow naturally from the earlier discussion of globalization as involving both 'extensive' and 'intensive' forms of interconnectedness (see § 1.2). The specific formulations of the tests of 'intensity' and 'comparative efficiency' are themselves adapted from current European discussion of the preconditions which ought to be met in order to justify EU involvement in the policy-making process (see Neunreither, 1993, esp. pp. 209–11, for a helpful discussion).

domains of authority, linked both vertically and horizontally, if it is to be a successful creator and servant of democratic practice, wherever it is located.[6]

In conclusion: the consolidation of democracy

The establishment of a cosmopolitan model of democracy is a way of seeking to strengthen democracy 'within' communities and civil associations by elaborating and reinforcing democracy from 'outside' through a network of regional and international agencies and assemblies that cut across spatially delimited locales. The impetus to the pursuit of this network can be found in a number of processes and forces, including: the development of transnational, grass-roots movements with clear regional or global objectives, such as the protection of natural resources and the environment, and the alleviation of disease and ill-health; the elaboration of new legal rights and duties affecting states and individuals in connection with the 'common heritage of humankind', the protection of the 'global commons', the defence of human rights and the deployment of force; and the emergence and proliferation in the twentieth century of international institutions to coordinate transnational forces and problems, from the UN and its agencies to regional political networks and organizations (see chapter 5; and Falk, 1991a). Accordingly, it can be argued, a political basis exists upon which to build a more systematic democratic future.

This future has to be conceived in cosmopolitan terms – a new institutional complex with global scope, given shape and form by reference to a basic democratic law, which takes on the character of government to the extent, and only to the extent, that it promulgates, implements and enforces this law. But however its institutions are precisely envisaged, it is a future built upon the recognition that democracy within a single community and demo-

[6] The principle that decisions about public affairs should rest with those significantly affected by them, or their representatives, will, of course, not always lead to clear demarcations among the appropriate levels of decision-making, even with the aid of the proposed filter principles and tests. Disputes about the appropriate jurisdiction of particular communities will in all likelihood be complex and intensive (as they are in the EU). Accordingly, 'issue-boundary' forums or courts will have to be created to hear cases concerning where and how a 'significant interest' in a public question should be explored and resolved (cf. n. 6, p. 206).

cratic relations among communities are deeply interconnected, and that new organizational and legal mechanisms must be established if democracy is to survive and prosper.

11

Markets, Private Property and Cosmopolitan Democratic Law

The least intrusive form of public power commensurate with the defence of individual rights, it has been argued, is the 'framework for utopia'. The author of this view, Robert Nozick, holds that we must get away from the idea that utopia represents *a* single conception of the best of all social and political arrangements (1974). There is no one type of community that will serve as an ideal for all people, because a wide range of conceptions of utopia exists. Provocatively, he wrote:

> Wittgenstein, Elizabeth Taylor, Bertrand Russell, Thomas Merton, Yogi Berra, Allen Ginsburg, Harry Wolfson, Thoreau, Casey Stengel, The Lubavitcher Rebbe, Picasso, Moses, Einstein, Hugh Heffner, Socrates, Henry Ford, Lenny Bruce, Baba Ram Dass, Gandhi, Sir Edmund Hillary, Raymond Lubitz, Buddha, Frank Sinatra, Columbus, Freud, Norman Mailer, Ayn Rand, Baron Rothschild, Ted Williams, Thomas Edison, H. L. Mencken, Thomas Jefferson, Ralph Ellison, Bobby Fischer, Emma Goldman, Peter Kropotkin, you, and your parents. Is there really one kind of life which is best for each of these people? (Nozick, 1974, p. 310)

A society in which utopian *experimentation* can be tried should be thought of as utopia. Utopia is a framework for utopias where people are 'at liberty to join together voluntarily to pursue and attempt to realize their own vision of the good life in the ideal community but where no one can *impose* his own utopian vision upon others' (Nozick, 1974, p. 312). Or, to put the point another way, utopia is the framework for liberty and experimentation (Nozick, 1974, pp. 333–4).

There is much to recommend this view; since individuals and peoples are extraordinarily diverse, no one kind of life seems best for all of them. An institutional arrangement which creates maximum space for initiative and autonomy, and minimum space for restriction and coercion, is, prima facie, highly appealing. But the questions are: how can individuals and groups make progress towards their chosen ends, whether these be social, political, cultural, economic or religious? How can radically different aspirations be both articulated and reconciled? How can self-determination be achieved without a framework of mutual accommodation? If people are to be self-determining, do they not require a common structure of political action to protect themselves as agents with an equal entitlement to self-determination? According to Nozick, the grounds for such a position are deeply suspect; the framework for utopia is properly conceived as 'libertarian and *laissez-faire*'. The only legitimate organization of human and material resources is that contingently negotiated by the unhindered activities of individuals in competitive exchanges with one another; and the only political institutions that can be justified are those that protect them against force, theft, fraud and the violation of contracts. The framework for utopia is inconsistent with 'planning in detail' and the active redistribution of resources.

Developing the emphasis on the centrality to liberty of individuals pursuing their ends in competitive exchanges with one another, Hayek insists that a free society is incompatible with the enactment of rules which specify how people should use the means at their disposal (1960, pp. 231–2). He seeks to specify strict limits on the possible use of political power, expounding a position I have characterized elsewhere as 'legal democracy' (see Held, 1987, ch. 8). In setting out the case for such a democracy, Hayek makes a number of distinctions which are important to consider in relationship to the possibility of a democratic legal framework and a cosmopolitan model of democracy. These distinctions are explored below (§ 11.1). Assessing them provides a useful background against which the connections of cosmopolitan democracy to the 'free market' and private property can be clarified (§ 11.2). It will be argued that cosmopolitan democratic law must be entrenched in market mechanisms and processes if different kinds of market are to flourish within the constraints of democratic processes and outcomes (§§ 11.3–11.6). In presenting this case, the democratic justification for political intervention in the economy will also be set out.

11.1 Law, liberty and democracy

In Hayek's view, unless the *demos* is constrained in its actions by general rules, there is no guarantee that what it commands will be good or wise. To the 'doctrinaire democrat', what the majority wants 'is sufficient ground for regarding it as good . . . the will of the majority determines not only what is law but what is good law' (Hayek, 1960, p. 103). This 'fetish' of democracy leads to the false suggestion that 'so long as power is conferred by democratic procedure, it cannot be arbitrary' (Hayek, 1976, p. 53). Democracy, Hayek rightly argues, is by no means infallible or certain. It is the case that 'democratic control *may* prevent power from becoming arbitrary, but it does not do so by its mere existence' (Hayek, 1976, p. 53).

Central to Hayek's argument is a particular distinction between liberalism and democracy. As he puts it, 'liberalism is a doctrine about what the law ought to be, democracy a doctrine about the manner of determining what will be the law' (Hayek, 1960, p. 103). While liberalism regards it 'as desirable that only what the majority accepts should in fact be law', its aim is 'to persuade the majority to observe certain principles' (Hayek, 1960, pp. 103–4). So long as there are general rules which constrain the actions of majorities and governments, the individual need not fear coercive power. Hayek makes a further important distinction between law (essentially fixed, general rules which determine the conditions of individuals' actions, including constitutional rules) and legislation (routine changes in the legal structure which are the work of most governments). Citizens can enjoy liberty only if the power of the state is circumscribed by law; that is, circumscribed by rules which specify limits on the scope of political activity – limits based upon the rights of individuals to develop their own views and tastes, to pursue their own ends and to fulfil their own talents and gifts (Hayek, 1976, pp. 11 and 63). The rule of law provides, in this account, the conditions under which individuals can decide how to use their energies and the resources at their disposal. It is, thus, the critical restraint on coercive power and the condition of individual freedom.

Hayek explains restrictions on the legislative scope of governments as follows:

> The Rule of Law . . . implies limits to the scope of legislation: it restricts it to the kind of general rules known as formal law, and excludes legislation either directly aimed at particular people, or at enabling anybody to use the coercive power of the state for the purpose of such discrimination. It means, not that everything is regulated by law, but, on the contrary, that the coercive power of the state can be used only in cases defined in advance by the law and in such a way that it can be foreseen how it will be used. (Hayek, 1976, pp. 62–3)

Legislators should not meddle with the rule of law; for such meddling leads generally to a diminution or loss of freedom.

Ultimately, Hayek's 'legal democracy' sets the contours for a free-market society and a 'minimal state' (cf. Nordhaus, 1975; Brittan, 1977). Such an order can be secured, he believes, only on the basis of 'catallaxy': 'the special kind of spontaneous order produced by the market through people acting within the rules of the laws of property, tort and contract' (1982, vol. II, p. 109). He does not refer to this order as *laissez-faire* because every state intervenes to a degree in the structuring of civil society and private life (Hayek, 1960, p. 231, 1976, pp. 60–1). The question is why, how and on what basis states intervene to condition economic and social affairs. In order to be consistent with the rule of law, intervention must be restricted to the provision of rules which can serve individuals as instruments in the pursuit of their various ends. Like Nozick, Hayek holds that it is only in specifying 'the means capable of serving a great variety of purposes' that agreement among citizens is possible (Hayek, 1976, p. 45). Like Nozick, he takes these means to be broadly synonymous with non-intrusive, non-directive organizations which provide a stable and predictable framework for the coordination of individuals' activities. But unlike Nozick, who appeals to inalienable (natural) rights as the basis for this position, Hayek argues essentially epistemologically; we know and can only know a very little about the needs and wants of those immediately around us, let alone of millions of people and how one might go about weighting their various aims and preferences (Hayek, 1976, p. 44). Any systematic attempt to regulate the lives and activities of individuals is perforce oppressive and an attack on their knowledge and freedom: a denial of their ability and right to be the ultimate judges of their own ends.

The prime example Hayek gives of coercive political action is legislation which attempts to alter 'the material position of particular people or enforce distributive or "social" justice', nationally or internationally (Hayek, 1960, p. 231). Distributive justice always imposes on some another's conception of merit or desert. It requires the allocation of resources by a central authority acting as if it knew what people should receive for their efforts and how they should behave. The value of individuals' services can, however, only be determined justly by their fellows in and through a decision-making system which does not interfere with their knowledge, choices and decisions. And there is only one sufficiently sensitive mechanism for determining 'collective' choice on an individual basis – the free market. No system can provide a mechanism of collective choice as dynamic, innovative and responsive as the operations of the free market.

The free market does not always operate perfectly; but, Hayek insists, its benefits radically outweigh its disadvantages (1960, 1976; and see Rutland, 1985). The market system is the basis for a genuinely free order; for economic freedom is, as Friedman put it, 'an essential requisite for political freedom' (1980, p. 21). In particular, the market can ensure the coordination of the decisions of producers and consumers without the direction of a central authority; the pursuit by everyone of his or her own ends with the resources at his or her disposal; the development of a complex economy without an elite that claims to know how it all works. Politics, as a governmental decision-making system, will always be a radically imperfect system of choice when compared to the market. Thus, 'politics' or 'state action' should be kept to a minimum – to the sphere of operation of an 'ultra-liberal' state (Hayek, 1976, p. 172). An 'oppressive bureaucratic government' is the almost inevitable result of deviation from this prescription. By contrast, a public authority which acts within this framework – preserving the rule of law, providing a limited number of public goods in the few cases where the market is an inefficient supplier, offering a 'safety net' for the clearly destitute, and maintaining collective security against external threats – will be not only a 'limited government' but a 'decent government' as well (1982, vol. II, p. 102; cf. 1982, vol. III, pp. 102–27).

It is important to note that Hayek is adamant that his argument should not be interpreted in nationalistic terms. He attacks preferences for national markets and national states (often championed by conservative and national liberal thinkers), maintaining that markets know no national boundaries and operate most effectively if unhindered by such artificial constraints. He argues for a market order based on the principles of free trade and minimum regulation. For him, liberty is a feature, ultimately, of an international market order and a network of ultra-liberal states. His preferred international system is a *federation* of ultra-liberal states where all interaction is conducted between individuals unimpeded by state boundaries (1976, pp. 220, 232 and 243). Such a federation would be bound by a 'higher' authority which would specify and help guarantee the rules of international trade and commerce. This 'authority' would be above particular interests in the sense that it would have no power to legislate about the specific ends of individuals; its entire brief would be restricted to ensuring the possibility of the rule of law in international terms. Hayek does not believe that such an agency can be created on a truly transnational basis in the short term; but he does believe a group of like-minded nations can begin to create such an agency. In the first instance, what would be created would be a regional authority – a first but nonetheless important step to a peaceful and truly global liberal order.

11.2 The economic limits to democracy?

Hayek's arguments include a number of elements which are important to consider in a re-examination of the relation between politics, law and the market. Those of particular note include his stress on protecting individual autonomy against coercive political power; limiting the scope and form of state action by means of the rule of law; restricting democracy by constitutional means in order that democracy might function effectively; and thinking beyond national borders while assessing the proper locus of the political and economic good. However, there are many grounds for pausing before equating the framework for utopia with legal democracy. Not only does Hayek's conception of the rule of law drastically restrict consideration of the proper form and scope of democracy, but it also removes (by design) consideration of the impact of key sites and sources of power on the possibility of democracy. Far from seeking a basis to protect people's equal interest in autonomy through the specification of a common structure of political action, the rule of law, as specified by Hayek, hinders and undermines deliberation about the impact of power on autonomy in the public realm; and it does this in the name of freedom itself. There are several major difficulties with these aspects of Hayek's thought.

In the first instance, Hayek's model of the liberal free-market order is fundamentally at odds with the modern corporate capitalist system. The idea that modern society approximates, or could progressively approximate, to a world where producers and consumers meet on an equal basis seems, to say the least, implausible. The reality of the 'free market' is marked by complex patterns of market formation, oligopolistic structures, and the economic rivalry of regional power blocs. In addition, while it is wrong to regard multinational corporations as simply 'footloose', they have developed a remarkable ability – helped by the new global communication networks and the extensive integration of the world financial markets – to transfer resources rapidly from one national jurisdiction to another and to seek out the most favourable economic conditions available for their own development. Moreover, in an international monetary system that fosters vast, instantaneous movements of short-term capital, a complex system of economic constraints is in force which impinges strongly on national governments (see § 6.2: the discussion of disjuncture 5; and cf. Evans, 1992; Hutton, 1993). This is not a world in which it is at all straightforward to claim that markets are free, responsive mechanisms of collective choice. Hayek in particular, and neo-liberalism in general, project an image of markets as 'powerless' mechanisms of coordination and in so doing neglect the distorting nature of economic power in relation to democracy (see Vajda, 1978).

These general reflections can be broken down further into a number of different elements. First, there are significant areas of market failure, recognized by many conventional economists, which need to be borne in mind when analysing the relationship of autonomy to market forces, including: the problem of externalities (for example, the environmental externalities produced by economic growth); the persistent dependence of market economies on *non*-market social factors which alone can provide an effective balance between 'competition' and 'cooperation' (and, thus, ensure an adequate supply of necessary 'public goods' such as education, trained labour and market information); the tendency towards the 'concentration' and 'centralization' of economic life (marked by patterns of oligopoly and monopoly); the propensity to 'short-termism' in investment strategy as fund holders and fund corporations operate policies aimed at maximizing immediate income return and dividend results; and the underemployment or unemployment of productive resources in the context of the demonstrable existence of urgent and unmet need (see Miller, 1989; Cohen, G. A., 1991; Hirst, 1993; Pierson, 1993; Evans, 1992; and, on the last point, see § 9.3).

Second, some of the main threats to autonomy in the contemporary world can be related not to demands for equality or the ambitions of the majority to level social difference, as thinkers from Tocqueville to Hayek have feared, but to inequality, inequality of such magnitude as to create significant violations of political liberty and democratic politics (Held, 1987, pp. 90ff; § 8.4 in this volume; and see Dahl, 1985, pp. 50 and 60). Hayek neglects to inquire into the extent to which market relations are themselves power relations that can constrain the democratic process. He does not ask whether systematic asymmetries in income, wealth and opportunity may be the outcome of the existing form of market relations – capitalist market relations – and whether one particular form of autonomy – the autonomy to accumulate unlimited economic resources and to organize productive activity into hierarchically governed enterprises and highly mobile units – poses a fundamental challenge to the extent to which autonomy can be enjoyed by all citizens; that is, the extent to which citizens can act as equals in the political process. Economic organizations are cooperative ventures governed by rules, policies and strategies, but they remain ventures in which most employees have no democratic stake, despite the fact that each employee is expected to operate for the mutual advantage of all others, and that the decisions, policies and strategies of these ventures have a major influence on other sites of power, from health and welfare to politics (see § 8.3; and Cohen, J., 1988). Economic nautonomy creates strict limits on the development of a common structure of political action and on the available set of participative opportunities.

Third, the stratification of autonomy produced by modern corporate capitalism goes beyond the immediate impact of economic inequalities on the capacities of citizens to participate as equals in their collective associations. For the very capacity of governments to act in ways that interest groups may legitimately desire is, as previously noted, constrained. Lindblom has explained the point well:

> Because public functions in the market system rest in the hands of businessmen, it follows that jobs, prices, production, growth, the standard of living, and the economic security of everyone all rest in

> their hands. Consequently government officials cannot be indifferent to how well business performs its functions. Depression, inflation, or other economic disasters can bring down a government. A major function of government, therefore, is to see to it that businessmen perform their tasks. (Lindblom, 1977, pp. 122–3)

The constraints on governments and state institutions systematically limit policy options. The system of private property and investment creates objective exigencies that must be met if economic growth and development are to be sustained. Accordingly, governments must take action to help secure the profitability and prosperity of the private sector: they are dependent upon the process of capital accumulation which they have for their own stability to maintain, which means, at the minimum, ensuring the compatibility of economic policies with the imperatives of the corporate sector and/or of the international capital markets. Government legitimacy, furthermore, is thoroughly bound up with the success of these measures. For governments are also dependent upon the private sector to meet the demands of their consumers (see Evans, 1992). If they fail in this regard, their electoral support can quickly melt away. A government's policies must, thereby, follow a political agenda that is at least favourable to, that is, biased towards, the development of the system of private enterprise and corporate power.

Democratic theory and practice are, thus, faced with a major challenge; the business corporation or multinational bank enjoys a disproportionate 'structural influence' over the polity and, therefore, over the nature of democratic outcomes. Political representatives would find it extremely difficult to carry out the wishes of an electorate committed to reducing the adverse effects on democracy and political equality of corporate capitalism. (For an account of some past attempts, see Coates, 1980; Ross, Hoffmann and Malzacher, 1987; cf. Hall, P., 1986.) Democracy is embedded in a socio-economic system that grants a 'privileged position' to certain interests. Accordingly, individuals and interest groups cannot be treated as necessarily equal, and the state cannot be regarded as a neutral arbiter among all interests.

If a state or set of regulative agencies is separate from the associations and practices of everyday life, then it is plausible to see it as a special kind of apparatus – a 'protective knight', 'umpire' or 'judge' – which the citizen ought to respect and obey. But if states and governing agencies are enmeshed in these associations and practices, then the claim that they constitute 'independent authorities' or 'circumscribed impartial powers' is compromised, as thinkers on the left have traditionally maintained (see § 1.1). This is unsettling for the whole spectrum of questions concerning the nature of public power, the relation between the 'public' and the 'private', the proper scope of politics and the appropriate reach of democratic governments (Pateman, 1985, pp. 172ff).

Furthermore, if states are, as a matter of routine, neither 'separate' nor 'impartial' with respect to society, then citizens will not be treated as equally free. If the 'public' and 'private' are interlocked in complex ways, then formal elections will always be insufficient as mechanisms to ensure the accountability of the forces actually involved in the 'governing' process. Moreover, since the 'meshing' of state and civil society leaves few, if any, realms of 'private life' untouched by 'politics', and vice versa, the question of the proper form of the state, law and democratic regulation is posed acutely. *Pace* Hayek, if the rule of law does not involve a central concern with distributional questions and matters of social justice, it cannot be satisfactorily entrenched, and the principle of autonomy and democratic accountability cannot be realized adequately.

The above arguments stress a number of sources of tension between democracy and capitalism. Even when taken together, however, they by no means amount to a straightforward critique of the latter. While granting priority to the right to self-determination entails recognizing the importance of introducing limits on the right to, and on the rights of, productive and financial property, the exact implications of this viewpoint remain obscure. It would be quite foolish to suggest that there are simple alternatives, which are both feasible and desirable, to the existing system of corporate capitalism. For instance, the notion that the tensions between democracy and capitalism can be overcome by the introduction of a planned economy, as classical Marxists have traditionally argued, suffers from two decisive problems that render it implausible and, for most people, unappealing. To begin with, in its technocratic-elitist form, expressed most clearly in the Soviet conception of a command economy, the planned economy has failed as a political and economic project. This is so for many of the reasons Hayek proffered; these include an arrogant and misplaced presumption of knowledge about people's needs and wants, a crisis of 'excessive information' which could not be properly evaluated in the absence of market prices and costs, and the pursuit of coercive political programmes in diverse domains, from economic management to cultural life. The command economy was the epitome of the 'oppressive bureaucratic state'. Secondly, all those who have sought to articulate the notion of a planned economy with democracy – defending the idea of a self-managed economic system, for instance – have so far failed to elaborate a fully convincing alternative political economy to capitalism (cf. Callinicos, 1993; Held, 1993b). At the present juncture, there does not seem to be a viable alternative economics to capitalism, but this does not mean, of course, that one might not be forthcoming. Nor does it mean that the question of 'alternatives' is an insignificant matter – far from it.

But the whole question of capitalism and its alternatives is wholly misstated by putting the issue, as Marxism has consistently done, as one between capitalism and something different in all fundamental respects. Just as there is more than one socialism, so there is more than one capitalism. Capitalism is not a single, homogeneous system the world over; there are different capitalisms with different capacities for reform and adaptation. The United States, Japan and Sweden, for instance, embody quite different models of economic development, production, labour-market regulation and welfare regimes (see Esping-Andersen, 1990; Allen, 1992). In addition, capitalism, in the context of democratic constitutional societies, has strengths as well as weaknesses – strengths that need to be recognized and defended as well as extended and developed (cf. Habermas, 1992).

Accordingly, if the implications of the arguments about the tensions between democracy and capitalism are to be pursued, it needs to be on terms which break with the simple and crude juxtaposition of capitalism with planning, or capitalism with systems of collective ownership and control, and in terms which are more cautious and experimental. In order to consider these matters further, it is necessary to relate them to a broader and more systematic framework of assessment – that provided by the arguments for democratic autonomy and cosmopolitan democracy.

11.3 The rationale of political intervention in the economy

To create a framework for utopia demands not an abdication of politics in the name of liberty and experimentation, but a distinctive logic of political intervention. The rationale for this logic does not derive, first and foremost, from the domain of political control; that is, from a desire to plan and regulate economic and social affairs. Rather, the rationale derives from the requirement to ensure that the conditions are met for the democratic regulation of sites of power in all their forms. The requirement of a common structure of political action, the entrenchment of cosmopolitan democratic law, provides a direction for public policy and for its proper form and limits. Political intervention is justified when it upholds and furthers this law.

A 'legal state', therefore, can never simply be a minimum national state or a federation of minimal states. For the rationale of political intervention lays upon the polity – at local, national, regional and global levels – the responsibility to promote and defend democratic autonomy. Hayek's distinction between 'law' and 'legislation' is important provided that 'law' is understood as cosmopolitan democratic law and 'legislation' is geared into the promotion of this law. The 'impartiality' of a system of political power, and the extent to which it remains 'depersonalized' and 'circumscribed', can be judged in relationship to the degree to which it enhances democratic autonomy and breaks down systems of nautonomy.

It follows from this that political intervention in the economy is warranted when it is driven by the objective of overcoming those consequences of economic interaction, whether intended or unintended, which generate damaging externalities such as environmental pollution threatening to health. And it is warranted when it is driven by the need to ensure that the basic requirements of autonomy are met both within and outside of the firm. The roots of such intervention lie in the indeterminacy of the market system itself (see Sen, 1985, p. 19). Market economies can only function in a manner commensurate with democratic autonomy if this indeterminacy is addressed systematically and if the conditions of democratic autonomy are approximated or met (see Pierson, 1993, pp. 191–2; cf. Miller, 1989, p. 123). The market system has to be entrenched in the rights and obligations clusters of democratic law.

None of this is an argument for abandoning the market system as such. The latter has distinct advantages, as Hayek has emphasized, over all known alternative economic systems as an effective mechanism to coordinate the knowledgeable decisions of producers and consumers over extended territories. But it is an argument for 'reframing' the market. The underlying purpose of democratic political intervention is, thus, not a will to control or run all things, but a will to ensure the conditions for the pursuit of individual or collective projects with minimum risk of intrusion by coercive powers, whether these be economic, political or social.

However, the exact priorities for public policy cannot be specified independently of public deliberation orientated towards reaching a political decision, with the democratic good in mind. Views as to the desirability and feasibility of particular policies will differ. But these differences do not amount, as previously noted, to a vicious circle in democratic reasoning; rather, they are the expression of clashes of interpretation which are part of an inevitable hermeneutic circle in politics (see § 9.4). Likewise, the question of at what level political intervention should take place raises issues of political judgement about the appropriate domain of application of the principle of democratic intervention. This judgement can be aided by the 'filter principles' and the tests of 'extensiveness', 'intensity' and 'comparative efficiency' (pp. 236–7). Although the latter do not provide definitive strategies for determining the level of political negotiation and change, they do constitute guiding orientations to help channel public deliberation and decision-making.

11.4 The entrenchment of democracy in economic life

Democracy is challenged, it has been argued in this chapter, by powerful sets of economic relations and organizations which can – by virtue of the bases of their operations – systematically distort democratic processes and outcomes. Accordingly, there is a case that, if democracy is to prevail, the key groups and associations of the economy will have to be rearticulated with political institutions so that they become part of the democratic process – adopting, within their very *modus operandi*, a structure of rules, principles and practices compatible with democracy. The corporate capitalist system requires constraint and regulation to compensate for the biases generated by the pursuit of the 'private good'. At issue is the establishment of an economic system that is neither simply planned nor merely market orientated but, rather, open to organizations, associations and agencies pursuing their own projects, subject to the constraints of a common structure of political action and democratic processes.

The possibility of such a system depends upon groups and

economic associations functioning within agreed and delimited frameworks. Companies may be conceived as real entities or 'legal persons' with legitimate purposes of their own, without surrendering the idea of a shared framework of action (cf. Hirst, 1990, pp. 75–8). Economic enterprises need to be able to initiate their own activities, develop their own strategies, create their own organizational and operational procedures, trade or barter as appropriate and pursue their own interests if they are to operate knowledgeably and independently in a market context. A democratic legal order must, therefore, recognize enterprises as well as individual citizens as part of its constitutive domain. But such recognition can be warranted and extended only so long as the principle of autonomy and its seven clusters of rights and obligations are not undermined. In other words, democratic autonomy, and the cosmopolitan model of democracy, require the enforcement of the principle of autonomy and these seven clusters within the realms of political and economic affairs. This requires the inscription of the principles, rules and procedures of the seven clusters into the organizational rules and procedures of companies, and of all other forms of economic association. There is no necessary reason why such organizations, large or small, cannot entrench the rules and procedures of the principle of autonomy into their own articles of association.

If democratic legal relations are to be sustained, corporations will have to uphold, *de jure* and *de facto*, a commitment to the requirements of autonomy. What this entails is that companies, while pursuing strategic objectives and profit goals, must operate within a framework which does not violate the requirement to treat their employees and customers as free and equal persons, as specified by democratic public law (see § 9.1). Within their sphere of competence, that is to say, companies would have to pursue working conditions and practices which sustained health and safety, learning and welfare, the ability to engage in discussion and criticism (including of the company and its staff), and the capacity to join independent associations (in this case, trade unions and professional organizations). But the entrenchment of democratic public law within companies would mean, above all, a commitment to surmounting the economic sources of nautonomy and, thereby, to a 'basic income' and 'access avenues' to productive and financial property (see pp. 197–8).

A commitment to a basic income is a commitment to the conditions for each employee's economic independence; that is, the conditions which are commensurate with an individual's need for material security and the independence of mind which follows from it (see Rousseau, 1968, p. 96; Connolly, 1981, ch. 7). Without a resource base of this kind, people remain highly vulnerable, dependent on others and unable to exercise fully their capacity to pursue different courses of action. The requirements of economic independence include a firm policy of 'minimum wages' at work, politically determined intervention to uphold such levels and a wider collective provision for those who, for whatever reason, fall outside the income-generating mechanisms of the market (see Jordan, 1985; Rogers and Streeck, 1994).[1] However, even more important for the form and character of economic associations is the commitment to 'access avenues' to the decision-making apparatus of productive and financial property; that is, to the creation of participative opportunities in firms and in other types of economic organization. Such opportunities do not translate straightforwardly into a right to social or collective ownership. For what is centrally at issue is an opportunity for involvement in the determination of the regulative rules of work organizations, the broad allocation of resources within them, and the relations of economic enterprises to other sites of power.

'Involvement' in firms entails more than conversation or consultation between management, labour and representatives of other parties significantly affected by an economic enterprise, including, for example, local communities, consumers and investment fund holders. It entails negotiation and bargaining between relevant groups to create decision frameworks on matters as diverse as employment prospects, work methods, investment opportunities, and income and dividend levels. If such frameworks are to be effective, they need to constitute the basis for a routine and durable understanding among economic partners, for without this it is hard to see how enterprises could function successfully in the context of economic competition and the need to raise funds, private or public, for their development. At stake is a balance between the requirements of participation in management and those of economic effectiveness, that is, a balance between the

[1] Or, as Galbraith boldly put it, 'there is, first, the absolute, inescapable requirement that everyone in the good . . . society has a basic source of income. And if this is not available from the market system . . . it must come from the state. Nothing, let us not forget, sets a stronger limit on the liberty of the citizen than a total absence of money' (1994, p. 2).

discipline of democracy and the discipline of the market (cf. Pierson, 1995). The question of particular forms of property right is not in itself the primary consideration (see § 11.6).

The transaction of all business would, in addition, have to be conducted in a manner which respected each and every person's right to lawful political relations and upheld the wider framework of cosmopolitan democratic law. This means that companies ought not to engage in activities, openly or covertly, which undermine the political choices of peoples as, for instance, some North American companies did in Chile in 1973 when they colluded in the downfall of the Allende regime, or as many companies do when they fund (typically centre-right) political parties in order to ensure electoral outcomes favourable to their interests. The private determination of election results, whether by force, fraud or funding, is ruled out by the requirements of democratic law with its insistence, in principle, on free and equal participative opportunities for all parties in the democratic process.

The entrenchment of democratic rights and obligations within economic organizations represents an extension of an established idea of using legislation to alter the background conditions of firms in the market-place. The Social Chapter of the Maastricht Agreement, for example, embodies principles and rules which are compatible with the notion of generating elements of a common structure of political action. If operationalized, the Social Chapter could, in principle, alter the structure and functioning of market processes in a number of distinct ways (Lebrun, 1990; Addison and Siebert, 1993). However, its provisions fall far short of the determination of what is necessary to secure a common structure of political action (see Hepple, 1993). Furthermore, the intensive arguments about the Social Chapter in Europe highlight a legitimate concern about an exclusively *European* attempt to address the social conditions of the market. It has rightly been objected that if some nation-states opt out of the Chapter, as Britain did prior to the ratification of the Agreement, it could force increased costs and regulations on some enterprises while leaving others – those in the opt-out nations – free of these, with the consequence that the latter become potentially a more attractive investment location for companies seeking to minimize their costs and responsibilities. It has also rightly been argued that a European social initiative of this kind which did not lead to parallel reforms and developments elsewhere might disadvantage European capital in competition with other regional economic zones and/or so weaken the European initiative that it would become either ineffective or unenforceable over time (see Addison and Siebert, 1993, pp. 29ff; cf. Balls, 1994).

It is desirable, therefore, that democratic public law is implemented as a cosmopolitan law which could entrench and enforce its provisions across economic life, nationally, regionally and globally. What is required, in essence, is the introduction of new clauses into the ground rules or basic laws of the free-market and trade system. Ultimately, this necessitates the stipulation of new democratic terms of economic organization and trade. While the advocacy of such a position would clearly raise enormous political, diplomatic and technical difficulties, and would need a substantial period to pursue and, of course, implement, this is a challenge that cannot be avoided if people's equal interest in self-determination is to be nurtured and fulfilled. Only by introducing new terms of empowerment and accountability throughout the global economic system, as a supplement and complement to collective agreements and welfare measures in national and regional contexts, can a new settlement be created between economic power and democracy (cf. Lipietz, 1992, pp. 119–24).

Such an extension of democracy would require 'framework legislation', above all, at the global level; that is, legislation which specifies the principles and objectives of cosmopolitan democratic law to be upheld, leaving the detailed implementation of these to those at 'lower' levels of governance (see § 10.3).[2] As part of this legislative initiative, restrictions could be imposed on the provision of capital for investment; for instance, the release of funds – whether public or private – to companies or governments could be linked directly to the latter respecting and satisfying the conditions of democratic autonomy. In this order, there would be no place for corporations or countries which flouted the terms of cosmopolitan democratic law; that is, which achieved economic success and competitiveness at the expense of the health, welfare and well-being of their workforce, or at the expense of the autonomy and independence of those in other places and countries. If disregard for the terms of cosmopolitan democratic law could be demonstrated, companies and even countries could be legitimately excluded from the new trade system; entered on a list of proscribed

[2] The idea of 'framework legislation', thus understood, underpinned the original notion of a 'directive' within the initial EC legislative armoury (see Neunreither, 1993).

economic partners, they could be temporarily or permanently banned from the system – a ban enforced by agencies which would monitor not just the rules of sound finance and market transaction but also the rules which specified the possibility of mutual respect for autonomy and self-determination (see § 11.5).[3] Without the first set of rules there could be no effective and efficient economic system; without the second set there could be no democratic order which embraces economic forces. What this amounts to, in other words, is a case for a new 'Bretton Woods' agreement – an agreement which would tie investment, production and trade to the conditions and processes of democracy.

A new agreement of this kind would seek to entrench not only the general conditions that are necessary for a common structure of political action in economic affairs, but also the conditions necessary for the pursuit of policies aimed at alleviating, in the short and medium terms, the most pressing cases of avoidable economic suffering and harm (see § 9.3). At a minimum, the latter would involve negotiation to reduce the economic vulnerability of many developing countries by reducing debt, decreasing the outflow of net capital assets from the South to the North,[4] and creating new economic facilities at organizations like the World Bank and the IMF for development purposes (see Lipietz, 1992, pp. 116ff; Falk, 1995, ch. 6). In addition, if such measures were combined with a consumption tax on energy usage and/or a shift of priorities from military expenditure to the alleviation of severe need, then the developmental context of Western and Northern nation-states could begin to be accommodated to those nations struggling for survival and minimum welfare.[5]

[3] The maintenance of democratic law might be monitored through the use of a 'democratic audit', which could investigate the extent to which democratic public law was implemented and assess the accountability of enterprises in much the same way as a financial audit oversees sound financial practices (see Beetham, 1993b).

[4] North/South patterns of indebtedness have produced a net outflow of capital from South to North of an estimated annual $50 billion; that is to say, the cost of servicing the debts of the South exceeds direct development assistance by that amount each year (see Falk, 1995, ch. 6; UNDP, 1992, p. 89).

[5] It has been estimated, for example, that a consumption tax 'of a dollar per barrel of oil, collected at source, would yield around $24 billion a year (73% from the industrial nations). An equivalent tax on coal would yield around $16 billion' (UNDP, 1992, p. 90). These

Moreover, 'zones of development', areas defined by the extensiveness of cases of urgent need (typically found in the South but also in parts of the North), could be established and formally demarcated. In such zones, the responsibility for the nurturing and enforcement of urgent levels of autonomy would not be left to the countries alone in which the zones were located, especially if particular rights clusters – for example, aspects of safety, welfare and a basic income – were demonstrably unfundable by those countries at that level. If this were the case, urgent levels of autonomy would have to be treated as targets for attainment by developing areas, rather than obligations which were legally binding and capable of immediate enforcement (see Wallace, W. et al., 1992, p. 17; and § 12.1 below). However, such a limited suspension of the enforcement of certain rights would need to be linked directly to the provision of additional resources by the international community to help promote local forms of industry and work. Such a 'double-sided' strategy could be expected to provide a significant impetus to self-generative activities; thus, hard-pressed nations or regions could find support from a policy context orientated towards mutual responsibility for autonomy, in the short and long runs.[6]

Entrepreneurs and executives appear to object less to regulation or reform *per se* than to the intrusion of regulatory mechanisms that upset 'the rules of the game' in some particular places or countries only. High direct-tax levels or tough equal-opportunities legislation, for example, are objectionable to companies if they handicap those companies' competitive edge on others from areas not subject to similar regulations. Under such circumstances, companies will do what they can to resist regulation or depart for more 'hospitable shores'. Accordingly, the rules of the game have, in principle, to be altered *tout court*, at regional and global levels, if capitalism is to be democratized and entrenched in a set of mechanisms and procedures that allow different kinds of market to flourish within the constraints of democratic processes. A democratic political economy can be envisaged as part of a 'democratic

are clearly substantial sums, reinforcing the view that development assistance is more a question of political will and judgement than of monetary resources *per se* (see § 9.3).

[6] In the long run, attainable levels of autonomy would become the attainment targets for development assistance across all regions, but these would need to be carefully negotiated and considered (see chapter 12).

alternative' to both state socialism and liberal democratic capitalist economies.

11.5 Forms and levels of intervention

Against this background, international organizations and institutions would be given new responsibilities to oversee the process of democratic entrenchment. Among their objectives would be to reduce the role of economic forces in delimiting democratic conditions and outcomes, while not eroding the role of market exchange, that is, the orientation of enterprises towards the effective use of their capacity to meet market demand (see Devine, 1991, pp. 211–12). To enhance the prospects of attaining this result, levels of public expenditure and public investment would need to be subject to public deliberation and decision, as would the broad aims of such investment. For example, the amount currently spent on the world's military exceeds the combined incomes of the poorest half of humanity (see UNICEF, 1992). With a reallocation of 10 per cent of the military expenditure in the developing world and 1 per cent in the industrialized world, there could be drastic reductions in malnutrition and disease and major strides towards the provision of a basic education for all. Accordingly, less investment in the arms industry and more spent directly on human capital would be a significant shift in the direction of the widespread development of some of the key conditions of human autonomy. Trade-offs such as these could be publicized and debated.[7] In the context of public decision-making orientated to the democratic good, priorities might be renegotiated and changed.

[7] In 1993 UNICEF estimated that an additional $25 billion per annum for a decade would be enough to bring to an end 'the age-old evils of child malnutrition, preventable disease, and widespread illiteracy' (1993, p. 1). Commenting on the sum of $25 billion, UNICEF noted that 'it is considerably less than the amount the Japanese Government has allocated this year to the building of a new highway from Tokyo to Kobe; it is [only] two or three times as much as the cost of the tunnel soon to be opened between the United Kingdom and France; it is less than the cost of the Ataturk Dam complex now being constructed in eastern Turkey; it is a little more than Hong Kong proposes to spend on a new airport; it is about the same as the support package that the Group of Seven has agreed on in 1992 for Russia alone; and it is significantly less than Europeans will spend this year for wine and Americans on beer' (1993, pp. 1–2).

Furthermore, decisions could be implemented by fixing the areas in which capital could be encouraged to deploy, and the terms on which it could be 'rented' (see Cohen, J., 1988, pp. 16–17). The management of interest rate levels to induce capital to invest in certain areas is clearly more justifiable in the case of social investment projects – or in what I would prefer to call 'social framework investments in the conditions of autonomy' – than in the case of particular economic sectors or industrial areas, where the track record of political bodies for second-guessing economic and technical change has generally been unimpressive.[8] The management of social and public investment in the infrastructure of autonomy is rightly undertaken publicly, whereas private investment in economic sectors is, as a working rule, best left to those in those sectors with the practical knowledge to make such decisions (see § 11.3). Of course, it is likely that there would be strong differences of view as to the scope and direction of public investment but, in a political system that welcomed open debate, these differences could be discussed and examined. If pressing and intermediate cases of autonomy are to be addressed, the scope and direction of such investment must be brought into the centre of democratic processes. In the absence of this, democracy is fundamentally handicapped.

It is hard to imagine how public expenditure and investment coordination could take place without a new, high-level, cooperative organization operating as a complement to, but reaching beyond, existing economic structures. New forms of economic coordination would be indispensable to overcome the fragmentation of policy-making which emerges in the context of organizations like the IMF, the World Bank, the Bank for European Reconstruction and Development, the Organization for Economic Cooperation and Development (OECD) and the Group of Seven – all operating with separate briefs. The possibility of creating a new coordinating economic agency, working at both global and regional levels, is not as fanciful as it might at first seem, especially in the light of the actual creation of new multilateral economic bodies after the Second World War – and most recently the World Trade Organization (1993), founded to oversee international commerce and to reduce tariffs. Where exactly a new economic coordinator should be located (whether it should be some form of

[8] One exception to this has been industrial sectors with high growth potential (see Hart, 1991).

Economic Security Council working at the UN, for instance) would need to be debated (see UNDP, 1993; and chapter 12). But this debate is of secondary importance. The primary issue is to recognize the need for a new transnational authority capable of deliberation about the broad balance of public investment priorities, expenditure patterns and emergency economic situations. The brief of such a body would be to fill a vacuum; that is, to become the coordinator for economic policy which is either set at global or regional levels or not set at all. It could, thereby, help establish targets for the deployment of funds in various policy areas, as well as create policies for economic domains which escape the jurisdiction of existing regulatory spheres, for instance, short-term international capital markets. Its task, therefore, would be to lay out broad policy frameworks which could act as points of orientation for those working at other levels of governance. To be effective, these frameworks would have to reflect the voices and interests of diverse national and regional groupings, bound by and committed to upholding cosmopolitan democratic law. Without such an orientation, agreement on such frameworks would, of course, be difficult, if not impossible.

The determination of general investment priorities – whether it be in public infrastructures, in systems to overcome serious externalities, or in major capital projects – is not the same thing, it should be emphasized, as the determination of how capital will actually be used in particular investments. Detailed public directives to companies, as Hayek has emphasized, will always be less knowledgeable than the directives generated by local managers and operatives. In this scheme, therefore, while a proportion of available income for public investment could be set aside for particular priorities or sector use, companies and other economic agencies would, where applicable, have to tender competitively for these funds, and the most effective and efficient ought to win them (subject to the proviso, of course, that they uphold democratic law).[9]

[9] A three-tiered institutional scheme to manage such an allocation of capital, suggested by Unger, might look something like the following, although it could take many different forms:

> the first tier would be a social investment fund [which could be developed at various levels: national, regional, global] that is controlled by democratically elected executive and representative bodies, that fixes the institutional and economic framework

Nonetheless, even with widespread support for a set of public investment priorities, it would be foolish to presuppose that major capital markets would simply accept and go along with these priorities. There has been many a reaction – including the flight of capital to 'safe havens' – against governments seeking to pursue social priorities for investment, sometimes despite clear mandates for such programmes. Further, in the era of the twilight of communism, it would also be unwise to think that there would not be clear and popular instances of resistance to programmes of public investment, especially if they involved a requirement to raise additional revenue. It is essential, therefore, that strategies of economic democratization, if they are to be feasible strategies, work, wherever possible, 'with the grain of private property rather than against it' (Beetham, 1993b, p. 69). Examples of such strategies include, for instance, the formulation of a general incomes policy which allows profits to rise while using increased taxation on a percentage of these to create social investment funds on a local, national or regional basis (Korpi, 1978); and/or the creation of special representative bodies at local, national and regional levels to control the investment of pension funds; and/or the alteration of company dividend policy to allow a proportion of profits to be set aside as shares or income for the collective control and future benefit of employees (Beetham, 1993b; see Dahl, 1985; cf. Adamson, 1990, pp. 56–71). Individually or together, such proposals would increase the possibility of the social determination of investment by creating further 'access avenues' to productive and financial resources.

Within the context of national, 'regional' (in this case subnational) and local markets, to the extent that they retain their separate identities, the erosion and break-up of nautonomic struc-

within which the rest of the order operates, and that lends capital to funds at the second tier. That tier, in turn, would be a system of subordinate investment funds controlled by semi-independent bodies that borrow from the central fund and lend to enterprises within the limits set by the central fund. The third tier would be composed of firms that borrow capital from the subordinate investment funds and that transact with one another within the rules fixed by the funds. A central aim of the system is to avoid direct links between the central fund and firms themselves. In the absence of such links, the central fund could not issue detailed directives to firms, thus institutionally limiting its capacity for political and economic domination. (Cohen, J., 1988, p. 22: see Unger, 1987, pp. 491–500 and 505–6)

tures could be further encouraged by the development of the non-market factors which impinge directly on the dynamics of market forces (see Reich, 1993). Such factors include the provision of public goods like education, the training of labour and market information.[10] In addition, the nurturing of 'regional' and local institutional contexts for the organization of economic activity, including the development of community-based mutual financial institutions (savings banks, local pension funds and industrial credit unions), provides a positive background for small- and medium-sized firms to develop (see Piore and Sabel, 1984; Best, 1990). Combined with effective local regulation, these firms can, individually and in combination, help generate the means of economic autonomy (see Hirst, 1993, pp. 125–30). In short, cooperation to enhance supply-side economic performance (nationally, 'regionally' and locally), commitment to policies which allow the adequate provision of public goods, and investment in human capital (alongside strategies of restraint in wage bargaining linked to investment in 'regional' and local areas) can all aid the development of the economic capacities of communities in an age in which national economic regulation and national demand management are increasingly ineffective alone. Along with the pursuit of greater political equity within companies and other forms of economic association, economies might be rebuilt or expanded neither simply from 'above' nor from 'below', but from within the framework of cosmopolitan law. Although none of this amounts, of course, to an economic policy *per se*, it does amount to the specification of certain parameters for economic activity, if the latter is to become part of the sphere of the political; that is, embedded in a framework for public deliberation and decision about the conditions of economic prosperity.

[10] The operation of corporate management in an economic environment preoccupied increasingly with short-term results and dividend performance means that governments alone can sustain the socio-economic conditions of economic prosperity. It is one of the paradoxes of modern capitalism that it depends on an institutional system, including education and long-term research, which can only survive with the aid of strong government (Evans, 1992, p. 7).

11.6 Private property, 'access avenues' and democracy

What are the implications of these arguments for the role of private property, and for the current system of corporate ownership and control? In the first instance, it is important to distinguish between different types of private property and, in particular, between productive and financial property, on the one hand, and consumption property, that is, items possessed for private use, on the other. While the principle of autonomy clearly requires the establishment of 'access avenues' to productive and financial property, it does not presuppose the pursuit of such conditions with respect to items we choose to consume in daily life, whether these are shirts, washing-machines or stereo systems. Individual consumption choices do not directly affect the conditions which determine the production and distribution of nautonomy, although they clearly help reproduce nautonomic stratification patterns once they are established.

An entitlement, as one commentator succinctly put it, 'to secure possession of the shirt on my back or the cash in my pocket' needs to be distinguished from a right to 'acquire shares in IBM and therewith the standard rights of ownership that shareholdings legally convey' (Dahl, 1985, pp. 74–5). If such a distinction is not made, it is not possible to grasp how particular systems of private property are implicated in the form and distribution of autonomy and democratic rule. A choice in favour of 'the standard rights of ownership' is a choice against political equality and a common structure of political action. If the latter are a requirement of democracy, so too is greater access to the conditions of productive resources. Without alterations in the system of private ownership and control, a necessary condition of democracy cannot be met.

But the pursuit of 'access avenues' to productive and financial property does not itself generate a simple and straightforward model of the proper form of such avenues. There are good reasons for criticizing systems of property composed exclusively of either private or state forms of ownership. As already argued, the power of private capital in the existing corporate system is a formidable obstacle to the possibility of democracy and an open, unbiased political agenda; and state forms of ownership and control face formidable objections concerning their propensity to monopolize power, misdirect resources and collapse into inefficiency (see, respectively, pp. 244–7 and 248–9). Other options, for instance cooperative forms of ownership, involving the collective possession of enterprises by work groups, are, in principle, attractive. But a thoroughly convincing case for cooperative ownership as a *generalized form of ownership* has yet to be made. Among the many questions which remain unanswered are: how exactly are the boundaries of an enterprise to be drawn? Would all existing companies have to be broken up into smaller units for cooperative ownership to be viable? How would those with interests in a company other than the workforce – for instance, the local community or providers of capital – secure a role in the key decision-making processes? How would the requirements of cooperative ownership be fully reconciled with the requirements of efficient management?

In addition, there is a plethora of programmes for the democratization of productive and financial property, from systems of 'negotiated coordination' to 'market socialism' and 'associationalism' (see, respectively, Devine, 1988; Miller, 1989; Hirst, 1993). It is unclear which, if any, of these is compatible with the programme of democratic autonomy and public deliberation, on the one hand, and sustainable in relation to international competition, changing divisions of labour and rapidly altering technologies, on the other. What the argument for democratic autonomy establishes is the necessity of extending democracy to the economy and the workplace; it sets down a direction of change, but leaves open the exact institutional model for such change to a process of public experimentation and testing.

If the suspicion is created thereby that this leaves a wholly indeterminate conclusion about the proper relationship between democracy and capitalism, it can quickly be dispelled. For criteria for the assessment of such experiments can be found in the theory of democratic autonomy and cosmopolitan democracy itself, with its emphasis on the importance of accountability to groups and interests – in this case, work-related groups and interests – significantly affected by an association or issue-area (see § 10.3). Further, the requirement on companies to uphold democratic public law means that experiments with different forms of ownership must also take account of how effective these are at delivering particular rights clusters, for instance, those of health and welfare. Or, to put the point somewhat differently, certain forms of ownership and control become relevant only in so far as they are obstacles to the entrenchment of the principle of autonomy and democratic legitimacy.[11] Moreover, in the agenda of economic democratization, these obstacles, it is worth bearing in mind, may be of secondary significance in comparison to finding ways of containing the huge, destabilizing flows of the international short-term capital markets, which can decisively restrict democratically formulated public policy (see § 6.2). Taxes on turnover in the foreign exchange markets, an increase in the amount of capital that banks are required to hold in support of their foreign exchange dealings, and the retention of capital controls as a policy option are among measures which also require urgent consideration if the wider framework of international economic transactions is to be amenable to democratic intervention at all (see Hutton, 1993, 1995). In short, the principle of autonomy requires the rigorous pursuit of a common structure of political action which is inseparable from a tough conception of distributive justice with respect to power and authority. But the aspiration to protect people's equal interest in the principle of autonomy does not translate into a straightforward conception of the proper form of ownership. While democratic autonomy and the existing distribution of resources are in marked tension, the exact form of ownership and private property must depend on experimentation within the framework of democratic autonomy and democratic public law.

The programme of bringing the economy into the 'sphere of democracy' creates new possible avenues of political participation, but it also raises a number of new risks for political life. Schumpeter rightly warned that an 'unbounded' concept of politics provides no clear-cut barrier between the polity, on the one hand, and the everyday life of citizens, on the other (1976, pp. 296–302). By making politics potentially coextensive with all realms of social and economic power, it opens these domains to public regulation and control. Schumpeter thought politics so conceived would offer an enormous temptation to those with resources, whether they be majorities or minorities, to control all aspects of life. Broad concepts of politics, he suggested, may become connected for many, in practice, to a diminution of freedom. But real though this risk is, the preference for democracy contains within itself obstacles to political hierarchy and unwarranted intrusion. It does so by the insistence that decisions be debated and taken by those who are

[11] I leave aside here the question of intellectual property rights and the protection of genetic patents.

immediately affected by them, and by the insistence that this process is compatible with respect for the rights and obligations of others. Political intervention, accordingly, finds its rationale in the pursuit and maintenance of the rule of democratic law; or, to recast the point, political issues and problems ought only to be pursued within and beyond particular associations if they deepen the entrenchment of this law. Thus, the framework for utopia is cosmopolitan democratic law – enhanced through its enactment in the agencies and organizations of economic life; through democratic deliberation and coordination of public investment priorities; through the pursuit of non-market policies to aid fair outcomes in market exchange, and through experimentation with different forms of the ownership and control of capital.

12

COSMOPOLITAN DEMOCRACY AND THE NEW INTERNATIONAL ORDER

In the contemporary world, democracy can only be fully sustained by ensuring the accountability of all related and interconnected power systems, from economics to politics. These systems involve agencies and organizations which form an element of and yet often cut across the territorial boundaries of nation-states. The possibility of democracy today must, accordingly, be linked to an expanding framework of democratic institutions and procedures – to what I have called the cosmopolitan model of democracy.

Parts I and II of this volume established that the meaning and place of democratic politics have to be rethought in relation to a series of overlapping local, regional and global processes. Three features of the latter have been emphasized: first, the way processes of economic, political, legal, military and cultural interconnectedness are changing the nature, scope and capacity of the sovereign state from above, as its 'regulatory' ability is challenged and reduced in some spheres; secondly, the way regional and global interconnectedness creates chains of interlocking political decisions and outcomes among states and their citizens, altering the nature and dynamics of national political systems themselves; and, thirdly, the way local groups, movements and nationalisms are questioning the nation-state from below as a representative and accountable power system. Democracy has to come to terms with all three of these developments and their implications for national and international power centres.

At least three distinct requirements arise: first, that the territorial boundaries of systems of accountability be recast so that those issues which escape the control of the nation-state – global financial flows, the debt burden of developing countries, environmental crises, elements of security and defence, new forms of communication and so on – can be brought under better democratic control; secondly, that the role and place of regional and global regulatory and functional agencies be rethought so that they might provide a more coherent and sharp focal point in public affairs; and thirdly, that the articulation of political institutions with the key groups, agencies, associations and organizations of the economy and civil society, national and international, be re-formed so that the latter become part of the democratic process – adopting a structure of rules and principles compatible with those of democracy.

How might this approach to democratic politics be further developed? Existing systems of geo-governance have failed to provide effective democratic mechanisms of political coordination and change. The Westphalian model, with its core commitment to the principle of effective power – that is, the principle that might eventually makes right in the international world – is at loggerheads with any requirement of sustained democratic negotiation among members of the international community. Moreover, the hierarchical structure of the states system itself has been disrupted by the emergence of the global economy, the rapid expansion of transnational relations and communications, the enormous growth of international organizations and regimes, and the development of transnational movements and actors – all of which challenge its efficacy. By contrast, the UN is a potential forum for deliberation about pressing international questions, but it has all too often been undermined as an autonomous agency (see § 4.2). Furthermore, although the post-Cold War era enhanced the possibility of a 'new international order' based on the extension of democracy across the globe and a new spirit of cooperation and peace, the enthusiasm with which this opportunity was greeted now seems far removed. The crises in Iraq, Bosnia, Somalia, Rwanda and elsewhere have brought many to the conclusion that the new world order is a new world disorder. Many UN initiatives in conflict management and resolution – initiatives which have all too often been contested, reactive and underfunded – face stagnation or defeat. The prospect is raised of an international community torn apart by the plurality of identities, of international public affairs as a quagmire of infighting among nations and groups wholly unable to settle pressing collective issues (see Archibugi and Held, 1995). Alternatively, steps could be taken towards the creation of an international democratic polity and culture. The international community is at a crossroads.

A first step in the direction of an international democratic polity, albeit a transitional step, lies within the grasp of the UN system, but would involve the latter actually living up to its Charter. Among other things, this would entail pursuing measures to implement key elements of the UN Rights Conventions, enforcing the prohibition of the discretionary right to use force, and activating the collective security system envisaged in the Charter itself (see § 4.2). In addition, if the Charter model were extended – for example, by adding the requirement of compulsory jurisdiction in the case of disputes falling under the UN rubric, or by providing means of redress in the case of human rights violations through a new international human rights court, or by making a (near) consensus vote in the General Assembly a legitimate source of international law (and recognized as such by the World Court), or by modifying the veto arrangement in the Security Council and rethinking representation on it to allow for adequate regional accountability – a basis might be established for the UN Charter system to generate political resources of its own, and to act as a politically independent decision-making centre. Thus, the UN could take a vital step towards shaking off the burden of the much-heard accusation that it operates 'double standards', functioning typically on behalf of the North and West – for instance, when it insists on military intervention to protect the sovereignty and legal autonomy of Kuwait in 1990–1 because oil and energy policy are at stake, but leaves Bosnia to disintegrate in 1993–5; or when it fails to enforce UN resolutions against Israel while downplaying the case of the Palestinians (1967–93). If the UN gained the means whereby it could begin to shake off this heritage, an important step could also be taken towards establishing and maintaining the 'rule of law' and its impartial administration in international affairs.[1]

While each move in this direction would be significant, particularly in enhancing the prospects of a global peace, it would still

[1] There is little chance of this happening while the suspicion is encouraged that the US and UN are often interchangeable. Recent remarks by President Clinton in this regard are unfortunate. Reflecting on 'the lessons of Desert Storm', he affirmed that the US would continue to play 'its unique role of leadership in the world . . . through multilateral means, such as the UN, which spread the costs and express the unified will of the international community' (*Guardian*, 1993, p. 18).

represent, at best, a movement towards a very partial or incomplete form of democracy in international life. Certainly, each state would enjoy formal equality in the UN system, and regional interests would be better represented. But it would still be possible for a plethora of different kinds of political regime to participate on an equal footing in the Charter framework; the dynamics and logic of the inter-state system would still represent an immensely powerful force in global affairs, especially with its military machinery largely intact; the massive disparities of power and asymmetries of resource in the global political economy would be left virtually unaddressed; *ad hoc* responses to pressing international and transnational issues would remain typical; there would be no forum for the pursuit of global questions directly accountable to the subjects and agencies of civil societies; transnational actors, civil associations, non-governmental organizations and social movements might still have a marginal political role; and the whole question of the wider accountability of international organizations and global bodies would remain unresolved. This governance system would remain, then, a state-centred or sovereignty-centred model of international politics, and would lie at some considerable distance from what might be called a 'thicker' democratic ordering of global affairs. Furthermore, it would lie at some distance from an adequate recognition of the transformations being wrought in the wake of globalization – transformations which are placing increasing strain on both the Westphalian and Charter conceptions of international governance.

12.1 Rethinking democracy and the international order: the cosmopolitan model

The essential characteristics of an alternative to the dominant models of geo-governance have been laid down in previous chapters, especially in chapters 7–11, and they can now be presented in summary form: see table 12.1. Table 12.1 sets out the key features of the cosmopolitan model, in a form which allows clear comparison with the Westphalian and UN models (see, respectively, pp. 77–9 and 85–7). However, its institutional components require further specification if its nature and scope are to be clarified fully.

How can cosmopolitan democratic law be maintained and

Table 12.1 The cosmopolitan model of democracy

1 The global order consists of multiple and overlapping networks of power involving the body, welfare, culture, civic associations, the economy, coercive relations and organized violence, and regulatory and legal relations. The case for cosmopolitan democracy arises from these diverse networks – the different power systems which constitute the interconnections of different peoples and nations.

2 All groups and associations are assumed to have a capacity for self-determination which can be specified by a commitment to the principle of autonomy and specific clusters of rights and obligations. These clusters cut across each network of power and are subsumed under the following categories: health, social, cultural, civic, economic, pacific and political. Together, they form the basis of an empowering legal order – a cosmopolitan democratic law.

3 Legal principles are adopted which delimit the form and scope of individual and collective action within the organizations and associations of state, economy and civil society. Certain standards are specified for the treatment of all, which no political regime or association can legitimately violate.

4 Law-making and law enforcement can be developed within this framework at a variety of locations and levels, along with an expansion of the influence of regional and international courts to monitor and check political and social authority.

5 The defence of self-determination, the creation of a common structure of political action and the preservation of the democratic good are the overall collective priorities; the commitment to democratic autonomy creates both an agenda of long-term change and a programme of urgent priorities, focused on transforming the conditions of those whose circumstances fall radically short of equal membership in the public realm.

6 Determinate principles of social justice follow: the *modus operandi* of the production, distribution and the exploitation of resources must be conducive to, and compatible with, the democratic process and a common structure of political action.

7 The principle of non-coercive relations governs the settlement of disputes, though the use of force must remain a collective option of last resort in the face of clear attacks to eradicate cosmopolitan democratic law. Cosmopolitan democracy might justify the deployment of force, after all other forms of negotiation and sanction have been exhausted, in the context of a threat to international democracy and a denial of democratic rights and obligations by

TABLE 12.1—*continued*

tyrannical regimes, or by circumstances which spiral beyond the control of particular peoples and agents (such as the disintegration of a state).

8 People can enjoy membership in the diverse communities which significantly affect them and, accordingly, access to a variety of forms of political participation. Citizenship would be extended, in principle, to membership in all cross-cutting political communities, from the local to the global.

upheld? Who can guard this law? On the face of it, only the participants in a democratic political system can be its 'guardians', for only they can judge whether the terms of democratic public law have been systematically flouted and assess what the institutional consequences and risks of this might be. But participants act in institutional milieux and the nature of these is, of course, of the utmost significance in the determination of political processes and outcomes. Several institutional clusters are of particular importance to help nurture and protect cosmopolitan law. These can be thought of as the necessary minimum components of an institutional solution to the problems of democracy in the global order.

In the first instance, the cosmopolitan model of democracy would seek the entrenchment of cosmopolitan democratic law in order to provide shape and limits to political decision-making. This requires that it be enshrined within the constitutions of parliaments and assemblies at the national and international level; and that the influence of international courts is extended so that groups and individuals have an effective means of suing political authorities for the enactment and enforcement of key rights and obligations, both within and beyond political associations. Democratic law, thus, creates the constitutive basis of modes of interaction and dispute settlement; its entrenchment could not be envisaged without the requirement of compulsory jurisdiction in the case of disputes falling under its rubric, and without providing means of redress in the case of rights violations (cf. Kelsen, 1944; Ferrajoli and Senese, 1992).

Hand in hand with these developments the cosmopolitan model would seek the creation of an effective transnational legislative and executive, at regional and global levels, bound by and operating within the terms of the basic democratic law. This would involve the creation of regional parliaments (for example, in Latin America and Africa) and the enhancement of the role of such bodies where they already exist (the European Parliament) in order that their decisions become recognized, in principle, as legitimate independent sources of regional and international regulation. Alongside the establishment of these bodies, the model anticipates the possibility of general referenda cutting across nations and nation-states in the case of contested priorities concerning the implementation of democratic law and the balance of public expenditure, with constituencies defined according to the nature and scope of disputed problems. In addition, the opening of international governmental organizations to public scrutiny and the democratization of international 'functional' bodies (on the basis perhaps of the creation of elected supervisory boards which are in part statistically representative of their constituencies) would be significant. Extensive use of referenda, and the establishment of the democratic accountability of international organizations, would involve citizens in issues which profoundly affect them but which – in the context of the current lacunae and fragmentation of international organizations – seem remote. These mechanisms would help contribute, thereby, to the preservation of the ideal of a rightful share in the process of governance, even in contexts where dispute settlement and problem resolution would inevitably be at some considerable distance from local groups and assemblies.

But the full implementation of cosmopolitan democracy would also require the formation of an authoritative assembly of all democratic states and agencies – a reformed General Assembly of the United Nations, or a complement to it. The UN, as previously noted, is an inter-state organization with all the strengths and limits that this implies. While to a degree effective as an agency to organize and further the aims and interests of governments and states, particularly those of the most powerful countries, it cannot, almost by definition, be an effective institutional framework to represent the peoples and movements of the world, many of whom require protection from their states and governments. The establishment of an independent assembly of democratic peoples, directly elected by them and accountable to them, is an unavoidable institutional requirement. To begin with at least, such an assembly is unlikely to be an assembly of all nations; for it would be an assembly of democratic nations, which would, in principle, draw in others over time. Accordingly, the new assembly in its early stages can best be thought of as a complement to the UN, which it would either replace in the long term or accept in a modified form as a 'second chamber' – a necessary meeting place for all states irrespective of the nature of their regimes.

Agreement on the terms of reference of an international democratic assembly would be difficult, to say the least. Among the difficulties to be faced would be the rules determining the assembly's representative base (cf. McLean, 1991, pp. 190–6; Burnheim, 1985, pp. 82–124). One nation, one vote? Representatives allocated according to population size? Would major international functional organizations be represented?[2] But if its operating rules could be agreed – preferably, in an international constitutional convention involving states, IGOs, INGOs, citizen groups and social movements – the new assembly could become an authoritative international centre for the examination of those pressing global problems which are at the heart of the very possibility of the implementation of cosmopolitan democratic law – for instance, health and disease, food supply and distribution, the debt burden of the 'Third World', the instability of the hundreds of billions of dollars that circulate the globe daily, global warming, and the reduction of the risks of nuclear and chemical warfare.

Of course, the idea of a new democratic international assembly is open to a battery of objections commonly put to similar schemes (see Archibugi, 1993, 1995). Would it have any teeth to implement decisions? How would cosmopolitan democratic law be enforced? Would there be a centralized police and military force? While these concerns are significant, many of them can be met and countered. For example, it needs to be stressed that any global legislative institution should be conceived above all as a 'framework-setting' institution. Although a distinction ought to be made between legal instruments concerned with the core issues of cosmopolitan democratic law which would have the status of law independently of any further negotiation on the part of a region or state or local government and instruments which would require further discussion with them, the implementation of a broad range of

[2] For an elaborate proposal for a 'Second Assembly' – an Assembly of Peoples – with significant support among many international non-governmental organizations, see Segall 1990, 1991. Segall's proposal includes an electoral system which is similar to that of the European Parliament, with representatives allocated in proportion to population size and safeguards for the populations of the smallest countries.

recommendations would be a matter for non-global levels of governance.[3]

International agreements about rules or resources often have significant normative implications, establishing a political 'marker' for a future change in institutions or customary practice; but without the means of implementation, they are, as one recent survey of such agreements put it, of 'little value, since they either are not legally binding or lack timetables and cash commitments' (Wallace, W. et al., 1992, p. 22).[4] Clearly, different types of legal arrangement require different forms of enactment and enforcement. This is true even in the case of cosmopolitan democratic law itself. The clusters of rights and obligations it embraces are not all realizable by the same means and by the same timetable. While the seven clusters are constitutive of the possibility of a common structure of political action, the distinction between ideal, attainable and urgent levels of autonomy is the interpretative grid that has to be borne in mind if the agenda for democracy is to be clearly framed and practical (see § 9.3). Thus, while the cosmopolitan democratic legal framework sets down an axial principle of public policy, some of its components will not be enforceable at attainable (let alone ideal) levels in the short term, even in some of the wealthiest countries. Health, social and welfare rights, for instance, require substantial financial resources to implement them, and these may not always be available if the targets for attainment are what is considered 'best practice' in comparative perspective.

However, if democratic rights and obligations are recognized as integral to the protection of people's equal interest in the principle of autonomy and treated as something other than open-ended commitments, then the international community will have to move to make them legally binding. Accordingly, they will have to be divided into those rights which can be made binding and which define cases of urgent need, entailing immediate responsibilities for action by particular national groups as well as by the inter-

[3] European Union law embodies a range of relevant distinctions among legal instruments and types of implementation which are helpful to reflect on in this context (see Hartley, 1988; Pinder, 1992, chs 1–2).

[4] The recent agreements at the Earth Summit – the treaties on biodiversity and on climate change, the set of principles for sustainable forestry, the agreement on the need for a future international convention on desertification, and 'Agenda 21', the guide for environmentally sustainable development – are troubling cases in point.

national community; those rights which can be made binding in principle because they represent attainable targets but from which certain zones, including 'zones of development', will be exempted for a negotiated period; and those rights which represent ideal orientations – statements of guiding intent which create an order of priorities but which are unenforceable in the short term (see §§ 9.3 and 11.4; cf. Wallace, W. et al., 1992). The democratic good is the frame of reference for the making of public policy, but the dialectic between the ideal and real, ideal and attainable and ideal and pressing autonomy will continue to determine degrees of contingent outcome, which will always be the stuff of everyday, practical democratic politics at diverse levels.

Considerations of law enforcement in an international context inevitably raise questions about the role of coercive power at regional and global levels. Although these are highly complex practical matters, they are not beyond resolution in principle; a proportion of a nation-state's military (perhaps a growing proportion over time) could be 'seconded' to the new international authorities and, once moulded into coherent units, placed at their disposal on a routine basis (cf. Grove, 1993). Or, preferably, these authorities could increase enforcement capabilities by creating a permanent independent force recruited directly from among individuals who volunteer from all countries (see Johansen, 1993b, p. 477). To this end, avenues could be established to meet the concern that 'covenants, without the sword, are but words' (Hobbes).

It is tempting to conceive of new international democratic organizations as potentially self-regulating and not requiring the backing of any form of coercive power (see Archibugi, 1995). But this is mistaken and dangerously over optimistic (see Shaw, 1991). It is mistaken because unless there is a general check on the right of states to go to war, the cosmopolitan model of democracy cannot be adequately secured: it would continue to be thwarted by the logic of state conflict and violence, as the UN is today. The durability of the existing war system is related to the reluctance of states to submit their disputes with other states to arbitration by a 'supreme authority'. Unless this reluctance is challenged, the cosmopolitan model is likely to be stillborn. In addition, it is dangerously over optimistic to conceive the cosmopolitan model without coercive powers, because tyrannical attacks against democratic law cannot be ruled out. One of the abiding lessons of the twentieth century must surely be that history is not closed and that human progress remains an extraordinarily fragile achievement. After all, fascism, Nazism and Stalinism came close to obliterating democracy in the West only fifty years ago. Without the means of law enforcement, the institutional framework for a new democratic international order cannot be properly conceived.

On the other hand, only to the extent that the new forms of military arrangement are locked into an international democratic framework would there be good grounds for thinking that a new settlement could be created between coercive power and accountability. If such a settlement sounds like a 'pipe dream', it should be emphasized that it is a 'pipe dream' to imagine that one can advocate democracy today without engaging with the range of issues elaborated here. If the new, emerging global order is to be democratic, these issues have to be confronted even if their details are open to further discussion.

The achievement of autonomy cannot be conceived as simply based, as it is in the doctrines of liberal thinkers such as Nozick and Hayek, on a set of checks and balances upon coercive power, which has its anchor in the right to private property and the resources citizens can accumulate to pursue their projects independently of the polity. Nor can it be conceived as based on the highly tenuous hope, maintained by many Marxists, that such checks and balances are unnecessary – on the assumption, in other words, of an ultimate 'harmony of interests' achieved at 'the end of politics', which apparently makes all forms of coercive political power redundant. Rather, the achievement of autonomy, as argued in chapters 10 and 11, must be conceived as based on the *multiple lodging* of the rights and obligations of democratic law in the organizational charters of the agencies and associations which make up the spheres of politics, economics and civil society. The liberal principle that a system of countervailing power is an essential component of any open and accountable political order must be affirmed while being recast and rearticulated.

Thus, an expanding democratic network of states and societies is incompatible with the existence of powerful social relations and economic organizations which can, by virtue of the very bases of their operations, systematically distort democratic conditions and processes. At issue are, among other things, the curtailment of the power of corporations to constrain and influence the *political* agenda (through the diverse measures suggested in chapter 11), and the restriction of the activities of powerful interest groups to pursue their goals unchecked (through, for example, the regulation of bargaining procedures to minimize the use of 'coercive tactics' within and between public and private associations). If individuals and peoples are to be free and equal in the determination of the conditions of their own existence, there must be an array of spheres, from privately and cooperatively owned firms to independent communications media and autonomously run cultural centres, which allow their members control of the resources at their disposal without direct interference from political agencies or other third parties. A cosmopolitan democracy must always be an ensemble of organizations, associations and agencies pursuing their own projects, whether these be economic, social or cultural; but these projects must always also be subject to the constraints of democratic processes and a common structure of political action.

12.2 Cosmopolitan objectives: short- and long-term

The cosmopolitan model of democracy presents a programme of possible transformations with short- and long-term political implications. It does not present an all-or-nothing choice, but rather lays down a direction of possible change with clear points of orientation. See table 12.2.

If the history and practice of democracy have been centred until now on the idea of locality and place – the city-state, the community, the nation – is it likely that in the future it will be centred exclusively on the international or global domain, if it is to be centred anywhere at all? To draw this conclusion is to misunderstand the nature of contemporary globalization and the arguments being presented here. Globalization is, to borrow a phrase, 'a dialectical process'; local transformation is as much an element of globalization as the lateral extension of social relations across space and time (Giddens, 1990, p. 64). New demands are unleashed for regional and local autonomy as groups find themselves buffeted by global forces and by inappropriate or ineffective political regimes (see §§ 4.3 and 6.1). While these circumstances are clearly fraught with danger, and the risk of an intensification of a sectarian politics, they also present a new possibility: the recovery of an intensive and participatory democracy at local levels as a complement to the deliberative and representative assemblies of the wider global order (see § 10.3). That is, they contain the possibility of a

TABLE 12.2 Objectives of the cosmopolitan model of democracy: illustrative issues

Short-term	*Long-term*
	Polity/governance
1 Reform of UN Security Council (to give developing countries a significant voice and effective decision-making capacity)	1 Entrenchment of cosmopolitan democratic law: new Charter of Rights and Obligations locked into different domains of political, social and economic power
2 Creation of a UN second chamber (following an international constitutional convention)	2 Global parliament (with limited revenue-raising capacity) connected to regions, nations and localities. Creation of a public issue Boundary Court
3 Enhanced political regionalization (EU and beyond) and the use of transnational referenda	3 Separation of political and economic interests; public funding of deliberative assemblies and electoral processes
4 Compulsory jurisdiction before the International Court. Creation of a new, international Human Rights Court	4 Interconnected global legal system, embracing elements of criminal and civil law. Establishment of an international Criminal Court
5 Foundation of a new coordinating economic agency at regional and global levels	5 Establishment of the accountability of international and transnational economic agencies to parliaments and assemblies at regional and global levels
6 Establishment of an effective, accountable, international, military force	6 Permanent shift of a growing proportion of a nation-state's coercive capability to regional and global institutions, with the ultimate aim of demilitarization and the transcendence of the war system

TABLE 12.2—*continued*

Economy/civil society	
1 Enhancement of non-state, non-market solutions in the organization of civil society	1 Creation of a diversity of self-regulating associations and groups in civil society
2 Systematic experimentation with different democratic organizational forms in the economy	2 Multisectoral economy and pluralization of patterns of ownership and possession
3 Introduction of strict limits to private ownership of key 'public-shaping' institutions: media, information, and so on	3 Social framework investment priorities set through public deliberation and government decision, but extensive market regulation of goods and labour remain
4 Provision of resources to those in the most vulnerable social positions to defend and articulate their interests	4 Guaranteed basic income for all adults, irrespective of whether they are engaged in market or household activities

political order of democratic associations, workplaces and cities as well as of nations, regions and global networks.[5]

[5] It is possible to conceive of different types of democracy as forming a continuum from the local to the global, with the local marked by direct and participatory processes while larger areas with significant populations are progressively mediated by representative mechanisms. The possibilities for direct participatory democracy in communities and workplaces are clearly extensive compared to those which exist in highly differentiated social, economic and political circumstances (see Held, 1987, chs 8 and 9; see also Beetham, 1993b; Phillips, 1993). However, the simple juxtaposition of participatory with representative democracy is now in flux given developments in information technology, which put simultaneous two-way communication within reach of larger populations. The merits of direct participatory democracy have to be re-examined now its technical feasibility is closer at hand. As Budge has recently argued, it is unacceptable to dismiss all types of direct democracy as if they could be realized only through 'unmediated popular voting on a take it or leave it basis'; for direct democracy can take several different institutional forms, just as liberal representative democracy does (1993, pp. 136–49). While

To lay out the objectives of a cosmopolitan model of democracy is not to claim that they can all be immediately realized – of course not! But who imagined the peaceful unification of Germany just a few years ago? Who anticipated the fall of the Berlin Wall and the retreat of communism across Central and Eastern Europe? The political space for a cosmopolitan model of democracy has to be made – and is being made by the numerous transnational movements, agencies and institutional initiatives pursuing greater co-ordination and accountability of those forces which determine the use of the globe's resources, and which set the rules governing transnational public life (see Commission on Global Governance, 1995). Those seeking to advance greater equity throughout the world's regions, peaceful dispute settlement and demilitarization, the protection of human rights and fundamental freedoms, sustainability across generations, the mutual acknowledgement of cultures, the reciprocal recognition of political and religious identities, and political stability across political institutions are all laying down elements essential to a cosmopolitan democratic community (cf. Reich, 1993, pp. 309–15). Further, it is not inconceivable that additional space for cosmopolitan democracy will be made in the wake of, for instance, a severe crisis of the global financial system, or of the environment, or of war. Political change can take place at an extraordinary speed, itself no doubt partially a result of the process of globalization.

Of course, it could be objected that the meaning of some of the core concepts of the international system are subject to deep conflicts of interpretation; and that globalization in the domains of communication and information, far from creating a sense of common purpose, has arguably served to reinforce the significance

---

some of these forms are open to serious reservations, it is possible to conceive, for instance, a type of party-based direct democracy in which the electorate would be able, in the first instance, to choose among competing parties for office and, in the second, to act like a parliamentary assembly – voting directly and regularly on proposed legislation set out and advocated by the party in office. The stability of such a political system would require a complex set of rules and procedures to be in place, but these are not in principle difficult to specify (see Budge, 1993, pp. 136–55). In practice, of course, a great many issues remain unresolved and, at the time of writing, they are clearly open to extensive debate. (For a range of views on this matter, see Held, 1993c, pt 2; Fishkin, 1991.)

of identity and difference in some regions, stimulating further, as noted earlier, the 'ethnicization' and 'nationalization' of politics (see §§ 4.3 and 6.1). Hence, the political and cultural obstacles to the realization of a cosmopolitan community remain formidable. But while few could seriously doubt the nature of these obstacles, their meaning should not be overstated either.

In the first instance, scepticism and dissent about the value of ideas such as rights is often related to the experience of Western hegemony. Political and civil rights discourse is frequently rejected along with the rejection of Western dominance, especially in those countries which have been deeply affected by the reach of Western empires. There are many understandable reasons for this. Understandable as they are, however, these reasons are insufficient to provide a well-justified critique: it is a mistake to throw out the language of self-determination and autonomy because of its contingent association with historical configurations of Western power. A distinction must be made between those discourses of rights and autonomy which obscure or underpin particular interests and power systems and those which seek explicitly to test the generalizability of interests and to render power, whether it be political, economic or cultural, accountable.

Moreover, a cosmopolitan democratic community does not require political and cultural integration in the form of a consensus on a wide range of beliefs, values and norms. For part of the attraction of democracy lies in its emphasis on the primacy of those political preferences generated by people themselves and on the public settlement of differences. Democracy has an appeal as the 'grand' or 'meta-political' narrative in the contemporary world because it offers a legitimate way of framing and delimiting the competing 'narratives' of the good. It is particularly important because it holds out the prospect of the constitution of the political good as the democratic good – the pursuit of the 'good life' defined under free and equal conditions of participation. Thus, the resolution of value conflicts becomes a matter of participating in public deliberation and negotiation, subject, of course, to provisions protecting the shape and form of these processes themselves. However, what is clearly also required is a 'commitment' to democracy, for without this there can be no sustained public deliberation, democracy cannot function as a decision-making mechanism, and divergent political aspirations and identities are unlikely to reach an accommodation.

Distinctive national, ethnic, cultural and social identities are part of the very basis of people's sense of being-in-the-world; they provide deeply rooted comfort and distinctive social locations for communities seeking a place 'at home' on this earth. But these identities are always only one possible identity, among others. They are historically and geographically contingent; for each individual, a different birthplace or social location could have produced a different national or cultural identity. Accordingly, for a plurality of identities to persist and to be sustained over time, each has to recognize the other as a legitimate presence with which some accommodation must be made; and each must be willing to give up exclusive claims upon the right, the good, the universal and the spatial. Without a politics of coercion or hegemony, the only basis for nurturing and protecting cultural pluralism and a diversity of identities is through the implementation of cosmopolitan democratic law: the constructive basis for a plurality of identities to flourish within a structure of mutual toleration, development and accountability. A commitment to this structure is a commitment to a form of life which each person could find equally good grounds to honour.

12.3 Concluding reflections

Would a cosmopolitan model of democracy have the organizational resources – procedural, legal, institutional and military – to alter the dynamics of resource production and distribution, and of rule creation and enforcement, in the contemporary era? It would be deeply misleading to suggest that it would initially have these capabilities. Nevertheless, the commitment to the extension and deepening of mechanisms of democratic accountability across major regions and international structures would help to regulate the forces which are already beyond the reach of national democratic mechanisms and movements. And the commitment to the protection and strengthening of democratic rights, and to the further development of a regional and international court system, would aid the process whereby individuals and groups could sue their governments for the enactment of key rights and political opportunities.

In addition, the establishment of regional authorities as major independent voices in world politics might contribute further to the erosion of the geopolitical divisions which dominated the world from 1945 to 1989. Likewise, the new institutional focus at the global level on major transnational issues would go some way towards eradicating sectarian approaches to these questions, and to countering some of the major asymmetries in life-chances and participative opportunities. Finally, new sets of regional and global rules and procedures might help lift public affairs out of the quagmire of infighting among nation-states unable to settle pressing collective issues. Of course, there would be new possible dangers – no political initiative is free from such risks. But what would be at issue would be the beginning of the creation of a new transnational democratic order – set off from the partisan claims of nations and nation-states.

To avoid some possible misunderstandings, it might be useful to emphasize the terrain occupied by the arguments offered here and the ground they reject. This can be done by assessing critically a number of conceptual polarities frequently found in political discourse: globalization versus cultural diversity; constitutionalism versus politics; the hierarchical ordering of states versus the durability of reform; political ambition versus political feasibility; participatory or direct democracy versus liberal representative democracy; and global governance from above versus the extension of grass-roots associations from below. Although these polarities provide much of the tension which charges the debate about the possibility of democracy beyond borders, there are good reasons for doubting their coherence.

To begin with, globalization and cultural diversity are not simply opposites. For global interconnectedness is already forming a dense web of relations linking cultures one to another. The issue is how and in what way cultures are linked and interrelated, through mutual accommodation, opposition or resistance, for example, not how a sealed cultural diversity can persist in the face of globalization.

Secondly, the juxtaposition of constitutionalism – or the elaboration of theoretical models of principles of political organization – with politics as a practical activity sets up another false polarity. Politics typically operates within a framework – albeit a shifting framework – of rules. Politics is rarely without some pattern, and is most often about the nature of the rules which will shape and delimit political activity. For politics is at root about the ways in which rules and resources are distributed, produced and legitimated. The question is whether politics will be shaped by an explicit, formal constitution or model which might, in principle, be open and contestable, or whether politics will be subject to an unwritten constitution, which is altogether more difficult to invoke as a defence in the face of unaccountable systems of power.

Thirdly, it is frequently argued that if the hierarchy of states is insufficiently acknowledged, then any reform of the global system of governance will, at best, be temporary (as happened in the case of the League of Nations). That is to say, if the hierarchy of state power is not built into political reforms, all such reforms will fail to survive beyond a short period. The problem with this point, thus put, is that the system of nation-states, while it, of course, persists, is already articulated with complex economic, organizational, military, legal and cultural processes and structures which limit and erode its power. And if these processes and structures are not acknowledged and brought into the political process themselves, they will tend to bypass or circumvent the states system. If the efficacy of democratic reform is at stake, the issue is how, not whether, these power systems can be brought into the democratic sphere.

Fourthly, the question of political feasibility cannot simply be set up in opposition to the question of political ambition. For what is ambitious today might be feasible tomorrow. Few, if any, political commentators foresaw the collapse of the Soviet Union and the many remarkable changes which followed in the main peacefully in 1989 and 1990. The growing interconnectedness between states and societies is generating consequences, intended and unintended, for the stability of regimes, governments and states. While the question of political feasibility is of the utmost significance, it would be naive to juxtapose it simply with programmes of political ambition.

Fifthly, versions of participatory democracy cannot simply be opposed to liberal representative democracy. Programmes of participatory or direct democracy are fraught with complexities and questions. Likewise, liberal representative democracy does not simply mean one set of possible institutions or forms. The nature of liberal democracy is itself an intensely contested issue. So while there seem to be good grounds for accepting the liberal distinction between state and civil society, there are not equally good grounds for uncritically accepting either of these in their traditional liberal cast. The juxtaposition of participation with liberal representative democracy leaves most of political analysis to one side.

Sixthly, the problems of global governance from above cannot be solved through the extension of grass-roots democracy alone. For the questions have to be posed: which grass-roots, and which democracy? There are many social movements – for instance, right-wing nationalist movements or the eugenics movement – which highlight how the very nature of a grass-roots movement can be contested and fought over. Grass-roots movements are by no means merely noble or wise (cf. §§ 2.2 and 7.2). Like most social, economic or political forms, they can appear in a variety of shapes, with a variety of patterns of internal organization. An appeal to the nature or inherent goodness of grass-roots associations and movements bypasses the necessary work of theoretical analysis.

Today, any attempt to set out a position of what could be called 'embedded utopianism' must begin both from where we are – the existing pattern of political relations and processes – and from an analysis of what might be: desirable political forms and principles (cf. Falk, 1991a, pp. 8–10). If utopia is to be embedded, it must be linked into patterns and movements as they are. But if this context of embeddedness is not simply to be affirmed in the shapes and patterns generated by past groups and movements, it has to be assessed according to standards, criteria and principles. These, it has been argued, follow from a theory of cosmopolitan democracy which places at its centre the principle of autonomy. To argue for this theory is to locate the political theorist as advocate, seeking to advance an interpretation of politics against countervailing positions. While advocacy is without guarantees, the very indeterminacy of this state of affairs creates the possibility of a new political understanding.

ACKNOWLEDGEMENTS

Some sections of this book have been adapted from previously published essays. While the content of each of these essays has been substantially modified and developed for the purposes of this volume, the details of the original publications are as follows:

'Democracy: From City-States to a Cosmopolitan Order?' In D. Held (ed.), *Prospects for Democracy: North, South, East, West*. Cambridge: Polity Press, 1993, pp. 13–52. An adapted version of sections of this essay forms parts of chapters 1 and 4.

'The Development of the Modern State'. In S. Hall and B. Gieben (eds), *Formations of Modernity*. Cambridge: Polity Press, 1992, pp. 71–119. Parts of this essay informed chapters 2 and 3.

'Democracy, the Nation-state and the Global Order'. In D. Held (ed.), *Political Theory Today*. Cambridge: Polity Press, 1991, pp. 197–235. Sections of this essay form parts of chapters 5 and 6.

References and Select Bibliography

Abu-Lughod, J. 1989: *Before European Hegemony.* Oxford: Oxford University Press.

Adamson, W. L. 1990: Economic democracy and the expediency of worker participation. *Political Studies*, 38.

Addison, J. T. and Siebert, W. S. 1993: *Social Engineering in the European Community.* London: Institute of Economic Affairs.

Allen, J. 1992: Post-industrialism and post-Fordism. In S. Hall, D. Held and T. McGrew (eds), *Modernity and its Futures*. Cambridge: Polity Press.

Almond, A. and Verba, S. 1963: *The Civic Culture: Political Attitudes and Democracy in Five Nations*. Princeton, N.J.: Princeton University Press.

Almond, A. and Verba, S. 1980: *The Civic Culture Revisited*. Boston: Little, Brown.

Amin, S. 1972: *Accumulation on a World Scale*. New York: Monthly Review Press.

Amin, S. 1990: *Delinking*. London: Zed Press.

Anderson, B. 1983: *Imagined Communities*. London: Verso.

Anderson, P. 1974a: *Passages from Antiquity to Feudalism*. London: New Left Books.

Anderson, P. 1974b: *Lineages of the Absolutist State*. London: New Left Books.

Andreski, S. 1968: *Military Organization and Society.* Berkeley, Calif.: University of California Press.

Archibugi, D. 1992: Models of international organization in perpetual peace projects. *Review of International Studies*, 18.

Archibugi, D. 1993: The reform of the UN and cosmopolitan democracy. *Journal of Peace Research*, 30, 2.

Archibugi, D. 1995: From the United Nations to cosmopolitan democracy. In D. Archibugi and D. Held (eds), *Cosmopolitan Democracy: An Agenda for a New World Order*. Cambridge: Polity Press.

Archibugi, D. and Held, D. (eds) 1995: *Cosmopolitan Democracy: An Agenda for a New World Order*. Cambridge: Polity Press.

Archibugi, D. and Michie, J., 1995: Myths and realities of the globalisation of technology: a re-examination of the evidence. *Cambridge Journal of Economics*, 19, 1.

Arendt, H. 1961: The crisis in culture. In *Between Past and Future: Six Exercises in Political Thought*. New York: Meridian.

Arendt, H. 1963: *On Revolution*. New York: Viking Press.

Aristotle 1981: *The Politics*. Harmondsworth: Penguin.

Aron, R. 1966: *Peace and War: A Theory of International Relations*. New York: Doubleday.

Ashford, D. 1986: *The Emergence of the Welfare State*. Oxford: Blackwell.

Babai, D. 1993a: International Monetary Fund. In J. Krieger (ed.), *The Oxford Companion to Politics of the World*. Oxford: Oxford University Press.

Babai, D. 1993b: World Bank. In J. Krieger (ed.), *The Oxford Companion to Politics of the World*. Oxford: Oxford University Press.

Bachrach, P. and Baratz, M. S. 1962: The two faces of power. *American Political Science Review*, 56, 4.

Baldwin, T. 1992: The territorial state. In H. Gross and T. R. Harrison (eds), *Jurisprudence: Cambridge Essays*. Oxford: Clarendon Press.

Balls, E. 1994: Looking beyond the flexibility rhetoric. *Guardian*, 6 June.

Barber, B. 1984: *Strong Democracy*. Berkeley, Calif.: University of California Press.

Barry, B. 1989: *Theories of Justice*. London: Harvester Wheatsheaf.

Beetham, D. 1981: Beyond liberal democracy. *Socialist Register 1981*. London: Merlin Press.

Beetham, D. 1984: The future of the nation-state. In G. McLennan, D. Held and S. Hall (eds), *The Idea of the Modern State*. Milton Keynes: Open University Press.

Beetham, D. 1985: *Max Weber and the Theory of Modern Politics*. Cambridge: Polity Press.

Beetham, D. 1993a: The democratic audit of the UK: key principles and indices of democracy. London: Charter 88 Trust.

Beetham, D. 1993b: Liberal democracy and the limits of democratization. In D. Held (ed.), *Prospects for Democracy: North, South, East, West*. Cambridge: Polity Press.

Beitz, C. 1979: *Political Theory and International Relations*. Princeton N.J.: Princeton University Press.

Beitz, C. 1991: Sovereignty and morality in international affairs. In D. Held (ed.), *Political Theory Today*. Cambridge: Polity Press.

Bellamy, R. 1993: Citizenship and rights. In R. Bellamy (ed.), *Theories and Concepts of Political Analysis: An Introduction.* Manchester: Manchester University Press.

Benhabib, S. 1992: *Situating the Self: Gender, Community and Postmodernism in Contemporary Ethics.* Cambridge: Polity Press.

Benhabib, S. 1994: Deliberative rationality and models of democratic legitimacy. *Constellations*, 1, 1.

Benn, S. I. 1967: Sovereignty. In *The Encyclopaedia of Philosophy.* New York: Macmillan.

Benn, S. I. 1995: The uses of sovereignty. *Political Studies*, 3, 2.

Benn, S. I. and Peters, R. S. 1959: *Social Principles and the Democratic State.* London: Allen & Unwin.

Bentham, J. 1838–43: *The Works of Jeremy Bentham*, 11 vols, ed. Jeremy Bowring. Edinburgh: W. Tait.

Bentham, J. 1838: *Principles of the Civil Code.* In *The Works of Jeremy Bentham*, vol. I, ed. Jeremy Bowring. Edinburgh: W. Tait.

Bentham, J. 1843: *Constitutional Code*, Book I. In *The Works of Jeremy Bentham*, vol. IX, ed. Jeremy Bowring. Edinburgh: W. Tait.

Bentham, J. 1960: *Fragment on Government*, ed. W. Harrison. Oxford: Blackwell.

Berlin, I. 1969: *Four Essays on Liberty.* Oxford: Oxford University Press.

Bernal, M. 1987: *Black Athena*, vol. 1. London: Free Association Books.

Best, M. 1990: *The New Competition.* Cambridge: Polity Press.

Black, A. 1992: *Political Thought in Europe 1250–1450.* Cambridge: Cambridge University Press.

Black, J. 1991: *A Military Revolution? Military Change and European Society 1550–1800.* London: Macmillan.

Blumenthal, W. M. 1987/8: The world economy and technological change. *Foreign Affairs*, 66, 3.

Bobbio, N. 1985: *Stato, Governo, Società: Per Una Teoria Generale della Politica.* Turin: Einaudi.

Bobbio, N. 1987: *Which Socialism?* Cambridge: Polity Press.

Bobbio, N. 1989: *Democracy and Dictatorship.* Cambridge: Polity Press.

Boden, D. 1992: Reinventing the global village. In A. Giddens (ed.), *Human Societies.* Cambridge; Polity Press.

Bodin, J. 1967: *Six Books of a Commonwealth*, trans. and ed. M. J. Tooley. Oxford: Blackwell.

Bozeman, A. B. 1984: The international order in a multicultural world. In H. Bull and A. Watson (eds), *The Expansion of International Society.* Oxford: Oxford University Press.

Bradley, H. 1992: Changing social divisions: class, gender and race. In R. Bocock and K. Thompson (eds), *Social and Cultural Forms of Modernity.* Cambridge: Polity Press.

Braudel, F. 1973: *Capitalism and Material Life*. London: Weidenfeld & Nicolson.

Brenner, R. 1977: The origins of capitalist development: a critique of neo-Smithian Marxism. *New Left Review*, 105.

Breuilly, J. 1982: *Nationalism and the State*. Manchester: Manchester University Press.

Brewer, A. 1982: *Marxist Theories of Imperialism*. London: Routledge.

Brittan, S. 1977: Can democracy manage an economy? In R. Skidelsky (ed.), *The End of the Keynesian Era*. Oxford: Martin Robertson.

Bromley, S. 1991: *American Hegemony and World Oil*. Cambridge: Polity Press.

Bromley, S. 1993: The prospects for democracy in the Middle East. In D. Held (ed.), *Prospects for Democracy: North, South, East, West*. Cambridge: Polity Press.

Brown S. 1988: *New Forces, Old Forces and the Future of World Politics*. Boston: Scott/Foreman.

Budge, I. 1993: Direct democracy: setting appropriate terms of debate. In D. Held (ed.), *Prospects for Democracy: North, South, East, West*. Cambridge: Polity Press.

Bull, H. 1977: *The Anarchical Society*. London: Macmillan.

Burnheim, J. 1985: *Is Democracy Possible?* Cambridge: Polity Press.

Burnheim, J. 1986: Democracy, the nation state and the world system. In D. Held and C. Pollitt (eds), *New Forms of Democracy*. London: Sage.

Buzan, B. 1991: *People, States and Fear*. Brighton: Harvester Press.

Buzan, B., Jones, C. and Little, R. 1993: *The Logic of Anarchy*. New York: Columbia University Press.

Callières, F. de 1963: *On the Manner of Negotiating with Princes*, trans. A. F. Whyte. Notre Dame: University of Notre Dame Press.

Callinicos, A. 1990: *Against Postmodernism*. Cambridge: Polity Press.

Callinicos, A. 1991: *The Revenge of History: Marxism and the East European Revolutions*. Cambridge: Polity Press.

Callinicos, A. 1993: Liberalism, marxism, and democracy: a response to David Held. *Theory and Society*, 22.

Campbell, D. 1984: *The Unsinkable Aircraft Carrier: American Military Power in Britain*. London: Michael Joseph.

Cantori, L. J. and Spiegel, S. 1970: *The International Politics of Regions: A Comparative Approach*. Englewood Cliffs, N.J.: Prentice Hall.

Capotorti, F. 1983: Human rights: the hard road towards universality. In R. St J. Macdonald and D. M. Johnson (eds), *The Structure and Process of International Law*. The Hague: Martinus Nijhoff.

Carr, E. H. 1946: *The Twenty Years Crisis 1919–1939*. London: Macmillan.

Cassese, A. 1986: *International Law in a Divided World*. Oxford: Clarendon Press.

Cassese, A. 1988: *Violence and Law in the Modern Age*. Cambridge: Polity Press.

Cassese, A. 1991: Violence, war and the rule of law in the international community. In D. Held (ed.), *Political Theory Today*. Cambridge: Polity Press.

Childers, E. 1993: *In a Time Beyond Warnings*. London: CIIR.

Clark, I. 1989: *The Hierarchy of States: Reform and Resistance in the International Order*. Cambridge: Cambridge University Press.

Coates, D. 1980: *Labour in Power*. London: Longman.

Cohen, G. A. 1989: On the currency of egalitarian justice. *Ethics*, 99, July.

Cohen, G. A. 1991: The future of a disillusion. *New Left Review*, 190.

Cohen, J. 1988: The material basis of deliberative democracy. *Social Philosophy and Policy*, 6, 2.

Cohen, J. 1989: Deliberation and democratic legitimacy. In A. Hamlin and P. Pettit (eds), *The Good Polity: Normative Analysis of the State*. Oxford: Blackwell.

Cohen, J. and Rogers, J. 1983: *On Democracy*. New York: Penguin.

Cohen, J. and Rogers, J. 1992: Associations and democratic governance. *Politics and Society*, 20, 4.

Commission on Global Governance 1995: *Our Global Neighbourhood*. Oxford: Oxford University Press.

Commission on Social Justice 1993: *The Justice Gap*. London: IPPR.

Conference on Security and Co-operation in Europe (CSCE) 1992: *Helsinki Declaration*. Helsinki: CSCE.

Connolly, W. 1981: *Appearance and Reality*. Cambridge: Cambridge University Press.

Cooper, R. N. 1986: *Economic Policy in an Interdependent World*. Cambridge: MIT Press.

Coote, A. (ed.) 1992: *The Welfare of Citizens: Developing New Social Rights*. London: IPPR/Rivers Oram Press.

Coote, A. 1994: Types of rights, forms of decision-making: a commentary. In D. Miliband (ed.), *Rethinking the Left*. Cambridge: Polity Press.

Corcoran, P. E. 1983: The limits of democratic theory. In G. Duncan (ed.), *Democratic Theory and Practice*. Cambridge: Cambridge University Press.

Cox, R. W. 1987: *Production, Power and World Order: Social Forces in the Making of History*. New York: Columbia University Press.

Cox, R. W. 1992: Multilateralism and world order. *Review of International Studies*, 18, 2.

Cranston, M. 1968: Introduction to Rousseau. In J.-J. Rousseau, *The Social Contract*. Harmondsworth: Penguin.

Crawford J. 1994: *Democracy in International Law*. Inaugural lecture. Cambridge: Cambridge University Press.

Crompton, R. 1993: *Class and Stratification*. Cambridge: Polity Press.
Cronon, W. 1983: *Changes in the Land: Indians, Colonists and the Ecology of New England*. New York: Hill and Wang.
Crosby, A. J. 1986: *Ecological Imperialism: The Biological Expansion of Europe 900–1900*. Cambridge: Cambridge University Press.
CSCE 1992: *Helsinki Declaration*. Helsinki: CSCE.
Dagger, R. 1989: Rights. In T. Ball, J. Farr and R. L. Hanson (eds), *Political Innovation and Conceptual Change*. Cambridge: Cambridge University Press.
Dahl, R. A. 1956: *A Preface to Democratic Theory*. Chicago: University of Chicago Press.
Dahl, R. A. 1957: The concept of power. *Behavioural Science*, 2, 3.
Dahl, R. A. 1961: *Who Governs? Democracy and Power in an American City*. New Haven, Conn.: Yale University Press.
Dahl, R. A. 1971: *Polyarchy: Participation and Opposition*. New Haven, Conn.: Yale University Press.
Dahl, R. A. 1978: Pluralism revisited. *Comparative Politics*, 10, 2.
Dahl, R. A. 1979: Procedural democracy. In P. Laslett and J. Fishkin (eds), *Philosophy, Politics and Society, Fifth Series*. New Haven, Conn.: Yale University Press.
Dahl, R. A. 1985: *A Preface to Economic Democracy*. Cambridge: Polity Press.
Dahl, R. 1989: *Democracy and its Critics*. New Haven, Conn.: Yale University Press.
Delphy, C. and Leonard, D. 1992: *Familiar Exploitation*. Cambridge: Polity Press.
Devine, P. 1988: *Democracy and Economic Planning*. Cambridge: Polity Press.
Devine, P. 1991: Economy, state and civil society. *Economy and Society*, 20, 2.
Dominelli, L. 1991: *Women Across Continents*. Hemel Hempstead: Harvester Wheatsheaf.
Doyal, L. and Gough, I. 1991: *A Theory of Human Need*. London: Macmillan.
Doyle, M. W. 1983: Kant, liberal legacies and foreign affairs, parts I and II. *Philosophy and Public Affairs*, 12, 3 and 4.
Dunn, J. 1969: *The Political Thought of John Locke*. Cambridge: Cambridge University Press.
Dunn, J. 1979: *Western Political Theory in the Face of the Future*. Cambridge: Cambridge University Press.
Dunn, J. 1980: *Political Obligation in its Historical Context: Essays in Political Theory*. Cambridge: Cambridge University Press.
Dunn, J. 1984: *Locke*. Oxford: Oxford University Press.
Dunn, J. 1990: *Interpreting Political Responsibility*. Cambridge: Polity Press.

Dunn, J. (ed.) 1992: *Democracy: The Unfinished Journey, 508 BC to AD 1993*. Oxford: Oxford University Press.

Dworkin, R. 1977: *Taking Rights Seriously*. Oxford: Duckworth.

Dworkin, R. 1978: Liberalism. In S. Hampshire (ed.), *Public and Private Morality*. Cambridge: Cambridge University Press.

Ekins, P. 1992: *A New World Order*. London: Routledge.

Elster, J. 1988: Introduction. In J. Elster and R. Slagstad (eds), *Constitutionalism and Democracy*. Cambridge: Cambridge University Press.

Elster, J. and Slagstad, R. (eds) 1988: *Constitutionalism and Democracy*. Cambridge: Cambridge University Press.

Erikson, R. and Goldthorpe, J. H. 1986: National variation in social fluidity. CASMIN Project Working Paper, no. 9. Mannheim: Institut für Sozialwissenschaft, University of Mannheim.

Esping-Andersen, G. 1990: *The Three Worlds of Welfare Capitalism*. Cambridge: Polity Press.

Evans, R. W. 1992: *Coming to Terms: Corporations and the Left*. London: IPPR.

Falk, R. 1969: The interplay of Westphalia and Charter conceptions of international law. In C. A. Black and R. Falk (eds), *The Future of the International Legal Order*, vol. 1. Princeton N.J.: Princeton University Press.

Falk, R. 1970: *The Status of Law in International Society*. Princeton, N.J.: Princeton University Press.

Falk, R. 1975a: *A Global Approach to National Policy*. Cambridge, Mass.: Harvard University Press.

Falk, R. 1975b: *A Study of Future Worlds*. New York: Free Press.

Falk. R. 1986: *Reviving the World Court*. Charlottesville, Va:. University Press of Virginia.

Falk, R. 1990: Economic dimensions of global civilization: a preliminary perspective. Working paper prepared for the Cairo meeting of the Global Civilization Project. Princeton, N.J.: Princeton University, Center for International Studies.

Falk, R. 1991a: Positive prescriptions for the near future. World Order Studies Program Occasional Paper, no. 20. Princeton, N.J.: Princeton University, Center for International Studies.

Falk, R. 1991b: Reflections on democracy and the Gulf War. *Alternatives*, 16, 2.

Falk, R. 1995: *On Humane Governance: Toward a New Global Politics*. Cambridge: Polity Press.

Ferguson, Y. and Mansbach, R. 1991: Between celebration and despair. *International Studies Quarterly*, 35.

Ferrajoli, L. and Senese, S. 1992: Prospettiva di riforma dell'ONU. *Democrazia e diritto*, 32,1.

Fieldhouse, D. K. 1966: *The Colonial Empires: A Comparative Survey*. London: Weidenfeld & Nicolson.

Figgis, J. N. 1913: *Churches in the Modern State*. London: Longman, Green.
Finley, M. I. 1963: *The Ancient Greeks*. Harmondsworth: Penguin.
Finley, M. I. 1972: Introduction to Thucydides. In Thucydides, *The Peloponnesian War*. Harmondsworth: Penguin.
Finley, M. I. 1973a: *The Ancient Economy*. London: Chatto & Windus.
Finley, M. I. 1973b: *Democracy Ancient and Modern*. London: Chatto & Windus.
Finley, M. I. 1975: *The Use and Abuse of History*. London: Chatto & Windus.
Finley, M. I. 1983: *Politics in the Ancient World*. Cambridge: Cambridge University Press.
Fishkin, J. 1991: *Democracy and Deliberation*. New Haven, Conn: Yale University Press.
Franklin, J. H. 1978: *John Locke and the Theory of Sovereignty*. Cambridge: Cambridge University Press.
Frieden, J. 1986: *Banking on the World*. New York: Basic Books.
Frieden, J. 1991: Invested interests: the politics of national economic policies in a world of global finance. *International Organization*, 45, 4.
Friedman, M. R. 1980: *Free to Choose: A Personal Statement*. Harmondsworth: Penguin.
Friedmann, W. 1964: *The Changing Structure of International Law*. London: Stevens and Son.
Fukuyama, F. 1989: The end of history? *The National Interest*, 16.
Fukuyama, F. 1989/90: A reply to my critics. *The National Interest*, 18.
Fukuyama, F. 1992: *The End of History and the Last Man*. London: Hamish Hamilton.
Furnivall, J. S. 1948: *Colonial Policy and Practice*. Cambridge: Cambridge University Press.
Gadamer, H.-G. 1975: *Truth and Method*. London: Sheed and Ward.
Galbraith, J. K. 1994: The good society. *Guardian*, 26 January.
Gallis, P. 1994: Partnership for peace. Congressional Research Report for Congress. Washington, D.C.: Library of Congress.
Galtung, J. 1994: *Human Rights in Another Key*. Cambridge: Polity Press.
Garrett, G. and Lange, P. 1991: Political responses to interdependence: what's left for the left? *International Organization*, 45, 4.
Garthoff, R. L. 1993: Warsaw Treaty Organization. In J. Krieger (ed.), *The Oxford Companion to Politics of the World*. Oxford: Oxford University Press.
Gellner, E. 1964: *Thought and Change*. London: Weidenfeld & Nicolson.
Gellner, E. 1983: *Nations and Nationalism*. Oxford: Blackwell.
Gerwith, A. 1978: *Reason and Morality*. Chicago: Chicago University Press.

Giddens, A. 1977: *Studies in Social and Political Theory*. London: Hutchinson.

Giddens, A. 1979: *Central Problems in Social Theory: Action, Structure and Contradiction in Social Analysis*. London: Macmillan.

Giddens, A. 1980: *The Class Structure of the Advanced Societies*, 2nd edn. London: Hutchinson.

Giddens, A. 1981: *A Contemporary Critique of Historical Materialism*, vol. I. London: Macmillan.

Giddens, A. 1984: *The Constitution of Society*. Cambridge: Polity Press.

Giddens, A. 1985: *The Nation-state and Violence*, vol. II of *A Contemporary Critique of Historical Materialism*. Cambridge: Polity Press.

Giddens, A. 1987: *Social Theory and Modern Society*. Cambridge: Polity Press.

Giddens, A. 1990: *The Consequences of Modernity*. Cambridge: Polity Press.

Giddens, A. 1991: *Modernity and Self-identity*. Cambridge: Polity Press.

Giddens, A. 1992: *The Transformation of Intimacy*. Cambridge: Polity Press.

Giddens, A. 1994: *Beyond Left and Right: The Future of Radical Politics*. Cambridge: Polity Press.

Giddens, A. and Held, D. (eds) 1982: *Classes, Power and Conflict*. London: Macmillan.

Gierke, O. 1987: *Political Theories of the Middle Ages*. Cambridge: Cambridge University Press.

Gilbert, F. 1965: *Machiavelli and Guicciardini*. Princeton, N.J.: Princeton University Press.

Gill, S. and Law, D. 1989: Global hegemony and the structural power of capital. *International Studies Quarterly*, 33, 4.

Gilpin, R. 1981: *War and Change in World Politics*. Cambridge: Cambridge University Press.

Gilpin, R. 1987: *The Political Economy of International Relations*. Princeton, N.J.: Princeton University Press.

Gilroy, P. 1987: *There ain't no Black in the Union Jack*. London: Hutchinson.

Girvan, N. 1980: Swallowing the IMF medicine in the seventies. *Development Dialogue*, 2.

Goldblatt, D., Held, D., McGrew, A. and Perraton, J., forthcoming: *What is Globalization? Concepts, Theories and Evidence*. Cambridge: Polity Press.

Gordon, D. 1988: The global economy. *New Left Review*, 168.

Gourevitch, P. 1978: The second image reversed: the international sources of domestic politics. *International Organization*, 32, 4.

Gourevitch, P. 1986: *Politics in Hard Times*. New York: Cornell University Press.

Graham, H. 1984: *Women, Health and the Family*. Brighton: Wheatsheaf Books.

Gray, J. 1993: When no deal is a good deal. *Guardian*, 9 November.

Grove, E. 1993: UN armed force and the Military Staff Committee. *International Security*, 17, 4.

Guardian 1993: In the name of the UN stop it. 14 June.

Guardian 1994: Poverty threatens the future of one in four US children. 13 April.

Habermas, J. 1962: *Strukturwandel der Öffentlichkeit*. Neuwied: Luchterhand.

Habermas, J. 1971: *Towards a Rational Society*. London: Heinemann.

Habermas, J. 1973: Wahrheitstheorien. In H. Fahrenbach (ed.), *Wirchlichkeit und Reflexion*. Pfüllingen: Neske.

Habermas, J. 1976: *Legitimation Crisis*. London: Heinemann.

Habermas, J. 1984: *The Theory of Communicative Action*, vol. I. Cambridge: Polity Press.

Habermas, J. 1988: *Theory and Practice*. Cambridge: Polity Press.

Habermas, J. 1989: *The Structural Transformation of the Public Sphere*. Cambridge: Polity Press.

Habermas, J. 1990: *Moral Consciousness and Communicative Action*. Cambridge: Polity Press.

Habermas, J. 1992: What does socialism mean today? In R. Blackburn (ed.), *After the Fall*. London: Verso.

Habermas, J. 1994: Three models of democracy. *Constellations*, 1, 1.

Habermas, J. 1996: *Between Facts and Norms: Contributions to a Discourse Theory of Law and Democracy*. Cambridge: Polity Press.

Hall, J. 1993: Consolidations of democracy. In D. Held (ed.), *Prospects for Democracy: North, South, East, West*. Cambridge: Polity Press.

Hall, J. 1996: *International Orders: An Historical Sociology of State, Regime, Class and Nation*. Cambridge: Polity Press.

Hall, J. and Ikenberry, P. 1989: *The State*. Milton Keynes: Open University Press.

Hall, P. 1986: *Governing the Economy*. Cambridge: Polity Press.

Hall, R. H. 1990: *Health and the Global Environment*. Cambridge: Polity Press.

Hall, S. 1992: The question of cultural identity. In S. Hall, D. Held and T. McGrew (eds), *Modernity and its Futures*. Cambridge: Polity Press.

Hall, S. and Gieben, B. (eds) 1992: *Formations of Modernity*. Cambridge: Polity Press.

Hall, S., Held, D. and McGrew, A. (eds) 1992: *Modernity and its Futures*. Cambridge: Polity Press.

Halsey, A. H., Heath, A. F. and Ridge, J. M. 1980: *Origins and Destinations*. Oxford: Oxford University Press.

Hansen, M. H. 1991: *The Athenian Democracy in the Age of Demosthenes.* Oxford: Blackwell.

Hanson, R. 1989: Democracy. In T. Ball, J. Farr and R. Hanson (eds), *Political Innovation and Conceptual Change.* Cambridge: Cambridge University Press.

Hart, J. 1991: *Rival Capitalists: International Competitiveness in the United States, Japan and Western Europe.* Ithaca, N.Y.: Cornell University Press.

Hartley, T. C. 1988: *The Foundations of European Law.* Oxford: Clarendon Press.

Harvey, D. 1989: *The Condition of Postmodernity.* Oxford: Blackwell.

Hawthorn, G. 1993: Sub-Saharan Africa. In D. Held (ed.), *Prospects for Democracy: North, South, East, West.* Cambridge: Polity Press.

Hayek, F. A. 1960: *The Constitution of Liberty.* London: Routledge & Kegan Paul.

Hayek, F. A. 1976: *The Road to Serfdom.* London: Routledge & Kegan Paul.

Hayek, F. A. 1978: *New Studies in Philosophy, Politics, Economics and the History of Ideas.* London: Routledge & Kegan Paul.

Hayek, F. A. 1982: *Law, Legislation and Liberty,* vols II and III. London: Routledge & Kegan Paul.

Heater, D. 1990: *Citizenship.* London: Longman.

Heath, A. 1981: *Social Mobility.* London: Fontana.

Hegel, F. 1975: *Lectures on the Philosophy of World History.* Cambridge: Cambridge University Press.

Held, D. 1980: *Introduction to Critical Theory: Horkheimer to Habermas.* London: Hutchinson.

Held, D. 1987: *Models of Democracy.* Cambridge: Polity Press.

Held, D. 1989: *Political Theory and the Modern State.* Cambridge: Polity Press.

Held, D. 1991a: Democracy, the nation-state and the global system. In D. Held (ed.) *Political Theory Today.* Cambridge: Polity Press.

Held, D. 1991b: Introduction. In D. Held (ed.), *Political Theory Today.* Cambridge: Polity Press.

Held, D. 1991c: The possibilities of democracy: a discussion of Robert Dahl, *Democracy and its Critics. Theory and Society,* 20.

Held, D. 1992a: The development of the modern state. In S. Hall and B. Gieben (eds), *Formations of Modernity.* Cambridge: Polity Press.

Held, D. 1992b: Democracy: from city-states to a cosmopolitan order? *Political Studies,* September, special issue.

Held, D. 1993a: Liberalism, Marxism and democracy. *Theory and Society,* 22.

Held, D. 1993b: Anything but a dog's life? Further comments on Fukuyama, Callinicos and Giddens. *Theory and Society,* 22.

Held, D. (ed.) 1993c: *Prospects for Democracy: North, South, East, West.* Cambridge: Polity Press.

Held, D., forthcoming: *Studies in Cosmopolitan Law.* Cambridge: Polity Press.

Held, D. and Leftwich, A. 1984: A discipline of politics? In A. Leftwich (ed.), *What is Politics?* Oxford: Blackwell.

Held, D. and McGrew, A. G. 1993: Globalization and the liberal democratic state. *Government and Opposition*, 28, 2.

Held, D. and Pollitt, C. (eds) 1986: *New Forms of Democracy.* London: Sage.

Hepple, B. 1993: *European Social Dialogue – Alibi or Opportunity?* London: Institute of Employment Rights.

Herz, J. H. 1976: *The Nation-state and the Crisis of World Politics.* New York: McKay.

Hesse, M. 1974: *The Structure of Scientific Inference.* London: Macmillan.

Hilferding, R. 1981: *Finance Capital.* 1st edn 1910. London: Routledge.

Hine, R. 1992: Regionalism and the integration of the world economy. *Journal of Common Market Studies*, 30, 2.

Hinsley, F. H. 1963: *Power and the Pursuit of Peace.* Cambridge: Cambridge University Press.

Hinsley, F. H. 1986: *Sovereignty*, 2nd edn. Cambridge: Cambridge University Press.

Hintze, O. 1975: *Historical Essays.* New York: Oxford University Press.

Hirst, P. (ed.) 1989: *The Pluralist Theory of the State.* London: Routledge.

Hirst, P. 1990: *Representative Democracy and its Limits.* Cambridge: Polity Press.

Hirst, P. 1993: Associational democracy. In D. Held (ed.), *Prospects for Democracy: North, South, East, West.* Cambridge: Polity Press.

Hirst, P. 1994: *Associative Democracy.* Cambridge: Polity Press.

Hobbes, T. 1968: *Leviathan*, ed. C. B. Macpherson. Harmondsworth: Penguin.

Hobsbawm, E. 1969: *Industry and Empire.* London: Pelican.

Hobsbawm, E. 1990: *Nations and Nationalism since 1780.* Cambridge: Cambridge University Press.

Hoffman, S. 1982: Reflections on the nation-state in Western Europe today. *Journal of Common Market Studies*, XXI, 1 and 2.

Hohfeld, W. 1964: *Fundamental Legal Conceptions.* New Haven, Conn.: Yale University Press.

Holloway, D. and Sharp, J. M. O. (eds) 1984: *The Warsaw Pact: Alliance in Transition?* London: Macmillan.

Holmes, S. 1988: Precommitment and the paradox of democracy. In J. Elster and R. Slagstad (eds), *Constitutionalism and Democracy.* Cambridge: Cambridge University Press.

Holsti, K. J. 1988: *International Politics: A Framework of Analysis*, 5th edn. Englewood Cliffs, N.J.: Prentice Hall.
Holsti, K. J. 1991: *Peace and War: Armed Conflicts and International Order, 1648–1989*. Cambridge: Cambridge University Press.
Hont, I. 1994: The permanent crisis of a divided mankind: 'contemporary crisis of the nation state' in historical perspective. *Political Studies*, 42, special issue.
Hornblower, S. 1992: Creation and development of democratic institutions in Ancient Greece. In J. Dunn (ed.), *Democracy: The Unfinished Journey, 508 BC to AD 1993*. Oxford: Oxford University Press.
Hourani, A. 1992: *History of the Arab People*. London: Faber.
Howard, M. 1981: *War and the Liberal Conscience*. Oxford: Oxford University Press.
Hultman, T. 1993: World Bank signals U-turn on African aid policy. *Guardian*, 24 May.
Hutton, W. 1993: Tokyo must curb rogue capital flows. *Guardian Weekly*, 11 July.
Hutton, W. 1995: *The State We're In*. London: Jonathan Cape.
Jackson, R. H. and Rosberg, C. G. 1982: Why Africa's weak states persist: the empirical and the juridical in statehood. *World Politics*, 17.
Janowitz, M. 1978: *The Last Half-Century*. Chicago: University of Chicago Press.
Jenks, C. 1963: *Law, Freedom and Welfare*. London: Stevens and Son.
Jenks, C. 1988: What must be equal for opportunity to be equal? In N. E. Bowie (ed.), *Equal Opportunity*. Boulder, Col.: Westview Press.
Jessop, B. 1990: *State Theory*. Cambridge: Polity Press.
Johansen, R. C. 1991: Real security is democratic security. *Alternatives*, 16, 2.
Johansen, R. C. 1993a: Military policies and the states system as impediments to democracy. In D. Held (ed.), *Prospects for Democracy: North, South, East, West*. Cambridge: Polity Press.
Johansen, R. C. 1993b: Japan as a military power? *Christian Century*, 5 May.
Jones, A. H. M. 1957: *Athenian Democracy*. Oxford: Blackwell.
Jordan, B. 1985: *The State: Authority and Autonomy*. Oxford: Blackwell.
Kaiser, K. 1972: Transnational relations as a threat to the democratic process. In R. O. Keohane and J. S. Nye (eds), *Transnational Relations and World Politics*. Cambridge, Mass.: Harvard University Press.
Kaldor, M. and Falk, R. (eds) 1987: *Dealignment*. Oxford: Blackwell.
Kant, I. 1956: *Critique of Pure Reason*. New York: St Martin's Press.
Kant, I. 1970: *Kant's Political Writings*, ed. and intro. H. Reiss. Cambridge: Cambridge University Press.

Keane, J. 1984: *Public Life and Late Capitalism*. Cambridge: Cambridge University Press.

Keane, J. 1988a: *Democracy and Civil Society*. London: Verso.

Keane, J. (ed.) 1988b: *Civil Society and the State*. London: Verso.

Kegley, C. W. and Wittkopf, E. R. 1989: *World Politics*. London: Macmillan.

Kegley, C. W. and Raymond, G. 1994: *A Multipolar Peace? Great-Power Politics in the Twenty-first Century*. New York: St Martin's Press.

Kelly, L. 1988: *Surviving Sexual Violence*. Cambridge: Polity Press.

Kelsen, H. 1944: *Peace Through Law*. Chapel Hill, N.C.: University of North Carolina Press.

Kennedy, P. 1988: *The Rise and Fall of the Great Powers: Economic Change and Military Conflict from 1500 to 2000*. London: Unwin Hyman.

Keohane, R. O. 1984a: *After Hegemony*. Princeton, N.J.: Princeton University Press.

Keohane, R. O. 1984b: The world political economy and the crisis of embedded liberalism. In J. H. Goldthorpe (ed.), *Order and Conflict in Contemporary Capitalism*. Oxford: Oxford University Press.

Keohane, R. O. 1986: *Neo-realism and its Critics*. New York: Columbia University Press.

Keohane, R. O. and Hoffmann, S. (eds) 1990: *The New European Community*. Oxford: Westview Press.

Keohane, R. O. and Nye, J. S. (eds) 1972: *Transnational Relations and World Politics*. Cambridge, Mass.: Harvard University Press.

Keohane, R. O. and Nye, J. S. 1989: *Power and Interdependence*, 2nd edn. Boston: Little, Brown.

Kiernan, V. G. 1982: *European Empires from Conquest to Collapse, 1815–1960*. London: Fontana.

Kim, S. S. 1984: Global violence and a just world order. *Journal of Peace Research*, 21, 2.

King, A. (ed.) 1991: *Culture, Globalization and the World System*. London: Macmillan.

King, P. 1974: *The Ideology of Order: A Comparative Analysis of Jean Bodin and Thomas Hobbes*. London: Allen & Unwin.

King, P. 1987: Sovereignty. In D. Miller, J. Coleman, W. Connolly and A. Ryan (eds), *The Blackwell Encyclopaedia of Political Thought*. Oxford: Blackwell.

King, R. 1995: Migrations, globalization and place. In D. Massey and P. Jess (eds), *A Place in the World? Culture, Places and Globalization*. Oxford: Oxford University Press.

Kitching, G. 1982: *Development and Underdevelopment in Historical Perspective*. London: Methuen.

Koblick, S. (ed.) 1975: *Sweden's Development from Poverty to Affluence: 1750–1970*. Minneapolis: University of Minnesota Press.

Kolko, J. 1988: *Restructuring the World Economy*. New York: Pantheon.

Korpi, W. 1978: *The Working Class in Welfare Capitalism*. London: Routledge & Kegan Paul.

Krasner, S. 1978: *Defending the National Interest*. Princeton, N.J.: Princeton University Press.

Krasner, S. 1983: *International Regimes*. Ithaca, N.Y.: Cornell University Press.

Krasner, S. 1988: Sovereignty: an institutional perspective. *Comparative Political Studies*, 21, 1.

Krouse, R. W. 1983: Classical images of democracy in America: Madison and Tocqueville. In G. Duncan (ed.), *Democratic Theory and Practice*. Cambridge: Cambridge University Press.

Kukathas, C. and Pettit, P. 1990: *Rawls: A Theory of Justice and its Critics*. Cambridge: Polity Press.

Lappé, F. M. and Collins, J. 1979: *Food First: Beyond the Myth of Scarcity*. New York: Ballantine.

Larsen, J. A. O. 1948: Cleisthenes and the development of the theory of democracy at Athens. In M. R. Konvitz and A. E. Murphy (eds), *Essays in Political Theory presented to George Sabine*. Post Washington, N.Y.: Kennikat Press.

Lash, S. and Urry, J. 1987: *The End of Organized Capitalism*. Cambridge: Polity Press.

Laski, H. 1932: *Studies in Law and Politics*. London: Allen & Unwin.

Laslett, P. 1963: Introduction to Locke. In Locke, *Two Treatises of Government*. Cambridge and New York: Cambridge University Press.

Lebrun, J.-F. 1990: Towards an economic and social area. *Social Europe*, 1.

Lee, D. 1974: Introduction to Plato. In Plato, *The Republic*. Harmondsworth: Penguin.

Leftwich, A. 1993a: Governance, democracy and development in the Third World. *Third World Quarterly*, 14, 3.

Leftwich, A. 1993b: Voting can damage your wealth. *Times Higher Education Supplement*, 13 August.

Leftwich, A. 1994: Governance, the state and the politics of development. *Development and Change*, 25, 2.

Lenin, V. I. 1947: *What is to be Done?* Moscow: Progress Publishers.

Lenin, V. I. 1971: *State and Revolution*. New York: International Publishers.

Lewis, P. 1990: Democratization in Eastern Europe. *Coexistence*, 27.

Lewis, R. 1991: The G7½ directorate. *Foreign Policy*, 85.

Lijphart, A. 1984: *Democracies*. New Haven, Conn.: Yale University Press.

Lindblom, C. E. 1977: *Politics and Markets*. New York: Basic Books.

Lipietz, A. 1992: *Towards a New Economic Order*. Cambridge: Polity Press.

Lively, J. 1975: *Democracy*. Oxford: Blackwell.

Locke, J. 1963: *Two Treatises of Government*. Cambridge and New York: Cambridge University Press.
Luard, E. 1977: *International Agencies: The Framework of Interdependence*. London: Macmillan.
Luard, E. 1990: *Globalization of Politics*. London: Macmillan.
Lukes, S. 1973: *Individualism*. New York: Harper & Row.
Lukes, S. 1974: *Power: A Radical View*. London: Macmillan.
Lukes, S. 1982: Of gods and demons: Habermas and practical reason. In J. B. Thompson and D. Held (eds), *Habermas: Critical Debates*. London: Macmillan.
Lukes, S. 1985: *Marxism and Morality*. Oxford: Oxford University Press.
Lukes, S. 1991: Equality and liberty: must they conflict? In D. Held (ed.), *Political Theory Today*. Cambridge: Polity Press.
Machiavelli, N. 1975: *The Prince*. Harmondsworth: Penguin.
Machiavelli, N. 1983: *The Discourses*. Harmondsworth: Penguin.
MacIntyre, A. 1966: *A Short History of Ethics*. New York: Macmillan.
Macpherson, C. B. 1962: *The Political Theory of Possessive Individualism*. Oxford: Clarendon Press.
Macpherson, C. B. 1966: *The Real World of Democracy*. Oxford: Oxford University Press.
Macpherson, C. B. 1968: Introduction to Hobbes. In T. Hobbes, *Leviathan*. Harmondsworth: Penguin.
Macpherson, C. B. 1973: *Democratic Theory: Essays in Retrieval*. Oxford: Clarendon Press.
Macpherson, C. B. 1977: *The Life and Times of Liberal Democracy*. Oxford: Oxford University Press.
Madison, J. 1966: *The Federalist Papers*. New York: Doubleday.
Madison, J. 1973: Reflecting on representation. In M. Meyers (ed.), *The Mind of the Founder: Sources of the Political Thought of James Madison*. Indianapolis: Bobbs-Merrill.
Maguire, J. M. 1978: *Marx's Theory of Politics*. Cambridge: Cambridge University Press.
Main, J. T. 1973: *The Sovereign States: 1775–1783*. New York: Franklin Watts.
Mancini, G. 1990: The making of a constitution for Europe. In R. O. Keohane and S. Hoffmann (eds), *The New European Community*. Oxford: Westview Press.
Manin, B. 1987: On legitimacy and political deliberation. *Political Theory*, 15, 3.
Mann, M. 1986: *The Sources of Social Power*, vol. I. Cambridge: Cambridge University Press.
Mann, M. 1987: Ruling strategies and citizenship. *Sociology*, 21, 3.
Mann, M. 1993: *The Sources of Social Power*, vol. II. Cambridge: Cambridge University Press.

Mansbach, R. W., Ferguson, Y. H. and Lampert, D. E. 1976. *The Web of World Politics*. Englewood Cliffs, N.J.: Prentice Hall.

Mansbridge, J. J. 1983: *Beyond Adversary Democracy*. Chicago: Chicago University Press.

Margolis, M. 1983: Democracy: American style. In G. Duncan (ed.), *Democratic Theory and Practice*. Cambridge: Cambridge University Press.

Marshall. T. H. 1973: *Class, Citizenship and Social Development*. Westport, Conn.: Greenwood Press.

Marx, K. 1844: Letter 2. In *Deutsch-Französische Jahrbücher*, Paris.

Marx, K. 1963a: *Economic and Philosophical Manuscripts*. In *Karl Marx: Early Writings*, ed. T. B. Bottomore. London: C. A. Watts.

Marx, K. 1963b: *The Eighteenth Brumaire of Louis Bonaparte*. New York: International Publishers.

Marx, K. 1963c: *The Poverty of Philosophy*. New York: International Publishers.

Marx, K. 1968: Value, price and profit. In K. Marx and F. Engels, *Selected Works*. New York: International Publishers.

Marx, K. 1970a: *The Civil War in France*. Peking: Foreign Languages Press.

Marx, K. 1970b: *The Critique of Hegel's Philosophy of Right*. Cambridge: Cambridge University Press.

Marx, K. 1971: Preface to *A Contribution to the Critique of Political Economy*. London: Lawrence and Wishart.

Marx, K. and Engels, F. 1969: *The Communist Manifesto*. In *Selected Works*, vol. I. Moscow: Progress Publishers.

Marx, K. and Engels, F. 1970: *The German Ideology*. London: Lawrence and Wishart.

Massey, D. 1991: A global sense of place. *Marxism Today*, June.

Mastanduno, M., Lake, D. A. and Ikenberry, G. J. 1989: Towards a realist theory of state action. *International Studies Quarterly*, 33, 4.

McCarthy, T. 1991: *Ideals and Illusions: On Reconstruction and Deconstruction in Contemporary Critical Theory*. Cambridge, Mass.: MIT Press.

McEvedy, C. 1961: *The Penguin Atlas of Medieval History*. Harmondsworth: Penguin.

McEvedy, C. 1982: *The Penguin Atlas of Recent History: Europe since 1815*. Harmondsworth: Penguin.

McGrew, A. G. 1988: Conceptualizing global politics. In *Global Politics*, unit 1. Milton Keynes: Open University.

McGrew, A. G. 1992a: Conceptualizing global politics. In A. G. McGrew, P. G. Lewis et al., *Global Politics*. Cambridge: Polity Press.

McGrew, A. G. 1992b: A global society? In S. Hall, D. Held and A. McGrew (eds), *Modernity and its Futures*. Cambridge: Polity Press.

McLean, I. 1986: Mechanisms for democracy. In D. Held and C. Pollitt (eds), *New Forms of Democracy*. London: Sage.
McLean, I. 1991: Forms of representation and systems of voting. In D. Held (ed.), *Political Theory Today*. Cambridge: Polity Press.
McNeil, W. 1977: *Plagues and Peoples*. Oxford: Blackwell.
Mearsheimer, J. 1990: Back to the future. *International Security*, 15, 1.
Meyers, M. (ed.) 1973: *The Mind of the Founder: Sources of the Political Thought of James Madison*. Indianapolis: Bobbs-Merrill.
Meyrowitz, J. 1985: *No Sense of Place*. Oxford: Oxford University Press.
Michels, R. 1962: *Political Parties*. New York: Free Press.
Mill, J. 1828: Prisons and prison discipline. In *Essays on Government*. London: J. Innis.
Mill, J. 1937: *An Essay on Government*. Cambridge: Cambridge University Press.
Mill, J. S. 1862: Centralisation. *Edinburgh Review*, CXV.
Mill, J. S. 1951: *Considerations on Representative Government*. In H. B. Acton (ed.), *Utilitarianism, Liberty, and Representative Government*. London: Dent.
Mill, J. S. 1965: *Principles of Political Economy*. In *Collected Works of J. S. Mill*, vols. II and III. Toronto: University of Toronto Press.
Mill, J. S. 1976a: Chapters on socialism. In G. L. Williams (ed.), *John Stuart Mill on Politics and Society*. London: Fontana.
Mill, J. S. 1976b: M. de Tocqueville on democracy in America. In G. L. Williams (ed.), *John Stuart Mill on Politics and Society*. London: Fontana.
Mill, J. S. 1980: *The Subjection of Women*, ed. S. Mansfield. Arlington Heights, Ill.: AHM Publishing.
Mill, J. S. 1982: *On Liberty*. Harmondsworth: Penguin.
Miller, D. 1976: *Social Justice*. Oxford: Clarendon Press.
Miller, D. 1989: *Market, State and Community: Theoretical Foundations of Market Socialism*. Oxford: Clarendon Press.
Miller, D. 1993: Deliberative democracy and social choice. In D. Held (ed.), *Prospects for Democracy: North, South, East, West*. Cambridge: Polity Press.
Mitchell, B. R. and Deane, P. 1962: *Abstract of British Historical Statistics*. Cambridge: Cambridge University Press.
Mitchell, B. R. and Jones, H. G. 1971: *Second Abstract of British Historical Statistics*. Cambridge: Cambridge University Press.
Modelski, G. 1972: *Principles of World Politics*. New York: Free Press.
Mommsen, W. J. 1974: *The Age of Bureaucracy*. Oxford: Blackwell.
Montesquieu, B. de 1952: *The Spirit of Laws*. Chicago: William Benton.
Moore, H. 1987: *Feminism and Anthropology*. Cambridge: Polity Press.
Morgenthau, H. 1948: *Politics Among Nations*. New York: Alfred Knopf.
Morse, E. 1976: *Modernization and the Transformation of International Relations*. New York: Free Press.

Mosley, P., Toye, J. and Harrigan, J. 1991: *Aid and Power*, 2 vols. London: Routledge.

Mulhall, S. and Swift, A. 1992: *Liberals and Communitarians*. Oxford: Blackwell.

Murphy, C. N. 1994: *International Organization and Industrial Change: Global Governance since 1850*. Cambridge: Polity Press.

Myers, N. 1994: Gross reality of global statistics. *Guardian*, 2 May.

Neumann, F. 1964: *The Democratic and the Authoritarian State*. New York: Free Press.

Neunreither, K. 1993: Subsidiarity as a guiding principle for European Community activities. *Government and Opposition*, 28, 2.

Noel, J. 1989: The Single European Act. *Government and Opposition*, 24.

Nordau, M. 1968: *Degeneration*. 1st edn 1892. New York: Fertig.

Nordhaus, W. D. 1975: The political business cycle. *Review of Economic Studies*, 42.

Nordlinger, E. 1983: *On the Autonomy of the Democratic State*. Cambridge, Mass.: Harvard University Press.

Nove, A. 1983: *The Economics of Feasible Socialism*. London: Macmillan.

Nozick, R. 1974: *Anarchy, State and Utopia*. Oxford: Blackwell.

Øberg, J. 1983: Why disarmament and arms control negotiations will fail – and what can be done? *Bulletin of Peace Studies*, 14, 3.

O'Brien, R. 1992: *The End of Geography*. London: Routledge/RIIA.

Offe, C. 1984: *Contradictions of the Welfare State*. London: Hutchinson.

Offe, C. 1985: *Disorganized Capitalism*. Cambridge: Polity Press.

Okin, S. 1979: *Women in Western Political Theory*. Princeton, N.J.: Princeton University Press.

O'Neill, O. 1991: Transnational justice. In D. Held (ed.), *Political Theory Today*. Cambridge: Polity Press.

Oppenheim, L. 1905: *International Law*, vol. 1. London: Longmans.

Osiander, A. 1994: *The States of Europe, 1640–1990*. Oxford: Clarendon Press.

Oxford English Dictionary, 1971: *The Compact Edition*, vol. 1. Oxford: Oxford University Press.

Paine, T. 1984: *The Rights of Man*. Harmondsworth: Penguin.

Parekh, B. 1989: Between holy text and moral void. *New Statesman and Society*, 23 March.

Parekh, B. 1993: The cultural particularity of liberal democracy. In D. Held (ed.), *Prospects for Democracy: North, South, East, West*. Cambridge: Polity Press.

Parker, D. 1981: Law, society, and the state in the thought of Jean Bodin. *History of Political Thought*, 2.

Parkin, F. 1979: *The Marxist Theory of Class: A Bourgeois Critique*. London: Tavistock.

Pateman, C. 1970: *Participation and Democratic Theory.* Cambridge: Cambridge University Press.

Pateman, C. 1983: Feminism and democracy. In G. Duncan (ed.), *Democratic Theory and Practice.* Cambridge: Cambridge University Press.

Pateman, C. 1985: *The Problem of Political Obligation: A Critique of Liberal Theory.* Cambridge: Polity Press.

Pateman, C. 1988: *The Sexual Contract.* Cambridge: Polity Press.

Pelczynski, Z. A. (ed.) 1985: *The State and Civil Society.* Cambridge: Cambridge University Press.

Perez-Diaz, M. 1978: *State, Bureaucracy and Civil Society.* London: Macmillan.

Petchesky, R. 1986: *Abortion and Women's Choice.* London: Verso.

Peters, R. S. 1956: *Hobbes.* Harmondsworth: Penguin.

Phillips, A. 1993: Must feminists give up on liberal democracy? In D. Held (ed.), *Prospects for Democracy: North, South, East, West.* Cambridge: Polity Press.

Pierson, C. 1986: *Marxist Theory and Democratic Politics.* Cambridge: Polity Press.

Pierson, C. 1991: *Beyond the Welfare State?* Cambridge: Polity Press.

Pierson, C. 1993: Democracy, markets and capital: are there necessary economic limits to democracy? In D. Held (ed.), *Prospects for Democracy: North, South, East, West.* Cambridge: Polity Press.

Pierson, C. 1995: *Socialism after Communism: The New Market Socialism.* Cambridge: Polity Press.

Pinder, J. 1992: *European Community.* Oxford: Oxford University Press.

Piore, M. and Sabel, C. 1984: *The Second Industrial Divide.* New York: Basic Books.

Plamenatz, J. 1963: *Man and Society*, vol. 1. London: Longman.

Plant, R. 1985: Welfare and the value of liberty. *Government and Opposition*, 20, 3.

Plant, R. 1992: Citizenship, rights and welfare. In A. Coote (ed.), *The Welfare of Citizens.* London: IPPR/Rivers Oram Press.

Plato 1952: *The Statesman.* London: Routledge & Kegan Paul.

Plato 1970: *The Laws.* Harmondsworth: Penguin.

Plato 1974: *The Republic.* Harmondsworth: Penguin.

Pocock, J. G. A. 1975: *The Machiavellian Moment: Florentine Political Thought and the Atlantic Republican Tradition.* Princeton, N.J.: Princeton University Press.

Poggi, G. 1978: *The Development of the Modern State.* London: Hutchinson.

Poggi, G. 1990: *The State: Its Nature, Development and Prospects.* Cambridge: Polity Press.

Polan, A. J. 1984: *Lenin and the End of Politics.* London: Methuen.

Potter, D. 1993: Democratization in Asia. In D. Held (ed.), *Prospects for Democracy: North, South, East, West.* Cambridge: Polity Press.

Przeworski, A. 1985: *Capitalism and Social Democracy.* Cambridge: Cambridge University Press.

Rahe, P. A. 1994: *Republics Ancient and Modern*, vol. 2. Chapel Hill, N.C.: University of North Carolina Press.

Rawls, J. 1971: *A Theory of Justice.* Cambridge, Mass.: Harvard University Press.

Rawls, J. 1985: Justice as fairness: political not metaphysical. *Philosophy and Public Affairs*, 14, 3.

Rawls, J. 1993: *Political Liberalism.* New York: Columbia University Press.

Raz, J. 1986: *The Morality of Freedom.* Oxford: Oxford University Press.

Reich, R. B. 1993: *The Work of Nations.* London: Simon and Schuster.

Reiss, H. 1970: Introduction. In H. Reiss (ed.), *Kant's Political Writings.* Cambridge: Cambridge University Press.

Remington, R. A. 1971: *The Warsaw Pact: Case Studies in Communist Conflict Resolution.* Cambridge, Mass.: MIT Press.

Richelson, J. and Ball, D. 1986: *The Ties that Bind.* London: Allen & Unwin.

Robertson, R. 1991: Social theory, cultural relativity and the problem of globality. In A. King (ed.), *Culture, Globalization and the World System.* London: Macmillan.

Robins, K. 1991: Tradition and translation: national culture in its global context. In J. Corner and S. Harvey (eds), *Enterprise and Heritage: Crosscurrents of National Culture.* London: Routledge.

Rogers, J. and Streeck, W. 1994: Productive solidarities: economic strategy and left politics. In D. Miliband (ed.), *Reinventing the Left.* Cambridge: Polity Press.

Röling, B. 1960: *International Law in an Expanded World.* Amsterdam: Djambatan.

Rosecrance, R. 1992: A new concert of powers. *Foreign Affairs*, 71, 2.

Rosenau, J. 1980: *The Study of Global Interdependence.* London: Frances Pinter.

Rosenau, J. 1988: The state in an era of cascading politics. *Comparative Political Studies*, 21, 1.

Rosenau, J. 1990: *Turbulence in World Politics.* London: Harvester Press.

Rosenne, S. 1985: *The Law and Practice of the International Court*, 2nd edn, 2 vols. Leyden: Martinus Nijhoff.

Ross, G. 1995: *Jacques Delors and European Integration.* Cambridge: Polity Press.

Ross, G., Hoffmann, S. and Malzacher, S. 1987: *The Mitterand Experiment.* Cambridge: Polity Press.

Rousseau, J.-J. 1962: *The Political Writings of Jean-Jacques Rousseau.* Oxford: Oxford University Press.

Rousseau, J.-J. 1968: *The Social Contract.* Harmondsworth: Penguin.
Rousseau, J.-J. 1974: *Emile.* London: Dent.
Rueschemeyer, D., Stephens, E. H. and Stephens, J. D. 1992: *Capitalist Development and Democracy.* Cambridge: Polity Press.
Ruggie, J. G. 1982: International regimes, transactions and change: embedded liberalism in the post war economic order. *International Organization*, 36.
Ruggie, J. G. 1983: Human rights and the future of international community. *Daedalus*, 112, 4.
Rutland, P. 1985: *The Myth of the Plan.* London: Hutchinson.
Ryan, A. 1974: *J. S. Mill.* London: Routledge & Kegan Paul.
Ryan, A. 1983: Mill and Rousseau: utility and rights. In G. Duncan (ed.), *Democratic Theory and Practice.* Cambridge: Cambridge University Press.
Sabine, G. H. 1963: *A History of Political Theory.* London: Harrap.
Schama, S. 1989: *Citizens.* New York: Alfred A. Knopf.
Scharpf, F. 1991: *Crisis and Choice in European Social Democracy.* Cornell: Cornell University Press.
Schattschneider, E. F. 1960: *The Semi-Sovereign People: A Realist View of Democracy in America.* New York: Rinehart and Winston.
Schumpeter, J. 1976: *Capitalism, Socialism and Democracy.* London: Allen & Unwin.
Scott, J. 1991: *Who Rules Britain?* Cambridge: Polity Press.
Segall, J. 1990: Building world democracy through the UN. *Medicine and War*, 6.
Segall, J. 1991: A UN Second Assembly. In F. Barnaby, (ed.), *Building a More Democratic United Nations.* London: Cass.
Sen, A. 1981: *Poverty and Famine.* Oxford: Clarendon Press.
Sen, A. 1985: The moral standing of the market. *Social Philosophy and Policy*, 2, 2.
Shaw, M. 1991: *Post-military Society.* Cambridge: Polity Press.
Shue, H. 1988: Mediating ethics. *Ethics*, 98.
Sigler, J. 1983: *Minority Rights.* Westport, Conn.: Greenwood Press.
Siltanen, J. and Stanworth, M. (eds) 1984: *Women and the Public Sphere.* London: Hutchinson.
Sivard, R. 1989: *World Military and Social Expenditures*, 13th edn. Washington, D.C.: World Priorities.
Skinner, Q. 1978: *The Foundations of Modern Political Thought*, 2 vols. Cambridge: Cambridge University Press.
Skinner, Q. 1981: *Machiavelli.* Oxford: Oxford University Press.
Skinner, Q. 1989a: The state. In T. Ball, J. Farr and R. L. Hanson (eds), *Political Innovation and Conceptual Change.* Cambridge: Cambridge University Press.
Skinner, Q. 1989b: The idea of the modern state. Two lectures delivered October and November, Cambridge University.

Skocpol, T. 1977: Wallerstein's world capitalist system: a theoretical and historical critique. *American Journal of Sociology*, 82, 5.
Skocpol, T. 1979: *States and Revolutions*. Cambridge: Cambridge University Press.
Smith, A. D. 1986: *The Ethnic Origins of Nations*. Oxford: Blackwell.
Smith, A. D. 1990: Towards a global culture? *Theory, Culture and Society*, 7, 2–3.
Smith, D. 1984: States and military blocs: NATO. In *The State and Society*, 6, 27 (D209). Milton Keynes: Open University.
Smith, R. 1987: Political economy and Britain's exernal position. In *Britain in the World*. London: ESRC.
Smith, S. 1987: Reasons of state. In D. Held and C. Pollitt (*eds*), *New Forms of Democracy*. London: Sage.
Smith, S. 1989: The fall and rise of the state in international politics. In G. Duncan (ed.), *Democracy and the Capitalist State*. Cambridge: Cambridge University Press.
Soroos, M. 1986: *Beyond Sovereignty*. Columbia, S.C.: University of South Carolina Press.
Springborg, P. 1992: *Western Republicanism and the Oriental Prince*. Cambridge: Polity Press.
Staniland, J. 1985: *What is Political Economy?* New Haven, Conn.: Yale University Press.
Ste Croix, G. E. M. de 1981: *The Class Struggle in the Ancient Greek World*. London: Duckworth.
Strange, S. 1986: *Casino Capitalism*. Oxford: Blackwell.
Sunkel, O. and Fuenzelida, E. 1979: Transnationalization and its national consequences. In J. Villamil (ed.), *Transational Capitalism and National Development*. Brighton: Wheatsheaf Books.
Swaan, A. de 1988: *In Care of the State*. Cambridge: Polity Press.
Tandon, Y. 1994: Recolonization of subject peoples. *Alternatives*, 19, 2.
Taylor, C. 1967: Neutrality in political science. In P. Laslett and W. G. Runciman (eds), *Philosophy, Politics and Society*, 3rd ser. Oxford: Blackwell.
Therborn, G. 1977: The rule of capital and the rise of democracy. *New Left Review*, 103
Thompson, J. B. 1984: *Studies in the Theory of Ideology*. Cambridge: Polity Press.
Thompson, J. B. 1990: *Ideology and Modern Culture*. Cambridge: Polity Press.
Thompson, J. B. 1995: *The Media and Modernity*. Cambridge: Polity Press.
Thomson, J. A. 1983: Nuclear weapons in Europe. *Survival*, May/June.
Thucydides 1972: *The Peloponnesian War*. Harmondsworth: Penguin.
Tilly, C. 1975: Reflections on the history of European state-making.

In C. Tilly (ed.), *The Formation of National States in Western Europe*. Princeton, N.J.: Princeton University Press.
Tilly, C. 1981: *As Sociology Meets Men*. New York: Academic Press.
Tilly, C. 1990: *Coercion, Capital and European States, AD 990–1990*. Oxford: Blackwell.
Tocqueville, A. de 1968: *Democracy in America*, 2 vols. London: Fontana.
Tomalin, C. 1985: *Mary Wollstonecraft*. Harmondsworth: Penguin.
Townsend, P. 1987: Deprivation. *Journal of Social Policy*, 16, 2.
Tully, J. 1994: The crisis of identification: the case of Canada. *Political Studies*, 42, special issue.
Turner, B. S. 1986: *Citizenship and Capitalism*. London: Allen & Unwin.
Turner, B. S. 1990: Outline of a theory of citizenship. *Sociology*, 24, 2.
UNDP 1990: *Human Development Report 1990*. Oxford: Oxford University Press.
UNDP 1992: *Human Development Report 1992*. Oxford: Oxford University Press.
UNDP 1993: *Human Development Report 1993*. Oxford: Oxford University Press.
Unger, R. M. 1987: *False Necessity*. Cambridge: Cambridge University Press.
UNICEF 1987: *The State of the World's Children*. Oxford: Oxford University Press.
UNICEF 1990: *The State of the World's Children*. Oxford: Oxford University Press.
UNICEF 1992: *The State of the World's Children*. Oxford: Oxford University Press.
UNICEF 1993: *The State of the World's Children*. Oxford: Oxford University Press.
United Nations 1988: *Human Rights: A Compilation of International Instruments*. New York: United Nations Publications.
United Nations 1993: *Report of the United Nations Conference on Environment and Development*, 3 vols. New York: United Nations Publications.
Vajda, M. 1978: The state and socialism. *Social Research*, 4, November.
Vincent, J. 1986: *Human Rights and International Relations*. Cambridge: Cambridge University Press.
Vincent, J. 1992: Modernity and universal human rights. In A. G. McGrew, P. G. Lewis et al., *Global Politics*. Cambridge: Polity Press.
Walker, R. B. J. 1990: Sovereignty, identity, community: reflections on the horizons of contemporary political practice. In R. B. J. Walker and S. H. Mendlovitz (eds), *Contending Sovereignties*. London: Lynne Reiner.
Walker R. B. J. 1993: *Inside/Outside: International Relations as Political Theory*. Cambridge: Cambridge University Press.

Wallace, H. 1991: The Europe that came in from the cold. *International Affairs*, 67, 4.

Wallace, W. et al., 1992: *Beyond the Nation State*. London: Liberal Democrat Publications.

Wallace, W. 1994: Rescue or retreat? The nation state in Western Europe. *Political Studies*, 42, special issue.

Wallerstein, I. 1974a: *The Modern World-system*. New York: Academic Press.

Wallerstein, I. 1974b: The rise and future demise of the world capitalist system. *Comparative Studies in Society and History*, XVI, 4.

Wallerstein, I. 1979: *The Capitalist Economy*. Cambridge: Cambridge University Press.

Wallerstein, I. 1983: *Historical Capitalism*. London: Verso.

Wallerstein, I. 1990: *Antisystemic Movements*. London: Verso.

Wallerstein, I. 1991: *Geopolitics and Geoculture*. Cambridge: Cambridge University Press.

Waltz, K. 1979: *Theory of International Politics*. New York: Addison-Wesley.

Walzer, M. 1983: *Spheres of Justice*. New York: Basic Books.

Ware, A. 1992: Liberal democracy: one form or many? *Political Studies*, XL, special issue.

Warren, B. 1973: Imperialism and capitalist industrialization. *New Left Review*, 81.

Webb, C. 1991: International economic structures, government interests, and international co-ordination of macro-economic adjustment policies. *International Organization*, 45, 3.

Weber, M. 1923: *General Economic History*. London: Allen & Unwin.

Weber, M. 1971: *The Protestant Ethic and the Spirit of Capitalism*. London: Allen & Unwin.

Weber, M. 1972a: Politics as a vocation. In H. H. Gerth and C. W. Mills (eds), *From Max Weber*. New York: Oxford University Press.

Weber, M. 1972b: Science as a vocation. In H. H. Gerth and C. W. Mills (eds), *From Max Weber*. New York: Oxford University Press.

Weber, M. 1978: *Economy and Society*, 2 vols. Berkeley, Calif.: University of California Press.

Wight, M. 1986: *Power Politics*. Harmondsworth: Penguin.

Wight, M. 1987: An anatomy of international thought. *Review of International Studies*, 13.

Williams, H. 1994: International relations and the reconstruction of political theory. *Politics*, 14, 1.

Wollstonecraft, M. 1982: *Vindication of the Rights of Woman*. Harmondsworth: Penguin.

Wood, Gordon S. 1969: *The Creation of the American Republic*. Chapel Hill, N. C.: University of North Carolina Press.

World Bank 1988: *World Development Report 1988*. Oxford: Oxford University Press.
World Commission on Environment and Development 1987: *Our Common Future*. Oxford: Oxford University Press.
Young, O. 1972: The actors in world politics. In J. Rosenau, V. Davis and M. East (eds), *The Analysis of International Politics*. New York: Cornell University Press.
Young, O. 1989: *International Cooperation*. New York: Cornell University Press.
Zacher, M. W. 1993: International organizations. In J. Krieger (ed.), *The Oxford Companion to Politics of the World*. Oxford: Oxford University Press.
Zelikow, P. 1992: The new concert of Europe. *Survival*, 34, 2.
Zimmern, A. 1936: *The League of Nations and the Rule of Law*. London: Macmillan.
Zolberg, A. 1981: Origins of the modern world system: a missing link. *World Politics*, 33, 2.
Zolo, D. 1992: *Democracy and Complexity*. Cambridge: Polity Press.

INDEX

Note: page numbers in italics denote figures or tables.